Just As I Thought

"Just As I Thought"

Grace Paley

Farrar • Straus • Giroux

New York

Farrar, Straus and Giroux
19 Union Square West, New York 10003

Distributed in Canada by Douglas & McIntyre Ltd.
Printed in the United States of America
Designed by Jonathan D. Lippincott
First edition, 1998

Library of Congress Cataloging-in-Publication Data
Paley, Grace.
    [1st ed]
    Just as I thought / Grace Paley.
        p.   cm.
    ISBN 0-374-18060-1 (cloth : alk. paper)
    1. Paley, Grace—Biography.   2. Authors, American—20th century—
Biography.   I. Title.
PS3566.A46Z465   1998
    813'.54—dc21
[B]   97-37630

A publication history appears on page 331.

Dedication and Thank Yous

I want to thank the women and men, black and white, who in the middle of my life taught me about nonviolence as an art, a strategy, and a way to live in the dangerous world.

And the women who preceded me in this last-half-of-the-century women's movement. They were early in understanding and action, so that it was easier for me and others to cross the slippery streets of indifference, exclusion, and condescension.

And the women and men I worked with in the antiwar movement day by day and into long nights with a happy combination of high excitement and essential steadying tedium.

And Bob Nichols, who was one of those people and my own particular companion, without whom real life would be smaller and probably sad.

And my children and children-in-law and grandchildren, who are on my mind every day and cannot be deposed.

And Jess Paley, my first encourager and friend.

And my brother and sister and sister-in-law, who continue to lead me by fifteen years of information and remembrance.

And Jonathan Galassi and Elaine Markson for their patience and timely impatience, and Lynn Warshow, whose eye was on the pages.

And friends who took hours and days from their own work to help me get the book together, especially Beatrix Gates, Barbara Selfridge, Vera B. Williams, Ellie Siegel, and again Bob Nichols; and also Nora Paley, who keeps me straight.

Contents

Introduction

I've called this collection *Just As I Thought*. I've left the articles, reports, and prefaces pretty much as originally written. The transcribed talks are another matter. They've required correction, clarification as they came from my indistinct speech on tape to the transcriber. Still it wasn't hard to present them reasonably unchanged; I haven't unsettled my views of the American war in Vietnam, war in general, racism in particular, and as time increases its speed, I am more of a feminist than ever.

Though I myself began in the twenties, much of what this book is about began in the fifties. Apart from the fascinating, life-enhancing fact of my children, certain national and international events decided the work and friendships of my daily life for the next forty years. Of course I didn't realize it at the time. It just seemed like more bad news. I had begun to write stories about women and children which included men. I thought at the time they were probably too personal, but that's what engaged me.

In 1954, half the world away, the Vietnamese defeated the French at Dien Bien Phu, causing great anxiety in Washington (not yet to me). The United States had hoped that France would take care of Southeast Asia, save it from Russian or Chinese Communism, since we had problems closer to home. There were democracies in Guatemala and Iran (not so close, I guess) that had elected the wrong people and the wrong parties. With the help of the CIA, Arbenz in Guatemala and Mossadegh in Iran were deposed. This is not new information.

Once the French had gone back to France, the United States feared the Vietnamese would probably make the same electoral mistake. That had to be prevented and it was. Its cost was twenty years of unremitting war.

Happily for the people of the United States there was one great good event in that busy year—almost a century too late: the Supreme Court's decision in *Brown vs. Board of Education* ordered desegregation in American schools.

Most of the pieces in this book were written because I was a member of an American movement, a tide really, that rose out of the civil-rights struggles of the fifties, rolling methods and energy into the antiwar, direct-action movements in the sixties, cresting, ebbing as tides do, returning bold again in the seventies and eighties in the second wave of the women's movement—and from quite early on splashed and salted by ecological education, connection, and at last action.

Probably by the late seventies, movement people, that is folks from leftish to left, began to understand the connections between and among these essential struggles for justice, for peace, and for a living planet. Then they began to prioritize and suggest or, more often, accuse one another of being wrong on color, class, gender, or planetary loyalty. Actually, this was true in lots of cases. After all, some feminists were sometimes racist, some African Americans were sometimes misogynist, some Jews did sometimes act as though they were in charge of suffering, and almost everybody arrived too slowly at the reality of the destruction of species, water, and air.

I am not a journalist. In the following reports I don't cover all the aspects of that war or the antiwar movement or the women's movement. Not too many correspondents of that time did, either. Many, in retrospective smartness, saw it all. Not necessarily agreeing with me. In the columns for *Seven Days* and the prefaces to various War Resisters League calendars, I did try to invent a form in which the characters from my stories could give or argue useful information about Puerto Rico, neighborhood vigils, or demonstrations at the Seabrook nuclear plant. The Vietnam section of this book has its own introduction because a young person told me it happened so long ago and needed contextualization.

But the fact is, 1954 *was* a year in which much was set in motion. Enough certainly to add daily committed political work to family life, to a haphazard work schedule and evening struggles to write poems and stories. I was, with many of my friends, in my mid-forties, fifties, and then sixties—a time of great energy for women lucky enough to live those years during the "second wave" of the feminist movement.

This is not an autobiographical collection, but it is about my life. Many of the pieces are political even when they take on literary subjects—a reaction not unnatural to me or deliberate. I didn't have to work my way toward a sudden awakening in revolutionary amazement. I knew from an early age that my father had been imprisoned in common local jails in Russia and then in Siberia at Archangel, that my mother had been sent into exile, and that both were released when the Czar had a son. Prisoners under twenty-one were sent home—probably just in time for the 1905 revolution and more pogroms.

My parents seemed heroic to me, and if I was amazed, it was by their anger at me the times I was suspended: first from junior high for signing (probably) the Oxford Pledge against war when I was about twelve and suspended again in high school for something similar. In this country, they seemed to believe, education, once struggled for, came first—then socialism.

My brother, my sister, and I are often annoyed by our failure to have extracted much information from our parents and grandmother. Of course they may not have known much—but there is a world where some people publicly trace their past to medieval baronies and others, plain Jews like us, believe they are descended, through centuries of wandering, settlement, pogroms, immigration, from famous rabbis, princes of great cities full of Polish and Lithuanian Jews, not to mention the Spanish communities of the Marranos—well, my sister and brother and I, we feel kind of left out. Actually, I don't think any one of us wants to go that far back, but we did want to know why those old cities, Bachmut, Baku, and Mariupol, were mentioned from time to time in discontinued conversations or printed on the backs of old Russian photographs, some taken in the family photography establishment, Gutzeit. Our grandmother (from whom we might have learned a few facts) and our parents thought their European past a delta of muddy suffering, a swamp of despair, in which we could only sink. Maybe they just forgot, being so damn busy with learning English, school, work, family, life, death. Suddenly, before they could say more, the story ended.

My grandmother, called Babushka (I thought that was her name), certainly didn't tell me much. She never learned English, which was great for my Russian. She probably thought there was little point—she'd surely die soon enough of sorrow: one son killed at seventeen, another certain to be deported (he was deported the year I was born), a cranky unmarried daughter living with her in her room in another woman's house (my mother's). She knew Russian poems and said them to me and worked on my accent. I have the accent but not much vocabulary left. She read the Yiddish paper, *The Forward*, every day. She was sad and intelligent and lived solemnly to be ninety.

She did describe sometimes what supper was like in her house in Russia in the town of Uzovka in the earliest 1900s. It was an occasion for infuriated political argument between swallows of borscht or kotletki—my father, a socialist, my uncle Grisha an anarchist, Aunt Luba a Zionist, my youngest aunt, Mira, a Communist. My grandmother didn't say what Rusya was. He was murdered in 1904 or '05 carrying the red banner of the working class. For this reason Mira told me never to carry the flag in demonstrations. I've mentioned this in a couple of stories. She never married, which seemed to anger most people—Damnit, she doesn't know how, my father said. She loved us all—except my mother—and because of Mira I believe that the woman-aunt is essential to a child's life. (My sister has been that person in my children's lives.) Mira felt she'd been torn at 16 from Russia, her home. I sometimes teased her: Mira, it's a shame you missed the First and Second World Wars, the 1917 revolution, the civil wars; you even missed the Holocaust and the Russian camps. —Gracie, Gracie, you don't understand!

An extended family is wonderful for a child who is important to everybody's life; who is, in fact, its meaning—but often a terrible experience for the grownups who carry into the new country secret and bitter knowledge of one another and all the old insults.

My mother was a woman of unusual kindness. She loved my father, who was considered a difficult man. This made me very romantic. I began as soon as I could (around thirteen or so) my successful searches for difficult men of my own. She had been a photography retoucher when my older brother and sister were children. In my middle-class childhood she managed a household—my father's neighborhood medical practice on the first floor and the complicated family life upstairs. She was not liked by my grandmother or my aunt. She lived with them all her life. She died before they did. I could see they felt my mother's love for my father one-upped their love for him—at least it interfered with their serving him his evening tea or morning coffee. My daughter has pointed out that there were not enough love jobs to go around in this new world. In any event, I probably learned tolerance, maybe even literary affection for the person in the wrong historical moment, living such long, never to be mediated wars with other sufferers.

My mother died too early in my adult life to see clearly that I wasn't going to rack and ruin. She missed all the grandchildren but my brother's Frances. But tucked into my granddaughter's name, Laura Manya Paley, there she is: my mother, modest as usual, but present.

I / Beginning

I ought to say a few things about the pieces in this section. "In-justice" is about your typical socialist Jewish child. "Other Mothers" was written first for Esquire's *"Mom and Apple Pie" issue, then was reprinted in* Feminist Studies. *I think I did have those other mothers in mind, the way they seemed left behind; I could almost see them watching their sons disappear into America and that generation's misogyny. It may have been a good time for apple pie, but it was a hard time for mom. It seemed everything was her fault, her daughter's autism in the life of one friend, for another friend her son's schizophrenia. With this friend, I visited many head doctors whose authoritative voices I heard addressing her, explaining, more frequently accusing. "Jobs" is the best résumé I ever dreamed up, and the most accurate. It was done a long time ago, but not much has changed. I'm still a writer, sometimes a teacher, and have graduated to grandmotherness. I'm glad to have included the interview, "The Illegal Days," from* The Choices We Made, *though it is kind of discursive, partly because it's presented as a written piece. I love Angela Bonavoglia's persistence in putting that book together.*

"Six Days" and "Traveling" explain themselves pretty well (I think). As for the speech "Like All the Other Nations"—it was given at a Tikkun *magazine conference, actually at the conference dinner, one of those fund-raising dinners that must happen from time to time or important organizations would starve. I began with*

what might be called a story, "Midrash on Happiness" (I do tend to begin or end my talks with stories or poems). In this case, I wanted to tell how my serious atheistic Jewish parents gave me enough stories—biblical, historical—so that I grew up as a Jewish woman and liked it.

There is on page 36 an introduction to Peacemeal, *a Greenwich Village Peace Center cookbook, which describes the gang fights in the East Bronx as a tough struggle between the Third and Fourth Internationals. A friend reading it suggested that no one would know what I was talking about. So I will explain that the Third International, as we were raised to understand it, believed that Socialism could be successfully built in one country, and that country became the Soviet Union under Lenin, then Stalin. The Fourth International became itself, believing that the Soviet Union was not a Marxist or a historical possibility. It then became Trotskyism after Trotsky, who had fled Russia and was murdered in Mexico by Third Internationalists. For some reason Trotskyism was attractive to many American intellectuals. Though I seem too easy or wry in my comments, these serious factional furies had great influence on our American labor movement and our literary magazines, as well as on street corners in the Bronx.*

"The Unfinished Bronx" was originally a preface to a book of Mel Rosenthal's wonderful photographs. The book has not appeared yet—but here's the preface. It does tell something about my poor borough's hard life, its betrayal by the Lords of the City. My own street, however, has improved—little one-story family houses seem almost literally planted on one side of the street. But our old, short, fat, two-story red brick still sits there. Grass now grows on the dirty old corner lots. I drove by and stopped the other day, and I saw that change. The mother in the upstairs window, the little black boy on my childhood's excellent stoop probably waiting for his friends. "Can I help you, señora?"—two Puerto Rican men walking by saw my intense looking. "I used to live here," I said. "Oh, lady, lady, come back," they cried.

 *Injustice*

When I was about nine years old, I was a member of an organization called the Falcons. We were Socialist youths under twelve. We wore blue shirts and red kerchiefs. We met once a week (or was it once a month?). To the tune of "Maryland, My Maryland," we sang:

> *The workers' flag is deepest red*
> *it shrouded oft our martyred dead.*

With the Socialist ending, not the Communist one, we sang the "Internationale." We were warned that we would be tempted to sing the Communist ending, because at our occasional common demonstrations there were more of them singing. They would try, with their sneaky politics, to drown us out.

At our meetings we learned about real suffering, which was due to the Great Depression through which we were living that very year. Of course many of my friends already had this information. Their fathers weren't working. Their mothers had become so grouchy you couldn't ask them for the least little thing. Every day in our neighborhood there were whole apartments, beds, bureaus, kitchen tables out on the street. We understood that this was because of capitalism, which didn't care that working people had no work and no money for rent.

We also studied prejudice—now known as racism. Prejudice was particularly sad, since it meant not liking people for no reason at all, except the color of their skin. That color could happen to anyone if they'd been born to some other parents on another street. We ourselves had known prejudice—well, not us exactly. In Europe, that godforsaken place, our parents and grandparents had known it well. From a photograph over my grandmother's bed, my handsome uncle, killed at seventeen because of prejudice, looked calmly at me when I sought him for reminder's sake. Despite its adherence to capitalism, prejudice, and lynching, my father said we were lucky to be here in this America. We sometimes sang "America the Beautiful" at our meetings. Parents were divided on that.

At each meeting we paid 5¢ or 10¢—not so much to advance Socialism as to be able to eat cookies at four o'clock. One day at cookie-eating time, our comrade counselor teacher, a young woman about eighteen years old, announced that we were going to do a play. There would be a party, too. It would include singing and maybe dancing. We began to rehearse immediately. She had been thinking about all this for a couple of weeks. The idea had matured into practical action.

Our play was simple, a kind of agitprop in which a father comes home; he says, "Well, Sarah, the shop closed down today. No more work! And without warning!" The mother is in despair. How to feed the children! The children's breakfast bowls are empty. Some boys carry the furniture (lots of chairs from the meeting room) out to the hall. Eviction! In the second act, neighbors meet to drag the furniture back, proving working-class solidarity. They then hold a rally and march to City Hall at the back of the room, singing the "Internationale" all the way. The event would have to take place in the evening after supper in case some father or mother still had a job.

I was one of the little empty-bowl children. Every day after school I worked in the bathroom mirror at the creation of a variety of heartrending expressions. But my sweetest contribution would be the song

> *One dark night when we were all in bed*
> *Old mother Leary took a candle to the shed*
> *and when the cow tipped it over*
> *she winked her eye and said*
> *There'll be a hot time in the old town tonight.*

This song had been chosen to show we had fun, too; our childhood was being respected.

Before supper that important night, I decided to sing for my mother. When I finished, she said gently, lovingly, "Gracie darling, you can't sing. You know you can't hold the tune. The teacher in school, she even said you were a listener. Try again— a little softer . . ."

"I can so sing," I said. "I was picked. I wouldn't of been picked if I couldn't sing." I sang the song once more.

"No no," my mother said. "That girl Sophie, Mrs. Greenberg's Sophie? She has no idea. She has no ear. Maybe deaf even. No no, you can't sing. You'll make a fool of yourself. People will laugh. For Sophie maybe, the more laughing the better."

"I don't care. I have to go. I have to go in a half hour. I have two parts."

"What? And I'm supposed to sit in the audience and see how your feelings are hurt when they laugh at you. When Papa hears—well, he wouldn't go anyway. That Sophie, she's just a kid herself."

"But, Mama, I have to go."

"No no," she said. "No. You're not going. Just to be a fool. They'll have to figure out what to do."

Guiltless but full of shame, I never returned to the Falcons. In fact, in sheer spite I gave up my work for Socialism for at least three years.

Fifty years later I told my sister this story. She said, "I can't believe that of Mama—that she would prevent you from singing —especially if you had an obligation. She wasn't like that."

Well, I had developed a kind of class analysis, an explanation which I think is pretty accurate. Our parents, remarkable people, were also a couple of ghetto Jews struggling with hard work and intensive education up the famous American ladder. At a certain rung in that ladder during my childhood they appeared to have climbed right into the professional middle class. At that comfort-able rung (probably upholstered), embarrassed panic would be the response to possible exposure.

"Exposure to what? What are you talking about?" my sister asked. "You forget, really. Mama had absolutely perfect pitch. For a person like that, your wandering all over the scale must have been torture. I mean real physical pain. To her, you were just screeching. In fact," my sister said, "although you've im-proved, you still sound that way to me."

My sister has continued to be fourteen years older than I. Nei-ther of us has recovered from that hierarchical fact. So I said, "Okay, Jeanne."

But she had not—when she was nine—been a political person and she had never been a listener. She took singing lessons, then sang. She and my brother practiced the piano like sensible chil-dren. In fact, in their eighties they have as much musical hap-piness in their fingertips as in their heads.

As for my mother—though I had no ear and clearly could not sing, she thought I might try the piano. After all, we had one. There were notes on paper inside a nice yellow book that said *Inventions by Bach* on its cover. Since I was a big reader, I might be able to accomplish *something*. I had no gift. That didn't mean I must be a deprived person. Besides, why had the Enlightenment poured its seductive light all across the European continent right into the poor endangered households of Ukrainian Jews? Probably, my mother thought, so that a child, any child (even a tone-deaf one), could be given a chance despite genetic deficiency to become, in my mother's embarrassed hopeful world, a whole person.

—1995

"The Unfinished Bronx"

I remember the day that the East Bronx began to become the South Bronx, though no one realized it at the time. I was in kindergarten. My entire class, probably many other classes as well, walked all the way from our school, P.S. 50 on Vyse Avenue and East 173rd Street, east, east to the Bronx River. There the Mayor of the City of New York, Jimmy Walker, dedicated the East 174th Street Bridge. Dedicated to what?

Probably to real-estate development (bridges, roads, benign or sneaky, are good for that). Soon some little houses and big houses called tenements or apartment houses were established, much like those on our side of the river. But in only a few years out of the frantic good-time winds of the 1920s, the merciless Depression sprang forward, stalking money, houses, people.

Then everything was unfinished, even in our neighborhoods. There were empty lots on many street corners, rocky, hilly, good for games, but already jammed with garbage and rats (our mothers said). Someone must have owned those lots and was hoping for better days. They never came—to that neighborhood at least. Evictions were a daily fact. Many neighbors and most of my friends were on home relief. It was only the terrible war news from Europe and the beginning of a war economy, then war, that returned people to work, saving them, as well as the system called capitalism.

The Depression was the first great blow to the unfinished Bronx. There were demographic changes, too, as the Irish and Jews, recovering from the harsh 1930s, began to move out of the old tenements to the North and West Bronx, New Jersey, the Westchester suburbs. Puerto Rican families and African Americans had already begun to move up out of Manhattan hopefully to the Bronx. But normal American racism never did let everyone into the melting pot at the same time.

The second great blow from which the Bronx has never recovered was the Cross-Bronx Expressway, which was hacked across the borough east to west in order to get the automobiles of suburbanites and the huge trailer trucks of commerce from New England to New Jersey and the rest of the United States.

It was a conscious decision, made finally on all levels of government, to sacrifice the poor and middle class, the communities in change as well as the stable communities of the mid-Bronx, to the arrogant dreams of engineers, politicians, real-estate developers. They believed the bulldozers would follow the hackers and lo! great areas of brand-new land would appear. It didn't happen that way. The populations for blocks and blocks north and particularly south of the expressway were delivered to years, decades, of instability, abandonment, devastation, fire.

In this way, the East Bronx that Mel Rosenthal and I knew (about twenty years apart) became the South Bronx, one body of human suffering.

I left home in 1942. Several years later my mother died. My father sold his neighborhood medical practice and moved to Gun Hill Road, where there were elevator apartments. But that street between 172nd and 173rd was my childhood home. So I returned every few years sentimentally and out of persistent political interest.

At first the neighborhood seemed almost the same. Except for the fact that mothers called to their children in Spanish instead of Yiddish. The grocery store in which the Statman family had worked maybe twelve, fourteen hours a day had enslaved another family in what was now called a bodega. The little shul just two doors away from my house was still God's house—Iglesia Pentecostal. The children still owned the streets, but more dangerously. There were more cars. The second time I returned, I saw among a dozen buildings in fairly good shape at least two tenements that stood empty, five stories of broken, soot-blackened windows. My house sat, a kind of squat red brick, kids playing stoop ball on its excellent stoop.

By my third visit, absolute disaster had taken the street in its teeth and had been shaking it with fire, drugs, rage, leaving an occasional building untouched. The street was jagged with glass. A block north, a sheet hung from the fourth floor of a half-intact solitary building. In big black letters printed on it: PEOPLE STILL LIVE ON THIS GODFORSAKEN BLOCK.

Mel Rosenthal made this book of portraits and places for those people. Also for those he looked for everywhere, photograph in hand, who were no longer in the neighborhood. Often the neighborhood was gone, telling the awful success of the depopulation schemes called "planned shrinkage."

He brought with him to the Bronx not only his particular gifts but the real experience of working in Tanzania with Paolo Freire, whose *Pedagogy of the Oppressed* played an important role in the literacy programs of Latin America.

In a way he was lucky. He was a member of a generation that thought it was a good, even joyous, political idea to put its brains, energy, labor at the service of the people.

So he did.

—1996

" The Illegal Days "

It was the late thirties, and we all knew that birth control existed, but we also knew it was impossible to get. You had to be older and married. You couldn't get anything in drugstores, unless you were terribly sick and had to buy a diaphragm because your womb was falling out. The general embarrassment and misery around getting birth control were real.

There was Margaret Sanger at that time, and she had a clinic right here in Manhattan in a beautiful house on Sixteenth Street; I still walk past and look at it. As brave as the Margaret Sanger people were, they were under very tough strictures. It was scary to go there. I was eighteen, and it was 1940 when I tiptoed in to get a diaphragm. I said I was married.

When I was young, it really angered me that birth control was so hard to get. Kids who were not as sophisticated as we Bronx kids just didn't know what to do. But I never felt that this was happening just to me. I had a very good social sense then from my own political family. I also had a lot of good girl friends, and we used to talk about it together. We had in common this considerable disgust and anger at the whole situation.

I grew up in the Bronx in a puritanical, socialist, Jewish family. My mother was particularly puritanical, and all that sex stuff was very hard for her to talk about—so she didn't. My father was a doctor, but we still didn't talk about such things. I really never felt terribly injured by all that. It just seemed to be the way it was with all of my friends. We considered ourselves freethinkers —in advance of our parents.

Most of my friends married early. I married when I was nineteen; then my husband went overseas during the Second World War. I would have loved it if I had had a child when he went overseas, but we had decided against it.

When he came back, I was in my late twenties, and in the next couple of years, I had two children. When the children were one and a half and three, I got pregnant again. I don't remember if my birth control failed . . . I wasn't the most careful person in the world. Something in me did want to have more children, but since I had never gotten pregnant until I really wanted to—I was twenty-six and a half when I had my first child—I had assumed that that general mode would continue.

I knew I couldn't have another child. I was exhausted with these two tiny little kids; it was just about all I could do to take care of them. As a child, I had been sick a lot, and people were always thinking I was anemic . . . I was having bouts of that kind. I just was very tired, all the time. I knew something was wrong because my whole idea in my heart had always been to have five, six children—I *loved* the idea of having children—but I knew I couldn't have this kid.

Seeing the state I was in, even my father said, "You must not have another child." That gives you an idea of my parents' view. They didn't feel you had to just keep having babies if you had a lot to do, small children, and not a lot of money.

And my husband and I were having hard times. It was really rough. My husband was not that crazy about having children anyway; it was very low on his list of priorities. We lived where the school is now, right next door, and were supers of the rooming house. He was just beginning his career. He eventually made documentary films, but he'd come back from the Army and was getting it all together, like a lot of those guys. So anyway, it was financially hard. But it was mostly the psychological aspect of it that would have been hard for him.

In the 1930s, my late teens, I really didn't know a lot of people who had had abortions, but then later on—not much later, when I was a young married woman in the 1940s—I heard much more. People would talk about it. By then, women were traveling everywhere—to this famous guy in Pennsylvania, to Puerto Rico. And you were always hearing about somebody who once did abortions but wasn't there doing them anymore.

I didn't ask my father for help. I wasn't really a kid, stuck and pregnant and afraid that the world would fall down on me. I was a woman with two small children, trying to be independent. I didn't want to distress him. He already wasn't feeling very well; he had a very bad heart. And he really couldn't travel; he lived in the North Bronx, and I was living on Eleventh Street—it would have been a terrible subway trip. I just didn't want to bother him.

I talked the situation over with the women in the park where I used to hang out with the kids. None of them thought having an abortion was a terrible thing to do. You would say, "I can't have a kid now . . . I can't do it," and everybody was perfectly sympathetic. They said to me, "Ask So-and-so. She had one recently." I did, and I got a name. The woman didn't say anything about the guy; she just said, "Call." I assumed he was a real doctor, and he was. That may have been luck.

My abortion was a very clean and decent affair, but I didn't know until I got there that it would be all right. The doctor's office was in Manhattan, on West End Avenue. I went during the day, and I went with my husband. The doctor had two or three rooms. My husband sat and waited in one of them. There were other people waiting for other kinds of care, which is how this doctor did it; he did a whole bunch of things. He saw someone ahead of me, and when he put me in another room to rest for a few minutes afterward, I heard him talking to other patients.

The nurse was there during the procedure. He didn't give me an anesthetic; he said, "If you want it, I'll give it to you, but it will be much safer and better if I don't." It hurt, but it wasn't that painful. So I don't have anything traumatic to say about it. I was angry that I had to become a surreptitious person and that I was in danger, but the guy was very clean, and he was very good, and he was arrested within the next year. He went to jail.

I didn't feel bad about the abortion. I didn't have the feelings that people are always describing. I may have hidden some of the feelings, but having had a child at that time would have been so much worse for me. I was certainly scared, and it's not something you want necessarily to do, but I don't see it in that whole ethical or moral framework. I guess I really didn't think of the fetus as a child until it was really a child.

But you'll hear plenty of abortion stories. I will tell you what happened next after that was over, which is what I really want to talk about. I became pregnant again a couple of years later. I wanted to have the child, but my husband didn't. It was very hard; I didn't know what to do. I was kind of in despair.

I got three or four addresses, again from women in the park. My husband wasn't going to come with me. Partly I didn't want him to come; I probably was mad at him. I had this good friend, and she said, "You're not going alone." I was very grateful to her. She said, "I'll go with you," and she did.

I remember very clearly traveling to those places—to the end of Long Island and the end of Queens and the end of Brooklyn. I went to each one of these guys, but they wouldn't do it. One guy said, "Look, if you weren't married, I would risk it, but you're married and maybe you just have to make do." He felt I didn't need an abortion that much. I'll never forget. The only person we could find was some distance away and didn't sound very good to me at all. I was frightened . . . terribly frightened.

A week or two later, I remember, it was a freezing night; I was visiting people, and I ran home very fast. I was distraught and terrified because I was going to have to go either to Puerto Rico or someplace else. It was late in the pregnancy; it might have been the second trimester. That night I ran home at top speed—I can't tell you—in the cold, crying, from about eight blocks away. I ran all the way home and just fell into bed. I remember I had a terrible bellyache from the running.

When I woke up the next morning, I was bleeding fiercely. It seemed to me I was having a miscarriage. I'd had another miscarriage, and both my children were born early, so it was not a weird thing that this would happen to me.

So I called this doctor I'd been to several times before, and he said to me, "Did you do something?" I said, "No! It's just like the last time I had a miscarriage. I'm bleeding." And he said, "Call somebody in your family. Get some ergot [a drug that stops uterine contractions]." I said, "Don't you want me to come over?" and he said, *"No! Don't come."*

By this time my father had had a serious heart attack, so I didn't tell him anything about it. I continued to bleed. I bled and bled, for three, four days. I was really in terrible shape, and I couldn't get anyone to take care of me. On about the third or fourth day, my doctor finally said, "Come over." He had to do a D&C.

Sometime after that, when I spoke to my father about it, he said, "That doctor was being watched. There's no other explanation. He was a kind guy. He knew you. He must have recently done something, and he was scared."

These things are not talked about a lot, this kind of criminalization of the medical profession, the danger these doctors were in. It meant that they could not take care of you. It's not even about abortion.

A good friend had an even clearer experience with this. She also was bleeding at the wrong time, and it didn't stop. She went to the emergency room here at a Catholic hospital, and they refused to take care of her. They just flatly refused. They said she had to have a rabbit test to see if she was pregnant and the results would take a couple of days. They would not touch her because she *might* be pregnant, and they *might* disturb the child. She continued to bleed, and they would not take care of her. She was a little skinny woman; she didn't have that much blood. Well, she wasn't pregnant. It turned out she had a tumor. It was an emergency—she had to be operated on immediately.

Your life, a woman's life, was simply not the first thing that hospital had on its mind at all. Not only that: Even if the doctor had compassion—and in my friend's case, one of the doctors was very anxious about her—they couldn't do anything unless they were willing to risk a great deal.

I think women died all the time when abortions were illegal. The horrible abortions were one way; the other way was the refusal of institutions—medical, church, and state—to care for you, their willingness to let you die.

It's important to be public about the issue, and I have been for years. I helped organize one of the first abortion speak-outs in the country, which was held at the Washington Square Methodist Church in New York City back in the late sixties.

But I'll be very truthful. I never liked the slogan "Abortion on demand," and most of my friends hated it. We'd go on marches, and we could never say it. It's such a trivialization of the experience. It's like "Toothpaste on demand." If somebody said there should be birth control on demand, I would say yes. That would make a lot of sense. If I ask for a diaphragm, if I ask for a condom, I should just get it right off the bat.

But an abortion . . . After all, it's a surgical procedure and really a very serious thing to undertake. It's not a small matter. Just because I didn't suffer a lot around my abortion, suffering is not the only thing that makes something important. I didn't suffer, but it was important. And when you say "on demand," it ignores the real question, which is: Where are you in your pregnancy? If you're in the sixth month, it's probably not wise, not good for you, even dangerous. Not that I think if a woman goes to a clinic and wants to have an abortion, she shouldn't have it when she needs it. It's just that there's a lot to think about.

The last demonstration I went to was in Montpelier, Vermont (Mobilization for Women's Lives, November 12, 1989). There were about twenty-five hundred women and men. The governor spoke, a woman governor, Madeleine Kunin; and, one of the great highlights, an older woman—older than me, even (I'm sixty-seven)—from Catholics for a Free Choice spoke; and I spoke.

I said that abortion is only the tip of the iceberg. These guys who run at the clinics—and by the way, our Burlington clinic was really raided, with people knocked down—are point men who make the noise and false, hypocritical statements about human life, which they don't much care about, really. What they really want to do is take back ownership of women's bodies. They want to return us to a time when even our children weren't our own; we were simply the receptacles to have these children. The great novels of the nineteenth and early-twentieth centuries were often about women who knew that if they took one wrong step, their children would be taken from them.

And another point I made is that abortion isn't what they're thinking about; they're really thinking about sex. They're really thinking about love and reducing it to its most mechanical aspects—that is to say, the mechanical fact of intercourse as a specific act to make children in this world, and thinking of its use in any other way as wrong and wicked. They are determined to reduce women's normal sexual responses, to end them, really, when we've just had a couple of decades of admitting them.

My generation—and only in our later years—and the one right after mine have been the only ones to really enjoy any sexual freedom. The kids have to know that it's not just the right to abortion which is essential; it's their right to a sexual life.

—1991

Obviously, the AIDS epidemic had not yet assaulted that next generation when I spoke/wrote this piece.

 *Jobs*

These are the jobs I've had in the last thirty years. Some before the war, some after. (When I say "the war," I mean the Second World War, because if people in my generation were going to die in a war, that would be the war.)

This was the first job: door opener and telephone answerer for a doctor. All I had to say afternoon and evening was: Please come in and sit down. Also: Thank you, but call back at 6:30.

Of all the jobs I was ever to have, that one had the most thank you's.

Second job: This was an important and serious job for the Central Elevator Company. Six days a week, because the five-day week hadn't been invented yet. (Working people had heard of it and thought it was probably a good idea, but the employers didn't see how it could be useful.) I typed bills at this important job and I answered simple letters. Nobody gave me anything too hard to do because they could see I felt stupid. I was younger than everybody. They and I thought that meant extreme stupidity.

The fact is, I did make at least one mistake a week. I had to figure out the payroll. Each week I underpaid or overpaid at least one worker. Whoever this man was—usually one of the elevator mechanics—he would be kind and try to help me cover the error.

Whoever the man happened to be, he would usually say, "Don't feel bad, honey. You'll get smarter. It takes time."

(I have a friend in charge of payrolls right now. She is in charge of one big IBM-type machine and 12,000 paychecks for 12,000 people. She makes a mistake maybe only once a year or once in two years. Of course when that mistake is made, 12,000 men and women are overpaid or underpaid. Machines do things in a more efficient way.)

Then I was a telephone answerer again.

Then it was 1942, a year that happened before most people were born. I married a soldier and went down South with him to keep him company while he was training.

That was in time for my fourth job. I was a babysitter for a Southern family named Grimm, whose father was missing in action. I learned how to make hominy grits for the babies and corn mush. I have never made them since.

Then I was a 5&10 salesgirl, but not for long. The pay was 35 cents an hour. There weren't enough hours.

The next job was the best I ever have had. I was the secretary to the fire chief on the army post and in on all the fires. Most of them were brush and continued all summer in the North Carolina grass. An important part of my job was the ringing of the fire bell at noon. In order to ring it at the right time, I had to call the post switchboard operator at about ten or eleven. I asked her for the abso*lute*ly correct time. One day I called her and said, "Ellie, how do you know what the correct time is? Who tells *you*?" "Oh," she said, "I set my clock every day by the twelve noon fire bell."

Then the war ended and everything since has happened very quickly. Life starts off slow but gets faster and faster. I had the following jobs:

1. Secretary to a reinsurance company. They insured insurance companies. Anybody can go broke, that proves.

2. Secretary to the Southern Conference for Human Welfare.

They raised money to educate black and white Southerners to a little understanding of each other.

3. Secretary to the New York Tenants Association, which did just that—got tenants together for more hot water and hotter heat.

4. Superintendent in a rooming house, in charge of linens.

5. Part-time secretary to the professors of zirconium and titanium at Columbia University.

6. Then finally I was a teacher.

But during all those jobs, once I was married and after I had children, most of the day I was a housewife. That is the poorest-paying job a woman can hold. But most women feel gypped by life if they don't get a chance at it. And all during those jobs and all the time I was a housewife, I was a writer. The whole meaning of my life, which was jammed until midnight with fifteen different jobs and places, was writing. It took me a long time to know that, but I know it now.

—mid-1960s

Six Days: Some Rememberings

I was in jail. I had been sentenced to six days in the Women's House of Detention, a fourteen-story prison right in the middle of Greenwich Village, my own neighborhood. This happened during the American war in Vietnam, I have forgotten which important year of the famous sixties. The civil disobedience for which I was paying a small penalty probably consisted of sitting down to impede or slow some military parade.

I was surprised at the sentence. Others had been given two days or dismissed. I think the judge was particularly angry with me. After all, I was not a kid. He thought I was old enough to know better, a forty-five-year-old woman, a mother and teacher. I ought to be too busy to waste time on causes I couldn't possibly understand.

I was herded with about twenty other women, about 90 percent black and Puerto Rican, into the bullpen, an odd name for a women's holding facility. There, through someone else's lawyer, I received a note from home telling me that since I'd chosen to spend the first week of July in jail, my son would probably not go to summer camp, because I had neglected to raise the money I'd promised. I read this note and burst into tears, real running-down-the-cheek tears. It was true: thinking about other people's grown boys, I had betrayed my little son. The summer, starting that day, July 1, stood up before me day after day, steaming the city streets, the after-work crowded city pool.

I guess I attracted some attention. You—you white girl you—you never been arrested before? A black woman about a head taller than I put her arm on my shoulder. It ain't so bad. What's your time, sugar? I gotta do three years. You huh?

Six days.

Six days? What the fuck for?

I explained, sniffling, embarrassed.

You got six days for sitting down front of a horse? Cop on the horse? Horse step on you? Jesus in hell, cops gettin crazier and stupider and meaner. Maybe we get you out.

No, no, I said. I wasn't crying because of that. I didn't want her to think I was scared. I wasn't. She paid no attention. Shoving a couple of women aside—Don't stand in front of me, bitch. Move over. What you looking at?—she took hold of the bars of our cage, commenced to bang on them, shook them mightily, screaming, Hear me now, you motherfuckers, you grotty pigs, get this housewife out of here! She returned to comfort me. —Six days in this low-down hole for sitting front of a horse!

Before we were distributed among our cells, we were dressed in a kind of nurse's-aide scrub uniform, blue or green, a little too large or a little too small. We had had to submit to a physical in which all our hiding places were investigated for drugs. These examinations were not too difficult, mostly because a young woman named Andrea Dworkin had fought them, refused a grosser, more painful examination some months earlier. She had been arrested protesting the war in front of the U.S. Mission to the UN. I had been there, too, but I don't think I was arrested that day. She was mocked for that determined struggle at the Women's House, as she has been for other braveries, but according to the women I questioned, certain humiliating, perhaps sadistic customs had ended—for that period at least.

My cellmate was a beautiful young woman, twenty-three years

old, a prostitute who'd never been arrested before. She was nervous, but she had been given the name of an important longtermer. She explained in a businesslike way that she *was* beautiful and would need protection. She'd be okay once she found that woman. In the two days we spent together, she tried *not* to talk to the other women on our cell block. She said they were mostly street whores and addicts. She would never be on the street. Her man wouldn't allow it anyway.

I slept well for some reason, probably the hard mattress. I don't seem to mind where I am. Also, I must tell you, I could look out the window at the end of our corridor and see my children or their friends on their way to music lessons or Greenwich House pottery. Looking slantwise I could see right into Sutter's Bakery, then on the corner of Tenth Street. These were my neighbors at coffee and cake.

Sometimes the cell block was open, but not our twelve cells. Other times the reverse. Visitors came by: they were prisoners, detainees not yet sentenced. They seemed to have a strolling freedom, though several, unsentenced, unable to make bail, had been there for months. One woman peering into the cells stopped when she saw me. Grace! Hi! I knew her from the neighborhood, maybe the park, couldn't really remember her name.

What are you in for? I asked.

Oh nothing—well, a stupid drug bust. I don't even use—oh well, forget it. I've been here six weeks. They keep putting the trial off. Are you okay?

Then I complained. I had planned not to complain about anything while living among people who'd be here in these clanging cells a long time; it didn't seem right. But I said, I don't have anything to read and they took away my pen and I don't have paper.

Oh, you'll get all that eventually, she said. Keep asking.

Well, they have all my hairpins. I'm a mess.

No no, she said, you're okay. You look nice.

(A couple of years later, the war continuing, I was arrested in Washington. My hair was still quite long. I wore it in a kind of bun on top of my head. My hairpins gone, my hair straggled wildly every which way. Muriel Rukeyser, arrested that day along with about thirty other women, made the same generous sisterly remark. No no, Grace, love you with your hair down, you really ought to always wear it this way.)

The very next morning, my friend brought me *The Collected Stories of William Carlos Williams.* —These okay?

God! Okay. —Yes!

My trial is coming up tomorrow, she said. I think I'm getting off with time already done. Overdone. See you around?

That afternoon, my cellmate came for her things. —I'm moving to the fourth floor. Working in the kitchen. Couldn't be better. We were sitting outside our cells, she wanted me to know something. She'd already told me, but said it again: I still can't believe it. This creep, this guy, this cop, he waits, he just waits till he's fucked and fine, pulls his pants up, pays me, and arrests me. It's not legal. It's not. My man's so mad, he like to kill *me*, but he's not that kind of—he's not a criminal type, *my* man. She never said the word "pimp." Maybe no one did. Maybe that was our word.

I had made friends with some of the women in the cells across the aisle. How can I say "made friends"? I just sat and spoke when spoken to, I was at school. I answered questions—simple ones. Why would I do such a fool thing on purpose? How old were my children? My man any good? Then: you live around the corner? That was a good idea, Evelyn said, to have a prison in your own neighborhood, so you could keep in touch, yelling out the window. As in fact we were able to do right here and now, calling and being called from Sixth Avenue, by mothers, children, boyfriends.

About the children: One woman took me aside. Her daughter was brilliant, she was in Hunter High School, had taken a test. No, she hardly ever saw her, but she wasn't a whore—it was the drugs. Her daughter was ashamed; the grandmother, the father's mother, made the child ashamed. When she got out in six months it would be different. This made Evelyn and Rita, right across from my cell, laugh. Different, I swear. Different. Laughing. But she *could* make it, I said. Then they really laughed. Their first laugh was a bare giggle compared to these convulsive roars. Change her ways? That dumb bitch. Ha!!

Another woman, Helen, the only other white woman on the cell block, wanted to talk to me. She wanted me to know that she was not only white but Jewish. She came from Brighton Beach. Her father, he should rest in peace, thank God, was dead. Her arms were covered with puncture marks almost like sleeve patterns. But she needed to talk to me, because I was Jewish (I'd been asked by Rita and Evelyn—was I Irish? No, Jewish. Oh, they answered). She walked me to the barred window at the end of the corridor, the window that looked down on West Tenth Street. She said, How come you so friends with those black whores? You don't hardly talk to me. I said I liked them, but I liked her, too. She said, If you knew them for true, you wouldn't like them. They nothing but street whores. You know, once I was friends with them. We done a lot of things together, I knew them fifteen years, Evy and Rita maybe twenty, I been in the streets with them, side by side, Amsterdam, Lenox, West Harlem; in bad weather we covered each other. Then one day along come Malcolm X and they don't know me no more, they ain't talking to me. You too white. I ain't all that white. Twenty years. They ain't talking.

My friend Myrt called one day, that is, called from the street, called, Grace Grace. I heard and ran to the window. A policeman, the regular beat cop, was addressing her. She looked up, then walked away before I could yell my answer. Later on she told me that he'd said, I don't think Grace would appreciate you calling her name out like that.

What a mistake! For years, going to the park with my children, or simply walking down Sixth Avenue on a summer night past the Women's House, we would often have to thread our way through whole families calling up—bellowing, screaming to the third, seventh, tenth floor, to figures, shadows behind bars and screened windows, How you feeling? Here's Glena. She got big. Mami mami, you like my dress? We gettin you out baby. New lawyer come by.

And the replies, among which I was privileged to live for a few days, shouted down: —You lookin beautiful. What he say? Fuck you, James. I got a chance? Bye-bye. Come next week.

Then the guards, the heavy clanking of cell doors. Keys. Night.

I still had no pen or paper despite the great history of prison literature. I was suffering a kind of frustration, a sickness in the way claustrophobia is a sickness—this paper-and-penlessness was a terrible pain in the area of my heart, a nausea. I was surprised.

In the evening, at lights-out (a little like the Army or on good days a strict, unpleasant camp), women called softly from their cells. Rita hey Rita, sing that song—Come on, sister, sing. A few more importunings and then Rita in the cell diagonal to mine would begin with a ballad. A song about two women and a man. It was familiar to everyone but me. The two women were prison sweethearts. The man was her outside lover. One woman, the singer, was being paroled. The ballad told her sorrow about having been parted from him when she was sentenced, now she would leave her loved woman after three years. There were about twenty stanzas of joy and grief.

Well, I was so angry not to have pen and paper to get some of it down that I lost it all—all but the sorrowful plot. Of course she had this long song in her head, and in the next few nights she sang and chanted others, sometimes with a small chorus.

Which is how I finally understood that I didn't lack pen and paper but my own memorizing mind. It had been given away with a hundred poems, called rote learning, old-fashioned, backward, an enemy of creative thinking, a great human gift disowned.

Now there's a garden where the Women's House of Detention once stood. A green place, safely fenced in, with protected daffodils and tulips; roses bloom in it, too, sometimes into November.

The big women's warehouse and its barred blind windows have been removed from Greenwich Village's affluent throat. I was sorry when it happened; the bricks came roaring down, great trucks carried them away.

I have always agreed with Rita and Evelyn that if there are prisons, they ought to be in the neighborhood, near a subway— not way out in distant suburbs, where families have to take cars, buses, ferries, trains, and the population that considers itself innocent forgets, denies, chooses to never know that there is a whole huge country of the bad and the unlucky and the self-hurters, a country with a population greater than that of many nations in our world.

—1994

" Traveling "

My mother and sister were traveling south. The year was 1927. They had begun their journey in New York. They were going to visit my brother, who was studying in the South Medical College of Virginia. Their bus was an express and had stopped only in Philadelphia, Wilmington, and now Washington. Here, the darker people who had gotten on in Philadelphia or New York rose from their seats, put their bags and boxes together, and moved to the back of the bus. People who boarded in Washington knew where to seat themselves. My mother had heard that something like this would happen. My sister had heard of it, too. They had not lived in it. This reorganization of passengers by color happened in silence. My mother and sister remained in their seats, which were about three-quarters of the way back.

When everyone was settled, the bus driver began to collect tickets. My sister saw him coming. She pinched my mother: Ma! Look! Of course, my mother saw him, too. What frightened my sister was the quietness. The white people in front, the black people in back—silent.

The driver sighed, said, You can't sit here, ma'am. It's for them, waving over his shoulder at the Negroes, among whom they were now sitting. Move, please.

My mother said, No.

He said, You don't understand, ma'am. It's against the law. You have to move to the front.

My mother said, No.

When I first tried to write this scene, I imagined my mother saying, That's all right, mister, we're comfortable. I can't change my seat every minute. I read this invention to my sister. She said it was nothing like that. My mother did not try to be friendly or pretend innocence. While my sister trembled in the silence, my mother said, for the third time, quietly, No.

Somehow finally, they were in Richmond. There was my brother in school among so many American boys. After hugs and my mother's anxious looks at her young son, my sister said, Vic, you know what Mama did?

My brother remembers thinking, What? Oh! She wouldn't move? He had a classmate, a Jewish boy like himself, but from Virginia, who had had a public confrontation with a Negro man. He had punched that man hard, knocked him down. My brother couldn't believe it. He was stunned. He couldn't imagine a Jewish boy wanting to knock anyone down. He had never wanted to. But he thought, looking back, that he had been set down to work and study in a nearly foreign place and had to get used to it. Then he told me about the Second World War, when the disgrace of black soldiers being forced to sit behind white German POWs shook him. Shamed him.

About fifteen years later, in 1943, in early summer, I rode the bus for about three days from New York to Miami Beach, where my husband in sweaty fatigues, along with hundreds of other boys, was trudging up and down the streets and beaches to prepare themselves for war.

By late afternoon of the second long day, we were well into the South, beyond Richmond, maybe South Carolina or Georgia. My excitement about travel in the wide world was damaged a little by a sudden fear that I might not recognize Jess or he, me. We hadn't seen each other for two months. I took a photograph out of my pocket; yes, I would know him.

I had been sleeping waking reading writing dozing waking. So many hours, the movement of the passengers was something like a tide that sometimes ebbed and now seemed to be noisily rising. I opened my eyes to the sound of new people brushing past my aisle seat. And looked up to see a colored woman holding a large sleeping baby, who, with the heaviness of sleep, his arms so tight around her neck, seemed to be pulling her head down. I looked around and noticed that I was in the last white row. The press of travelers had made it impossible for her to move farther back. She seemed so tired and I had been sitting and sitting for a day and a half at least. Not thinking, or maybe refusing to think, I offered her my seat.

She looked to the right and left as well as she could. Softly she said, Oh no. I became fully awake. A white man was standing right beside her, but on the other side of the invisible absolute racial border. Of course, she couldn't accept my seat. Her sleeping child hung mercilessly from her neck. She shifted a little to balance the burden. She whispered to herself, Oh, I just don't know. So I said, Well, at least give me the baby. First, she turned, barely looking at the man beside her. He made no move. So, to my surprise, but obviously out of sheer exhaustion, she disengaged the child from her body and placed him on my lap. He was deep in child-sleep. He stirred, but not enough to bother himself or me. I liked holding him, aligning him along my twenty-year-old young woman's shape. I thought ahead to that holding, that breathing together that would happen in my life if this war would ever end.

I was so comfortable under his nice weight. I closed my eyes for a couple of minutes, but suddenly opened them to look up into the face of a white man talking. In a loud voice he addressed me: Lady, I wouldn't of touched that thing with a meat hook.

I thought, Oh, this world will end in ice. I could do nothing but look straight into his eyes. I did not look away from him. Then I held that boy a little tighter, kissed his curly head, pressed him even closer so that he began to squirm. So sleepy, he reshaped himself inside my arms. His mother tried to narrow herself away from that dangerous border, too frightened at first to move at all. After a couple of minutes, she leaned forward a little, placed her hand on the baby's head, and held it there until the next stop. I couldn't look up into her mother face.

I write this remembrance more than fifty years later. I look back at that mother and child. How young she is. Her hand on his head is quite small, though she tries by spreading her fingers wide to hide him from the white man. But the child I'm holding, his little face as he turns toward me, is the brown face of my own grandson, my daughter's boy, the open mouth of the sleeper, the full lips, the thick little body of a child who runs wildly from one end of the yard to the other, leaps from dangerous heights with certain experienced caution, muscling his body, his mind, for coming realities.

Of course, when my mother and sister returned from Richmond, the family at home wanted to know: How was Vic doing in school among all those gentiles? Was the long bus ride hard, was the anti-Semitism really bad or just normal? What happened on the bus? I was probably present at that supper, the attentive listener and total forgetter of information that immediately started to form me.

Then last year, my sister, casting the net of old age (through which recent experience easily slips), brought up that old story. First I was angry. How come you never told me about your bus ride with Mama? I mean, really, so many years ago.

I don't know, she said, anyway you were only about four years old, and besides, maybe I did.

I asked my brother why we'd never talked about that day. He said he thought now that it had had a great effect on him; he had tried unraveling its meaning for years—then life family work happened. So I imagined him, a youngster really, a kid from the Bronx in Virginia in 1927; why, he was a stranger there himself.

In the next couple of weeks, we continued to talk about our mother, the way she was principled, adamant, and at the same time so shy. What else could we remember . . . Well, I said, I have a story about those buses, too. Then I told it to them: How it happened on just such a journey, when I was still quite young, that I first knew my grandson, first held him close, but could protect him for only about twenty minutes fifty years ago.

—1997

Peacemeal

Because I believe in the oral tradition in literature, I have been opposed to cookbooks. But I must concede I missed my chance. My mother and grandmother died silent and intestate—as far as borscht and apple pie are concerned. Or is it possible that I wasn't listening, that I was down the block drinking chocolate sodas and watching gang fights, which, in my part of the Bronx, raged between the kids of the Third and Fourth International?

After that, there was the war, then at last the daily life of grown-ups for which supper is prepared every night. I entered that world without a cookbook, but with an onion, a can of tomato sauce, and a fistful of ground chuck. If I have progressed beyond that worried moment, it is not due to cookbooks but to nosiness and political friendships.

I know lots of these recipes, because in the forty-five minutes between work and a Peace Center meeting I have often had to call Mary or Karl and ask, "How the hell did you say I should do that fish?" I have also gathered some hot tips at the Resistance dinners, which we served once a week at the Peace Center to about a hundred young men who were *not* going to be part of the U.S. plan to torment and murder the Vietnamese people.

Certainly this cookbook is for people who are not so neurotically antiauthoritarian as I am—to whom one can say, "Add the juice of one lemon," without the furious response: "Is that a direct order?" This leads to the people who made this book. We are a local Peace Center in a public neighborhood. We have lived and worked in basements and lofts, churches and storefronts, and are now at St. Luke's Church.

Although I have not been very useful to the writing and editing of this cookbook, I now see it as a sensible action—since it's impossible to invite *everyone* to supper.

—1973

" Other Mothers "

The mother is at the open window. She calls the child home. She's a fat lady. She leans forward, supporting herself on her elbows. Her breasts are shoved up under her chin. Her arms are broad and heavy.

I am not the child. She isn't my mother. Still, in my head, where remembering is organized for significance (not usefulness), she leans far out. She looks up and down the block. The technical name of this first seeing is "imprint." It often results in lifelong love. I play in the street, she stands in the window. I wanted her to call me home to the dark mysterious apartment behind her back, where the father was already eating and the others sat at the kitchen table and waited for the child.

She was destined, with her meaty bossiness, her sighs, her suffering, to be dumped into the villain room of social meaning and psychological causation. When this happened to her, she had just touched the first rung of the great American immigrant ladder. Her husband was ahead of her, her intentional bulk kept him from slipping. Their children were a couple of rungs above them. She believed she would follow them all up into the English language, education, and respect.

Unfortunately, science and literature had turned against her. What use was my accumulating affection when the brains of the opposition included her son the doctor and her son the novelist? Because of them, she never even had a chance at the crown of apple pie awarded her American-born sisters and accepted by them when they agreed to give up their powerful pioneer dispositions.

What is wrong with the world? the growing person might have asked. The year was 1932 or perhaps 1942. Despite the world-wide fame of those years, the chief investigator into human pain is looking into his own book of awful prognoses. He looks up. Your mother, probably, he says.

As for me, I was not paying attention. I missed the mocking campaign.

The mother sits on a box, an orange crate. She talks to her friend, who also sits on an orange crate. They are wearing housedresses, flowered prints, large, roomy, unbelted, sleeveless. Each woman has a sweater on her lap, for coolness could arrive on an after-supper breeze and remain on the street for the summer night.

The first mother says, Ellie, after thirty you notice it? the years fly fast.

Oh, it's true, says the second mother.

I am so shocked by this sentence that I fall back against the tenement, breathing hard. I think, Oh! Years! The next sentence I remember is said about twenty minutes later.

Ellie, I'll tell you something, if you don't want to have so many children, don't sleep in a nightgown, sleep in pajamas, you're better off.

Sometimes even that doesn't help, says the second mother.

This is certainly an important sentence, I know. It is serious, but they laugh.

Summer night in the East Bronx. The men are inside playing pinochle. The men are sleeping, are talking shop. They have gone to see if Trotsky is still sitting on a bench in Crotona Park. The street is full of mothers who have run out of the stuffy house to look for air, and they are talking about my life.

At three o'clock in the autumn afternoon, the American-born mother opens the door. She says there is no subject that cannot be discussed with her because she was born in this up-to-date place, the U.S.A. We have just learned several words we believe are the true adult names of the hidden parts of our bodies, the parts that are unnameable. (Like God's name, says a brother just home from Hebrew school. He is smacked.) The American-born mother says those are the worst words of all, never to use them or think of them, but to always feel free to talk to her about anything else.

The Russian-born mother has said on several occasions that there are no such words in Russian.

At 3:45 the Polish-born mother stands at the kitchen table, cutting fine noodles out of dough. Her face is as white as milk, her skin is so fine you would think a Polish count had married an English schoolmistress to make a lady-in-waiting for Guinevere. You would think that later in life, of course.

One day an aunt tells us the facts, which are as unspeakable as the names of the body's least uncovered places. The grandfather of the Polish mother was a fair-haired hooligan. He waited for Easter. Through raging sexual acts on the body of a girl, his grief at the death of God might be modulated—transformed into joy at His Resurrection.

When you're home alone, lock the door double, said the milky Polish mother, the granddaughter of the fair hooligan.

On Saturday morning, at home, all the aunt-mothers are arguing politics. One is a Zionist, one is a Communist, one is a Democrat. They are very intelligent and listen to lectures at Cooper Union every week. One is a charter member of the ILGWU. She said she would leave me her red sash. She forgot, however. My friend and I listen, but decide to go to the movies. The sight of us at the door diverts their argument. Are you going out? Did you go to the bathroom first? they cry. We mean, did you go for *everything*? My friend and I say yes, but quietly. The married aunt with one child says, The truth, be truthful. Did you go? Another aunt enters the room. She has been talking to my own mother, the woman in whose belly I gathered flesh and force and became me. She says, There's real trouble in the world, leave the children alone. She has just come to the United States and has not yet been driven mad by all the requirements for total health and absolute sanitation.

That night, my grandmother tells a story. She speaks the common language of grandmothers—that is, not a word of English. She says, He came to me from the north. I said to him, No, I want to be a teacher. He said, Of course, you should. I said, What about children? He said, No, not necessarily children. Not so many, no more than two. Why should there be? I liked him. I said, All right.

There were six. My grandmother said, You understand this story. It means, make something of yourself.

That's right, says an aunt, the one who was mocked for not having married, whose beauty, as far as the family was concerned, was useless, because no husband ever used it.

And another thing, she said, I just reminded myself to tell you. Darling, she said, I know you want to go to the May Day parade with your friends, but you know what? Don't carry the flag. I want you to go. I didn't say you don't go. But don't carry the flag. The one who carries the flag is sometimes killed. The police go crazy when they see that flag.

I *had* dreamed of going forth with a flag—the American flag on July 4, the red flag of the workers on May Day. How did the aunt know this? Because I know you inside out, she said, since you were born. Aren't you *my* child, too?

The sister-mother is the one who is always encouraging. You can do this, you can get an A, you can dance, you can eat squash without vomiting, you can write a poem. But a couple of years later, when love and sex struck up their lively friendship, the sister was on the worried mother's side, which was the sad side, because that mother would soon be dying.

One evening I hear the people in the dining room say that the mother is going to die. I remain in the coat closet, listening. She is not going to die soon, I learn. But it will happen. One of the men at the table says that I must be told. I must not be spoiled. Others disagree. They say I have to go to school and do my homework. I have to play. Besides, it will be several years.

I am not told. Thereafter I devote myself to not having received that knowledge. I see that my mother gazes sadly at me, not reproachfully, but with an anxious look, as I wander among the other mothers, leaning on their knees, writing letters, making long phone calls. She doesn't agree with their politics, what will become of mine? Together with the aunts and grandmother she worked to make my father strong enough and educated enough so he could finally earn enough to take care of us all. She was successful. Despite this labor, time has passed. Her life is a known closed form. I understand this. Does she? This is the last secret of all. Then for several years, we are afraid of each other. I fear her death. She is afraid for my life.

Of which fifty years have passed, much to my surprise. Using up the days and nights in a lively manner, I have come to the present, daughter of mothers and mother to a couple of grown-up people. They have left home. What have I forgotten to tell? I have told them to be kind. Why? Because my mother was. I have told them when they drop a nickel (or even a shirt) to leave it for the gleaners. It says so in the Bible and I like the idea. Have I told them to always fight for mass transportation and not depend on the auto? Well, they know that. Like any decent kids of Socialist extraction, they can spot the oppressor smiling among the oppressed. Take joy in the struggle against that person, that class, that fact. It's very good for the circulation; I'm sure I said that. Be brave, be truthful, but do they know friendship first, competition second, as the Chinese say? I did say, Better have a trade, you must know something to be sure of when times are hard, you don't know what the Depression was like, you've had it easy. I've told them everything that was said *to* me or *near* me. As for the rest, there is ordinary place and terrible time—aunts, grandparents, neighbors, all my pals from the job, the playground and the PTA. It is on the occasion of their one hundred thousandth bicentennial that I have recalled all those other mothers and their histories.

—1975

Like All the Other Nations

I want to read this story to you first and then I want to say a few things. This is called "A Midrash on Happiness"; I don't think this is really a midrash, but I called it that.

What she meant by happiness, she said, was the following: she meant having (or having had) (or continuing to have) everything. By everything she meant, first, the children, then a dear person to live with, preferably a man, but not necessarily (by live with, she meant for a long time, but not necessarily). Along with and not in preferential order, she required three or four best women friends to whom she could tell every personal fact and then discuss on the widest, deepest, and most hopeless level the economy, the constant, unbeatable, cruel war economy, the slavery of the American worker to the idea of that economy, the complicity of male people in the whole structure, the dumbness of men (including her preferred man) on this subject. By dumbness, she meant everything dumbness has always meant: silence and stupidity. By silence, she meant refusal to speak; by stupidity, she meant refusal to hear. For happiness, she required women to walk with. To walk in the city arm in arm with a woman friend (as her mother had with aunts and cousins so many years ago) was just plain essential. Oh! those long walks and intimate talks, better than standing alone on the most admirable mountain or in the handsomest forest or hay-blown field (all of which were certainly splendid occupations for the wind-starved soul). More important even (though maybe less sweet because of age) than the old walks with boys she'd walked with as a girl, that nice bunch of worried left-wing boys who flew (always slightly handicapped by that idealistic wing) into a dream of paid-up mortgages with a small room for opinion and solitude in the corner of home. Oh, do you remember those fellows, Ruthy?

Remember? Well, I'm married to one.

But she had, Faith continued, democratically tried walking in the beloved city with a man, but the effort had failed since from about that age—twenty-seven or -eight—he had felt an obligation, if a young woman passed, to turn abstractedly away, in the middle of the most personal conversation, or even to say confidentially, Wasn't she something?—or clasping his plaid shirt, at the heart's level, Oh my God! The purpose of this: perhaps to work a nice quiet appreciation into thunderous heartbeat as he had been taught on pain of sexual death.

For happiness, she also required work to do in this world and bread on the table. By work to do, she included the important work of raising children righteously up. By righteously, she meant that along with being useful and speaking truth to the community, they must do no harm. By harm, she meant not only personal injury to the friend the lover the co-worker the parent (the city the nation) but also the stranger; she meant particularly the stranger in all her or his difference, who, because we were strangers in Egypt, deserves special goodness for life, or at least until the end of strangeness. By bread on the table, she meant no metaphor but truly bread, as her father had ended every single meal with a hunk of bread. By hunk, she was describing one of the attributes of good bread.

Suddenly she felt she had left out a couple of things: love. Oh yes, she said, for she was talking, talking all this time, to patient Ruth, and they were walking for some reason in a neighborhood where she didn't know the children, the pizza places, or the vegetable markets. It was early evening and she could see lovers walking along Riverside Park with their arms around one another, turning away from the sun, which now sets among the new apartment houses of New Jersey, to kiss. Oh, I forgot, she said, now that I notice, Ruthy I think I would die without love. By love, she probably meant she would die without being *in* love. By *in* love, she meant the acuteness of the heart at the sudden sight of a particular person or the way over a couple of years of interested friendship one is suddenly stunned by the lungs' longing for more and more breath in the presence of that friend, or nearly drowned to the knees by the salty spring that seems to beat for years on our vaginal shores. Not to omit all sorts of imaginings which assure great spiritual energy for months and, when luck follows truth, years.

Oh sure, love. I think so, too, sometimes, said Ruth, willing to hear Faith out since she had been watching the kissers, too, but I'm really not so sure. Nowadays it seems like pride, I mean overweening pride, when you look at the children and think we don't have time to do much (by time, Ruth meant both her personal time and the planet's time). When I read the papers and hear all this boom-boom bellicosity, the guys outdaring each other, I see we have to change it all—the world—without killing it absolutely—without killing it, that'll be the trick the kids'll have to figure out. Until that begins, I don't understand happiness— what you mean by it.

Then Faith was ashamed to have wanted so much and so little all at the same time—to be so easily and personally satisfied in this terrible place, when everywhere vast public suffering rose in reeling waves from the round earth's nation-states—hung in the satellite-watched air and settled in no time at all into TV sets and newsrooms. It was all there. Look up and the news of halfway round the planet is falling on us all. So for all these conscientious and technical reasons, Faith was ashamed. It was clear that happiness could not be worthwhile, with so much conversation and so little revolutionary change. Of course, Faith said, I know all that. I do, but sometimes walking with a friend I forget the world.

One of the things I did want to talk about is the moment at which in one's youth, or one's childhood even, one develops a kind of fidelity, or one is so struck by some event that one is changed by it. I think of this particularly when we talk of the Holocaust and its meaning to us all.

We seem to forget that our people really lived before the Holocaust and that they were also in a lot of hot water even before that. And I understood this first in a way that has never left me. This happened when I was about—well, what I remember is the size of the kitchen table. The table was just below eye level for me at the time. My mother was reading the newspaper, and she turned to my father—my father's name was Zenya (my parents were Russian Jews, like a lot of people)—she turned to my father and said, "Zenya, it's coming again."

Now, they had come to America in about 1905, and she said, "It's coming again." That's all I remember her saying. But I must have heard lots of other conversations. Because that was in the very beginning of the thirties, maybe earlier, and what she was talking about, of course, was the coming of Hitler. And she said, "It's coming *again*."

I think Marge Piercy has a poem about sleeping with your shoes under your pillow. Well, from that time on, in the middle of an extraordinarily happy childhood in a perfectly wonderful Jewish neighborhood with thousands of children and a first-class family quite friendly to my interests, and despite all the goodness, that incident at the kitchen table was so powerful that when I began to write, I thought, Should I really write in English? But since I didn't know any other language, there really was no choice.

The general feeling I had was that I might be forced to live somewhere else; and as a matter of fact, when my parents came to the United States, a lot of my mother's friends went to Argentina, and to Palestine, and to Brazil. So they had become Spanish or Portuguese speakers and writers. It didn't seem strange to me that I might live out my life in another country, and I think a lot of us must feel that way sometimes.

That moment at the kitchen table was one of the most striking events in my life. And who knows how I might have felt about things if that hadn't happened, because actually my family was a rather typical Socialist Jewish family. My father refused to go anywhere near a synagogue, although he allowed me to take my grandmother on holidays. On the other hand, we were clearly and peacefully Jewish, so there we were. I don't know in what direction my Judaism would have gone were it not for that moment.

I move from that to tell another story, or midrash, which I have talked about on various occasions. For those who grew up within that family there was, I suppose, a certain amount of feeling about being Jewish. I had a certain vanity about being Jewish. I thought it was really a great thing, and I thought this without any religious education. But I also really felt that to be Jewish was to be a socialist. I mean, that was my idea as a kid—that's what it meant to be Jewish. I got over that at a certain point, and so did a great many of my family members who were my age. But all this brought me to the story that I think of again and again. I don't understand why this story isn't told more often, especially in Israel. Or maybe it should be thrown away.

The story I'm referring to is about the judge and prophet Samuel (I think it's in Kings I). Samuel goes to speak to God and he says that the people want a king.

God says, "No no, that's wrong, it will be terrible for them if they have a king. They'll have this king, and they'll have to give up their vineyards and their concubines. They'll have a lot of trouble with this king, and they'll lose a great deal more than they'll gain."

So Samuel goes back, and he talks to the people. He tells them what God has said. But the people say, "No, we already told you what we want. We want a king."

So Samuel goes back to God and he says, "You know, they really want a king, but I think it's partly because they don't like me."

And God says, "No, that's not true; it's *me* they don't like."

Well, Samuel goes back to the people and tells them again that they really don't want a king. This time the people say, "Look, we want to tell you something. This is what we want. Listen: we want to be like all the other nations and have a king."

God hears this, and He understands they really mean it. And He sends Samuel on his way to look for Saul. So that's who they get: they get Saul.

I think of those lines again and again: "We want to be like all the other nations and have a king." And I think: We want to be like all the other nations and have great armies; we want to be like all the other nations and have nuclear bombs. I've told this story to other people, and asked them, What does that mean? We want to be like all the other nations and have these things—what does that mean? They say, "Why should Jews be better?"

I keep going back again to an idea, and it's a somewhat sentimental idea, but I'm stuck with it. And I'm entitled to be sentimental, since I'm already old, which you can tell because I'm up here. I had this idea that Jews *were* supposed to be better. I'm not saying they were, but they were *supposed* to be; and it seemed to me on my block that they often were. I don't see any reason in being in this world actually if you can't in some way be better, repair it somehow, and I think most of the people here feel something like that. So to be like all the other nations seems to me a waste of nationhood, a waste of statehood, a waste of energy, and a waste of life.

I want to say just two more things. First, I want to describe an experience I had in Israel about a year and a half ago. We visited a kibbutz, and we stayed a couple of nights with people there. All the members of this kibbutz were South African. They had come to this very kibbutz about thirty years ago. We found them interesting because they had come from South Africa. At one point I was talking with our hosts about what was happening in Israel, and this was a year and a half ago, not last week. Having lived on this kibbutz all these years, having raised their children there—their daughters now in the working world, their son in the army—the husband said to me, "I think we should talk to the PLO, and I really think we should get out of the territories."

I said, "Oh?" (I'm in another person's country, after all.)

And he said, "I never would have said anything like this two years ago, but I say it now because I don't like what's happening to my son and his friends. That's the main thing. Not just that they're in danger, but I don't like *what's happening* to them."

Well, we spoke a little further, and I was saying to him, "You're in danger, Israel is in great danger, and maybe the Diaspora is a kind of backup world for Jews," and so forth. And he looked at me and he said, "Ah, but who said that the Jews have to continue?"

Well, I was hit, stunned by that remark. And I was brought back to that day in my childhood when my mother spoke to my father at the kitchen table. Although it was a totally different sentence, it was one that I would not forget. He said to me, "Who says that we have to continue?" And such an idea had never occurred to me.

So I said to this man in Israel, this Israeli, and I spoke from the Diaspora, I said, "We *have* to." And now, two years later, I wonder, Yes, but how . . .

Now I just want to end with a short poem, which is about generations:

In my family
people who are 82 are very different
from people who are 92.

The 82-year-old people grew up
The year was 1914
This is what they knew   World War I
War   World War   War
That's why when they speak to the grandchild
they say   poor little one

The 92-year-old people grew up
The year was 1905
They went to prison
They went into exile
They said ah   soon
That's why when they speak to the grandchild
they say   first there will be revolution
then there will be revolution   then once more
then the earth itself will turn and turn
and cry out   Oh I have been made sick
Then you my little buds
will flower and save it.

—December 1988

II / Continuing

People, students particularly, tell me that Vietnam happened a long time ago. In the meantime, I have become old myself. Therefore it doesn't seem as long ago as some fairly recent events.

Unless one is a journalist or a soldier or a battered civilian, an American doesn't often have the opportunity to be present at a war. Of course, in the last couple of years interested men and women have visited, reported, and even entertained the wars in the Balkans. Several writers went to Hanoi before I did. A couple of them wrote books. Some were surprised later on that the Vietnamese did not turn out to be the absolutely intelligent reasonable people they seemed to be while being bombed.

But certainly the Vietnamese were naïve. They really believed— having fought beside the Allies as guerrillas during the Second World War, against the Vichy French; having witnessed in their Socialist youth the way the American Marshall Plan raised up defeated Germany—and having seen the financial if bossy way the Japanese were helped after their defeat—well, the Vietnamese assumed that the United States, once the war was over, would surely want to offer a little restitution, at least maybe make a few repairs to a hospital or a school, or send over some prostheses for the broken kids they didn't adopt.

Instead, an embargo was begun. The war continued with eco-

nomic assaults. If some early friends of Vietnam at war became disillusioned with Vietnam after the war, I want to suggest that the Vietnamese became embittered first.

In any event, I could hardly believe my extraordinary fortune in having been asked in 1969 to go to North Vietnam. I had been working against the war for about eight years by then. To see for myself! To understand! Of course, when you go to a foreign country where you don't know the language, you certainly can't see or hear too much "for yourself." On the long, long, twenty-six-hour flight I happened to notice a Diner's Club magazine in the seat pocket. In it I saw to my amazement a wonderful map of Vietnam—kind of skinny with a fat little Mekong Delta bottom. Along the coasts there were stars—or were they tiny hotels where mountain resorts with stunning views of the sea would be planted by American hotel companies once the war was over? This was in 1969.

So if my understanding of Vietnam was imperfect, my understanding of my own country was growing daily.

In the following articles, two of which were originally talks, I have described the nature and the disposition of our tasks. We were seven—five men and two women. We had not come to sightsee, but we did see the terrible topography of war from Hanoi to the Ben Hai River, the Demilitarized Zone, the DMZ. Three of us were filmmakers and made a film (impounded on our return). Four of us had the task of accompanying three POWs back home. The Vietnamese had agreed to return these men through the offices of the antiwar movement. But all this is described in the next few pages.

I should say that there are certain problems of what I'd call overlapping in the following reports—that is, repeated information, since I spoke these stories to different audiences. I have cut much of that kind of repetition out, but here and there kept some descriptions for emphasis. For instance, the greenness of Hanoi was described nostalgically by a Vietnamese woman I'd met in an airplane who had been sent south in 1954 along with her entire Cath-

olic school. It was what she dreamed of, that green, she said. And then the women who met me at the small Hanoi airport wanted to know if I had seen Hanoi's greenness. I thought it must be the way the New Yorker stumbling through slum side streets, truck-jammed avenues holds in her head the picture of the fish-shaped island city heavy with skyline at its gasping mouth. (My exiled city-loving head, anyway.)

A story that I've told many times, but didn't get to in immediate spoken reports: One does meet a few important people on journeys of this sort. You are assumed by your hosts to be an important person in your country, whereas you are really a kind of medium-level worker in one tendency in the nonviolent direct-action left wing of the antiwar movement. So it was that we seven met with Pham Van Dong, the second or third in power and authority in North Vietnam.

This is the way these meetings usually progressed: After people are seated in some order we are welcomed in the kindest way. Then one of us (we are also drinking tea) expresses our happiness to be here in the country of our imagination, at last. One of the young Vietnamese men says how happy they are to see us here. One of us remarks on the great courageous Vietnamese people and our shame at their suffering, for which we are responsible. No no, one or maybe two of them say, it is not your personal fault, we know the great American people would not permit it if they had the power. One of the young Vietnamese continues: Soon the war will be over and we will meet here or in the United States and our families will know one another. My own heart is quite full by then, and I assure them our children will certainly know one another, and we will dine in one another's houses—I see myself cooking up one of my good soups for Nhan and Phan (our translators), and so on and actually on.

Suddenly one of our number, a passionate young man, speaks up, wants to wash away all that cant, that false sentiment. He states, No no, you will not want to come to our country, it's a racist country, you will be looked down on for your color alone, it is a country with a violent tradition, you could not bear it, Vietnam is not its only terrible intervention. But one of the young Vietnamese is horrified to hear this speech, this disloyalty. He cries out, How can you talk about your own country like that? How can you say these things about your own country? Have you forgotten Emerson? Have you forgotten Whitman? Jefferson?

We are all silenced. Americans and Vietnamese. Our American friend is abashed. He sits quietly. He does not, as I feared he might, begin to explain cautious Emerson, slaveholding Jefferson.

A couple of days later in Quangbinh province, we are reminded that South Vietnam's Premier Diem and North Vietnam's General Giap both come from this beloved province of fire, one an American puppet, the other the genius general of Dien Bien Phu and—as it turns out—of the defeat of the United States six years later. We are expected to have learned something from this fact about the contradictory—even warring-to-the-teeth—factions in one's own indivisible always beloved country.

The poem "Two Villages" and the "Report from North Vietnam" are from a talk I gave at the Washington Square Methodist Church after returning from Vietnam. The year was 1969, the month August.

I didn't know it at the time but '69 was a key year, the one in which the war might have ended, but Nixon and Kissinger decided (while talking peace) to continue the war. (See Haldeman's diaries, also the resignation of Kissinger's key aides* over that decision.) When our little delegation stopped in Vientiane we were told by a young (at the time) fellow named, I believe, T. D. Allman, that B52 bombers were flying over Laos. We tried to talk about this at

---

* One of those who resigned is Anthony Lake, National Security head in the first Clinton administration, and recently tormented by the Senate Foreign Relations Committee in hearings about his possible new job as head of the CIA (which he didn't get).

press conferences in New York, but were not heard, or at least not taken seriously. By the spring of 1970, the destruction of Cambodia had begun.

I must mention Lady Borton here. She was, is, a Friend, a Quaker. Her job during the war was to fit prostheses on Vietnamese civilian amputees. She was the woman who brought a congressman and the press to My Lai. She's lived in both South Vietnam and North Vietnam. She published a book, Sensing the Enemy, *about the Vietnamese boat people.*

I wrote a preface to her most recent book, After Sorrow, *which is about living among Vietnamese families in the Mekong Delta in 1989 and '90. I haven't included it because almost everything in that preface appears in the early reports in this section. But attention to her and her work belong in this book. I often wish I could have done this world some good in that Lady Borton way, offering political understanding and labor* directly *to those whose suffering was surely my responsibility.*

I believe "Conversations in Moscow" needs no explanation. It seems fairly clear that we wanted Russian dissidents to know they had the active support of most of the antiwar movement. We hoped these remarkable people would recognize the troubles of those suffering U.S.-exported repression—Chile, Guatemala as examples. Of course, the Russians explained, that's what it said in Pravda, *too, so how could they believe it?*

 *Home*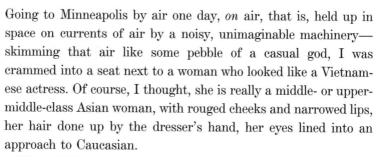

Going to Minneapolis by air one day, *on* air, that is, held up in space on currents of air by a noisy, unimaginable machinery— skimming that air like some pebble of a casual god, I was crammed into a seat next to a woman who looked like a Vietnamese actress. Of course, I thought, she is really a middle- or upper-middle-class Asian woman, with rouged cheeks and narrowed lips, her hair done up by the dresser's hand, her eyes lined into an approach to Caucasian.

Why did I think she was an actress? Because I've been in Vietnam. In 1969 I traveled by jeep on a dirt road called National Highway 1 from Hanoi to Vinh Linh, a tiny hamlet on the DMZ near the Ben Hai River. During this journey along the Vietnamese coast we traveled under what could be considered the American sky—since that's where Americans were seen, floating, flying, dropping tons of ordnance (bombs), sometimes even falling down out of their planes to death, injury, prison on the Vietnamese earth. We often stopped in villages or in fields that had been villages to see how people could live on the floor of blast and carnage. We saw rosy, rouged theater groups playing to the thin, pale people, making some kind of cheeriness in those caves and underground households. Since then, I never see an Asian woman

wearing lots of makeup without thinking, Ah! an actress! A theater person.

Naturally I wanted to speak to my neighbor; she had the window seat and there was no reason for her to turn toward me.
When we were about twenty-five minutes from Minneapolis, I
said, Excuse me, but where are you from? She looked at me out
of a half minute's silence. I'm Vietnamese, she said. Then I asked
her the following questions all at once, in rapid, nervous order:
What city are you from? What province? Do you have children?
Where do you live now? When did you come here—to this
country?

She answered in a friendly but factual way. I am from Saigon.
I have two children. I am here six months. My children are in the
Sisters School in Maryland, the nuns that helped us get here. My
husband is dead. He is an American. German. I live with his
family in Wisconsin.

Then I asked her: Was your husband a soldier? Were you born
in Saigon?

No. No, he was a businessman. He was much older than I. He
was very rich; real estate was only one of his businesses. He was
in Saigon from the late fifties. He died of a long illness. Oh, we
have lost over $200,000 in the rush to get here on time. No, I
was not born in Saigon. I was born in Hanoi.

We drank our pre-landing orange juice for a while. I had to
make a decision. Should I tell her that I had been in Hanoi, that
I had gone with others as a political antiwar woman to record
the devastation of American war and bring back (at the North
Vietnamese initiative) three American prisoners of war? I
thought, No. Better not. God knows, she could become angry and
attack me with the sorrow of her exile. Then I thought (since
opposing thoughts often succeed one another), Yes, I *will* tell her.
Otherwise this air talk will remain just another chitchat, nothing
moved further, no knowledge gained on either side. So I told her

I had been to Hanoi a few years earlier. I had been a guest of the North Vietnamese and I had worked against the war. With all my strength, I added.

You were in Hanoi? she asked, turning to me, probably to see my eyes which had seen her home. What was it like? How were the people? And the streets?

I told her I had walked every morning along the Lake of the Restored Sword. I had lived in the Hotel of Reunification.

What's that? she said with a little irritation. Then: What else?

I told her there were trolley tracks along the park and the cars were packed with people, stuffed, their heads and legs and arms stuck out of doors and windows. I told her I saw a military parade, but the lines were not straight, and children and women joined the march and then went off. I walked up and down streets of French Mediterranean houses.

She said, Most people think Saigon is much handsomer than Hanoi. They think Hanoi is gray. Was it much damaged?

I told her about the individual shelters sunk along the streets like big garbage cans for individuals caught in sudden bombing. In 1969 it had seemed a poor, bike-riding city. But the trees were wonderful, plane trees, and what was it—eucalyptus.

Yes, it's green; it is green.

Why did you leave? I asked.

Oh, long ago, she said. In '54, when the French left us, we were taken south, tens of thousands of schoolchildren, by the sisters—in trains and vans and buses. So that we should not grow up to become Communists and forget our Jesus. My father was already dead, but my mother—I never saw my dear mother again. I remember I looked back, she said, and in my mind it has remained always a mist of greenness.

In '69, my friends and I flew into Hanoi, from Phnom Penh, a big busy city, stinking of bad automobiles and, streaming among them, the Cambodian ricksha runners hauling upper blue-collar workers from office to lunch to home. We were greeted at the little hidden Hanoi airport by women and men, their arms full of flowers for us—Americans who amazingly hadn't flown all the way to Vietnam, 12,000 miles, just to kill Vietnamese.

The woman from the Women's Solidarity Committee took my arm. She spoke enough English to be able to ask, after embraces and the delivery of the flowers, and the taking of my arm as we walked, loving the sight of one another, toward the car, Grace, from the air, tell me, did you see our city, how beautiful and green it is, did you see our green Hanoi?

—1980

" Two Villages "

I

In Duc Ninh a village of 1,654 households
Over 100 tons of rice and casava were burned
18,138 cubic meters of dike were destroyed
There were 1,077 air attacks
There is a bomb crater that measures 150 feet across
It is 50 feet deep

Mr. Tat said: The land is more exhausted than the people
I mean to say that the poor earth
is tossed about
thrown into the air again and again
it knows no rest

whereas the people have dug tunnels
and trenches   they are able in this way
to lead normal family lives

II

In Trung Trach
a village of 850 households
a chart is hung in the House of Tradition

rockets	522
attacks	1201
big bombs	6998
napalm	1383
time bombs	267
shells	12291
pellet bombs	2213

Mr. Tuong of the Fatherland Front
has a little book
in it he keeps the facts
carefully added

—1969

"*Report from North Vietnam*"

Our interpreter Nhan said, "Grace, if you would stay another two weeks, I could teach you the tune of the language. Speaking is singing—a lot of up and down anyway. The word *Hoa* means flower, *Hoa* means harmony. The tune's important. Okay."

Our twenty-one days in Vietnam happened in three parts. The first—Hanoi, the city, the officials, the organizations, useful information, making friends. All necessary to the second part, a seven-day, 1,100-kilometer journey to the Ben Hai River, which is the seventeenth parallel, the riverbank of American power. We washed our hands and feet there, a lot of symbolism. Reality too, almost—the roadway was shelled right after we left. American reconnaissance planes which we'd seen above us had noticed a jeep or a movement.

A word about Hanoi. One of our hosts said, from the plane, "Did you see how green we are?" Yes. Old trees, parks, lakes, a beautiful city, old, much of it in bad shape, no new construction in the city. The suburbs had been built for the workers, and bombed flat by us. Hanoi was wildly defended—from the rooftops everywhere—one of seven pilots we talked to said, "Downtown Hanoi, the flak, you don't know what it was like—the air was absolutely black."

As we started from Hanoi on fair roads, immediately the de-

struction of public buildings, hospitals, schools was apparent. The
first city we came to—Phu Ly—totally destroyed. We were not
military men, not even people who'd been to wars, we weren't
bored by the repetition; we didn't even get used to it. So the
destruction we saw happened first to our eyes: the mud and straw
huts, and beyond them the cities, where a wall or two of small
brick stucco-covered houses remained, and maybe one wall of the
larger public buildings. And all the way on National Highway 1,
the people—something like Fourteenth Street in Manhattan for
about 650 kilometers—going back and forth, about their business
of life and repair, carrying on their backs, on bamboo poles, bal-
anced baskets of salt, water spinach, fertilizer, young shoots for
transplanting, mud and stones for the roads, firewood for cooking.
Bicycles doing the work of trucks. The children—little boys
lounging on water buffalo, fishing with nets like sails in the rivers
and ponds—and bomb craters. All this life moving on the road
and alongside the road, so that Ching, our driver, who looked like
a tough Puerto Rican kid, drove hundreds of miles with his fist
on the horn.

"Humans out of the way, here come the Progressive American
People, to view the insanity of their countrymen. Let them deal
with this disgust and shame."

South—past the Ham Rong Bridge, near Thanh Hoa—another pilot said, "What? It's still standing?" Yes, standing—
trucks, cars, bikes move over it continuously. We note its twisted
girders shot with holes.

The Ham Rong Bridge, the pride of the defenders of Thanh
Hoa, was the last bridge we saw that withstood the bombing. As
we moved farther south along the road, the American intention
was clear. The first order was to kill the bridges and destroy
transportation. On the reconnaissance maps, a bridge was a
bridge in some head, so for a couple of miles every river looked
as though maniacs had been let loose by a fool. Hundreds and
hundreds of bomb craters—whether the river (and bridge) was

2 feet wide or 1,000 feet wide. The next day, at whatever the small cost—$100 at most—a few planks restored traffic over the mountain streams. The craters—at a couple of thousand per bomb—cost the American taxpayer close to one million dollars.

The larger bridges were more of a problem, but we saw the remains of half a dozen bridges at some rivers. And the repairs varied—on occasion, bound bamboo pontoons; often the riverbed was raised with stones and we drove hubcap-deep across the river. But all along the roads piles of stones were prepared for the next attack of the madmen. Gangs of young girls working and boys, too—all of them, for no good reason, cheery and unbelieving at the sight of us.

Wherever we went, people said—greeting us hospitably, to put us at ease, guessing our shame—"We distinguish between the American imperialist war maker and the American people." The child in the street believes this. "It's not so hard to explain," Dang Thai Mai, a writer, one of our hosts, said. "After all, General Giap and Diem come from Quangbinh—from the same district."

Okay. So. Trying to be a logical American, I or we think, Well, of course it's a war and they are bombing communication, transportation. It's true, they are overkilling the Vietnamese countryside and the little brooks, but that's America for you, they have overkilled flies, bugs, beetles, trees, fish, rivers, the flowers of their own American fields. They're like overgrown kids who lean on a buddy in kindergarten and kill him.

Then we leave National Highway 1 and move into the villages to live for a few days in a guest house in a small field, which before we left was plowed, manured, and planted with groundnuts up to our door. I guess they expected no immediate guests. The villages. The village Trung Trach was in the Land of Fire. Mr. Tat said, "The Land of Fire for three reasons: first, the fire of the burning heat; second, the fire of continuous *day and night* American bombardment for three years, so that people never left their tunnels; and third, the fires of resistance that burned in the heart of the people."

In all of Quangbinh province, not one brick house stood. This is true of the cities on the main road, too. Hoxa, the beautiful city—there's nothing there—grass—some doorsteps. People in Hanoi asked in nostalgic pride, "Did you see Hoxa?" Donghoi— a city of 30,000—something like pictures of Pompeii. A city shaped like New York with its nose in the water, a great outdoor theater whose terraced seats remain, a magnificent blasted Catholic church (the French, in their war, spared the churches). Nobody lives in Donghoi. These cities will not be rebuilt until the Americans leave Vietnam. In the hills a new Donghoi will be built.

I return to the villages. The village Nien Trach Nuc Ninh, Trung Trach, and the village T and D in Vinh Linh Zone at the DMZ. It turned out that these villages far off the roads and highways were military targets, too. Each village had a House of Tradition, which kept the artifacts of other victories—the weapons with which they'd fought the French, Japanese, Chinese. Also deactivated CBUs, pellet bombs in one village, the belongings of the pilot Dixon, who is buried near the sea—with a cross over his grave—in case his mother should want to come see it after the war. It was in the bombed-out blasted torn-up villages where the entire population had been driven underground to live in tunnels for three years, to suffer in underground hospitals, to study in underground schools. It was into these villages that pilots floated or tumbled out of burning planes.

It's a people's war. The Army and the people are interchangeable in many cases. The Army sometimes works on the roads, the people in the self-defense units: the girls' militia, the old men's militia in the villages take to the artillery, to their rifles, to anything handy. The villages are bombed, restored in mud and thatch, to cultivate the land, to make paths between the craters which in one village had become duck ponds, fisheries, and irrigation sources. Water spinach, a wonderful vegetable, was planted in some. They could do this because nobody left the land or ran from the Land of Fire. They dug underground and lived in the rooms we saw, and crawled on hands and knees to other rooms and exits through supported tunnels—as we did. The people said, We could not have held out if we hadn't, in these tunnels, been able to lead a normal life. Normal life is very important, family life, children's education, care of the sick and old, rice culti- vation—along with the resistance." Threads were pulled, but the cloth of life mysteriously held. They are naturally proud to have held the greatest power in the world at bay.

I think they hide the cost—they did not, except in two or three cases, introduce us to the severely wounded or ill. The people we saw looked well after six, seven months of no bombing—or very little. The children, hundreds and hundreds, looked well. We did not visit hospitals. Bach Mai was bombed six months later.

So this is what we saw there: the destruction of the cities, roads, the bridges, and finally the villages. Some people do not like the word "genocide" and we will leave the word alone; still, in this kind of war, every person takes part, and the next thing a logical military brain hooks into is the fact that every person is a military target, or the mother of a military target, and they live in the same house; and since all military targets must be de- stroyed, it follows that the whole people must be destroyed. And that is what I think was attempted and that is what was abso- lutely thwarted.

The prisoners. The American war prisoners. This is what we were told about their treatment. When they first fall to the Vietnamese fields or dikes (which they've just bombed), they are taken into the care of the militia or self-defense unit, sometimes a couple of girls or a boy or two of sixteen. No abuse is permitted, and in only one case of seven men we talked to was any attempted.

One of the reasons Captain Wesley Rumble was so sick on the airplane on our return is that the Army doctors loaded him and his stomach was filled with Darvon and Librium for his worries.

From what he told us, he was used to traditional Vietnamese medicines for stomach ailments.

The third fact that emerged from our conversations with these men was the adequacy of the food. Almost all said that they were fed more than their guards—the Vietnamese think the Americans have large frames which must be served. The truth is, the men lost a tremendous amount of weight in the one to three years of imprisonment. The diet is mostly vegetable soup, with a little pork on occasion, and bread and some rice. Monotonous to an American but adequate. On a more varied Vietnamese diet, in three weeks we all lost weight. I lost eleven pounds.

Now, the Vietnamese say they release these men from time to time, as an act in their own humanitarian tradition. They *still* consider these Americans war criminals. They *hope* that some repentance has set in. They bring them news of the world, through occasional radios and books. The Americans all asked questions that showed they were somewhat informed but not well. I wish they could see more American periodicals or papers. The statements of congressmen and the tremendous feeling against the war, as reported in our own establishment press, would be more useful as propaganda. The pilots are sometimes taken to the places they bombed, so they can see the land and the people —who seem only to be things when viewed at 650 miles an hour from a height of thousands of feet.

The three prisoners we brought home were taken to the museums in Hanoi and to the zoo before they left with us.

There's no time and I want to tell two or three things about the prisoners. They said many things I haven't sorted out yet— some of which horrified us, such as, "To be truthful I really liked bombing." I don't understand this remark, and for now I don't intend to. "I wish I'd met you people in '66"—the same man. "I went into this a military man and that's how I'm coming out."

Talking to another Vietnamese military man, one who worked with the prisoners, I said, "You release these men and many of them may make bad propaganda. They say one thing to you, then another thing later on radio or television." "That's all right," he said. "We know they have terrible pressure from the American Army and Navy, but they know the truth." I press forward, because I'm anxious: "Yes, you feel close to them, but they may not say what they feel." He says, "That's all right. We know it. They will go out and say something on radio, they will say something on TV bad, but at night they will go home and they will whisper the truth to their wife."

—1969

Everybody Tells the Truth

Why did we older people waste time answering the ones who said, Who are you, you middle-aged do-gooders, to tell some kid he's better off in jail? We could have saved not only Bruce Anello* but the Vietnamese peasant he shot, who ran ahead of him across the field holding his ripped guts. We didn't work resistance hard enough. We didn't breathe with the hundreds of Vietnamese who would live if one American with his arms full of technology chose not to kill.

Now the dead and the living are telling us about the war. No matter whose side they're on, they tell the truth. When Lieutenant Robert Frishman, Navy airman, returned POW, runs around the country crying, "I was tortured, I was tortured," it is certainly true. He fell out of a plane from a great height. His elbow, with which he might have been a great warrior (and still may become an administrative admiral), was shattered. He is a tall, bossy person, and he was at the tough call of small, yellowish people, some no higher than his hip. He had to wear a collarless gown and pajama pants like hospital patients he may have re-

* Bruce Anello was a young soldier who kept a heartbreaking diary of his days in Vietnam and whom our movement was not strong enough to save from death—along with over 50,000 others.

membered. No brass buttons on this nightie, no cuffs, no neck buttons or tie to hold his throat, no way of being himself. When on his way home he cried out, tears included, to the State Department official, "I'm a military man, I've got to have my uniform," it was ordered at the Tel Aviv airport and practically stood by itself, waiting in Athens a couple of hours later, along with an assortment of naval attachés, old pals who understood.

In Vietnam he told us, "You know, compared to the Vietnamese, we pilots are living high on the hog . . . We eat better than the guards." Over an American steak, back home at last, it seemed to him he must have been starving, and that was true. In Vietnam he told Captain Than (who happily and innocently reported this to us) that he would "go home and work as a teacher, go deep into the study of social science, there is a need, biology, too." He spoke the truth; but he was being tortured. His brains were being washed, as they say in Central Intelligence, and it hurt. Thinking of the New Man they hoped to create someday, the Vietnamese were trying to turn Lieutenant Frishman into a useful citizen, which for him would be a 180-degree turn. In pain his mouth seized a couple of social options. But within four days, among his very own (I mean, me, Rennie Davis, Jimmy Johnson, Linda Evans, and the Newsreel gang—the delegation which had gone to North Vietnam to return the POWs to the United States), he began his cry—well, chant—which was "I came into this a military man, and I'm going out a military man."

Before we left the little Hanoi–Vientiane plane for the American world just outside Vietnam, all sorts of naval and U.S. state power climbed aboard, beefy, cheery in ordinary suits and summer mufti. Lieutenant Robert Frishman, former prisoner of the Vietnamese, new prisoner of the Americans, in a paroxysm of painful saluting said, "Sir! Sir! I have not been debriefed. When will you debrief me? I haven't said anything, sir. I won't talk until I've been debriefed." I am ashamed to say that I laughed at this fit before authority and saw the cocky, joyful meaning of my own pacifist anarchism. Still, I knew that his words proceeded from a head that had been nearly turned (tortured) and was turning back in pain.

Where had he bombed? He came down near Hanoi in the black flak he had dropped on the steel bridge at Thanh Hoa a number of times. He couldn't believe it was still standing. Though on the mountain not too far away it said in white stones, as large as a plane can see, DETERMINED TO WIN.

There were five other POWs we met in Hanoi in August '69. I want to tell who they were, where they came down, what their target areas looked like when they were finished. They made a few remarks to us when we talked about their first crash—contacts with the Vietnamese people. These are fairly verbatim—somewhat staccato, because my shorthand left out a lot of connective tissue in order to get the verbs and nouns right.

Most of them flew F105s out of the American sanctuary in Thailand; others, off carriers in the Gulf of Tonkin.

The first man is Robinson Reisner, Lieutenant Colonel, U.S. Air Force, shot down September 1965, ten miles north of Thanh Hoa.

"Down 16th September, 9:00 a.m. Had not reached target, treetops, to get away from fire. Saw smoke tracers, airplane received jolts, cockpit filled with smoke, only had time to get out. When I looked, plane hit ground burning. I landed on paddy wall. Jumped down, ligaments tore, rolled in rice field on shoulder . . . had drawn pistol, nearly fatal mistake. Looked around, saw civilians and military militia. Young man, a boy, ordered me to drop gun, raise hands. Obeyed order. Pleasant surprise. I was not abused, not manhandled. This was remarkable. We had dealt them a lot of misery. Heavy-hit people, they had right to intense feeling against me. They tied my arms, grimaced because of tight ropes. Man loosened them. A comfort . . . they weren't interested in abusing me, I started to learn. They led me to a hamlet court-yard. I took bath, washed, clean clothes. Food, tea next day. I was sick, shock, pain, back and knees. Wanted to give me rice. Doctor came, inoculation, treated wounds and pain. People came to look, no one threatening, raised voices. Strange behavior on part of people I had just been bombing. Acts of discipline. Seeing my discomfort, they raised my head. Just an act of kindness. Different."

Roger Dean Ingvalsen, Major, Air Force, F105 shot down May 28, 1968, in Quangbinh province near Donghoi.

"Hit by 37 mm. unit aircraft fire while strafing truck. Caught fire. Lost control, forced to eject. Boy sixteen years old captured me with three, four others. Didn't know how I'd be treated, scores angry inhabitants tried to punish me. Militiaman interfered, protected me. Gave me water. Was not wounded, no medical attention. 28 days to this city. Treated well by guards."

Donghoi in Quangbinh was a city of 33,000. It had been beautiful with a great, grass-terraced open theater, an ancient thousand-year-old wall. Like my city, New York, it lay with its nose in the water. No one lives in Donghoi, no houses in Donghoi. White doorsteps as though Baltimore had disappeared into grass.

Mr. Gnach, war crimes commission head of Quangbinh province, asked, "Why do Americans hate this province and this city so? They have even smashed the Catholic cathedral." We stood in the blue, pink, and orange rubble of a famous pagoda.

Then we stayed for a couple of days in little villages near Donghoi where families had lived underground for two years in tunnels because of day-and-night bombing. A Captain Boyd, speaking as a Winter Soldier witness a couple of weeks ago, explained, "I don't know why it was customary for us pilots to dump all unexpended ordnance on Donghoi. It wasn't an order. It was just customary."

Edwin Frankmiller, Lieutenant J.G., shot down May 22, 1968, photo reconnaissance west of Vinh.

"Had to eject, landed, dislocated knee. Captured soon by peasants in militia, carried me to hut. Given injections. Water. Medical man around put knee, back, and leg in cast. Okay for walking. When stationed on ship I thought if shot down I'd receive bad treatment, and I thought that was war. Little known historically. Medical treatment was good beginning."

Vinh City had been an industrial center of about 80,000. It existed powerfully in 1969 in decentralized settlements in the countryside. In one of these villages, a small, shy woman asked me, "How is Mrs. Morrison? Tell her we think always about Norman Morrison."*

Anthony Charles Andrews was a captain in the Air Force, shot down in October 1967.

"As I bailed out I said, what am I doing here? Bruises on leg from ejection seat. I landed in a rice field a hundred yards from village. Three young men immediately approached. One had rifle. Fired it. Being in a highly populated area I had no intentions. I surrendered at once. Young people there. Very excited. Big event in their life and mine. Wise to be placed in hands of military. They showed fair restraint in dealing. Concerned about conditions. Informed about how to treat military men. We were short

* In protest against the widening war, in 1965 Norman Morrison immolated himself.

time in the village. Young men and women took charge. I was impressed. Led from village for miles. Had no shoes. They'd been removed because of serious bruises. I made this known. Taken to bomb shelter, kept overnight. I did not expect to be shot at, but expected poor treatment. Close to target area. Many times their emotions were strong. People not friendly, some downright hostile. But their restraint . . ."

Thinking of Bruce Anello, I have written all this, because it seems likely that the troops will be brought home. (President Nixon also tells the truth.) The men who will not come home are the high-fliers, the meat-eating birds of our Air Force. Waiting in Thailand or Cambodia or Laos within easy devastation distance of all Indochina. The war will go on.

And that means, too, that 339 American pilots will spend many more years in exile, condemned by American anti-Communist insanity and the administration's perversion of their situation.

—1971

"The Man in the Sky Is a Killer"

There's a good deal of sentiment and dreamy invention attached to the American prisoners of war in North Vietnam. Politicians and newsmen often talk as though these pilots had been kidnapped from a farm in Iowa or out of a canoe paddling the waterways of Minnesota.

In reality, they were fliers shot down out of the North Vietnamese sky, where they had no business to be; out of that blueness they were dumping death on the people, the villages, the fields. And none of these men were forced into the job. They were not drafted, they volunteered. They were trained. Then, out of the American sanctuaries in Thailand, the carrier nests at sea, they rose, a covey of brilliant down-swoopers, high-fliers to do their work. Each one of these men may have accomplished half a dozen My Lais in any evening.

The Vietnamese have a saying: The man in the sky is a killer, bring him down; but the man on the ground is a helpless human being. The men who were shot down, the human beings who fell alive into the shallow paddies, on beaches, into villages they'd just bombed, became POWs. Their Vietnamese captors were often half their size, half-starved, stiff with the grief of continuous loss of dear family, but survivors with a determination to win. They shared their squash and water spinach with these captured Americans whose great frames immediately (it's been reported) suffered the lack of beefsteak.

Nine prisoners of war have been returned to the United States, the last in 1969. I was a member of the peace movement delegation which escorted the last three from Hanoi to home. While in North Vietnam we talked to four other prisoners. I believe that the Vietnamese had great hopes for this program of POW return. With obvious logic, the Vietnamese had asked that the United States government not use these returned pilots against them again. But the United States was not ready then for any easing of war or righteousness.

Therefore, at the present time, they are all in or associated with the armed forces. Some are training younger pilots to fly out again and again over that tortured country, that laboratory for American weapons engineers. Some are part of the propaganda mill that continues the air war and enlarged it to include Laos and Cambodia—that makes new POWs.

I submit that the families of these men who, on the ground, are human beings, whose time of life is being used up in prison camps—these families must know that their men will not come home until the war ends. Removing American ground troops from South Vietnam will not end the Indochina air war. Automating the battlefields will not end the Indochina air war. Propaganda and punishing war will not bring those men home.

I would like to add two recollections that are painful to me, but I want to share the recollections and the pain.

At a festive dinner in a Hanoi hotel, a celebration of departure after arduous years of imprisonment, one of the pilots turned his ingenuous American boy's face of about thirty to me. He said, "Gosh, Grace, to be truthful I really liked bombing."

One summer day before I left for North Vietnam, a woman called me at home. She was a pilot's wife. She had not heard from her husband in two and a half years. She asked me to get information about him in Hanoi, if any existed. I tried. But no one had seen or heard of him, neither the Vietnamese nor the pilots we talked to. When I came home I had to call and tell her this. She asked me why the Vietnamese insisted on keeping the pilots.

I explained that they were considered war criminals who had come 10,000 miles to attack a tiny country in an undeclared and brutal war.

She said, "Well, they're airmen. They're American officers."

I told her about the villagers living in wet dark tunnels for years, shattered by pellets, seared by napalm—I told her only what my own eyes had seen, the miles of maniac craters—

She said, "Oh, Mrs. Paley, villages and people! My husband wouldn't do that."

I held the phone for a while in silence. I took a deep breath. Then I said, "Oh? Well, I guess it must have been someone else."

—1972

Thieu Thi Tao is twenty-three years old—the age of my own American children. That coincidence helps me to think about her. As I write about Tao, I call up the lives my children have led these past six years and hold those images in mind; then I reflect on the fragments of information we have about Thieu Thi Tao.

Thieu Thi Tao has spent those six years as a prisoner. She was arrested in 1968, when she was seventeen, a student at Marie Curie High School in Saigon. We don't know the exact day.

The government of the Republic of Vietnam says it has no political prisoners. The United States ambassador says this must be true, since the government says it is true. But Thieu Thi Tao was arrested "for spreading Communist propaganda"; there is no other charge against her.

In prison, Thieu Thi Tao was beaten on the head with truncheons. Her head was locked between two steel bars. Water was forced down her throat. She was suspended above the ground.

Then, on November 20, 1968, she was transferred to national police headquarters. The Vietnamese Catholic priest Father Chan Tin, in a plea for international concern about her case, wrote that she was "further beaten and subjected to electric shock."

"She's become insane," Father Tin wrote, "unable to sleep for fifteen days, believing herself to be a pampered dog that could only eat bread and milk. Not being given these, she refused to eat and became so weak she couldn't talk. When the wind blew she wanted to fly."

Nothing like that has happened to my children.

Late in 1969, Thieu Thi Tao was transferred to the island prison of Con Son, along with her sister, Tan, who has since been released. We heard nothing for nearly a year, until July 2, 1970—an extraordinary day, when Don Luce managed to lead two United States congressmen into a forbidden section of Con Son, where prisoners were held in tiger cages.

There is a picture of the congressmen, William Anderson and Augustus Hawkins, looking down with Don Luce into the cages where some prisoners had lived for years, shackled, some to the point of being permanently deformed. On that day Thieu Thi Tao, who speaks English, described for the congressmen exactly what was happening to her and the other women.

She was one of five women in her cage. A bucket of lime stood above each cell. At different times, the women were doused with lime or sprayed with tear gas. During their menstrual periods, they were given no means to keep themselves clean.

Anderson and Hawkins reported what they had seen and heard; photographs and interviews were published; there was a great uproar, and it was assumed that the publicity would destroy the cages. But on January 17, 1971, the U.S. Navy gave a $400,000 contract to Raymount, Morrison, Knudson, Brown, Root and Jones to build 384 new "isolation cells"—two square feet smaller than the old ones.

Thieu Thi Tao lived three years in these cages. She had been sentenced to two years by the military court. But it was said of her, in 1971: "She is still obstinate."

Tao's mother was in Thu Duc Prison for Women at that time; she wrote this poem for her two daughters:

Dearest Children,

My heart is torn!
How I suffer in this lonely prison
How our love is severed.

I care nothing for myself
But for you, you at Con Son
   A place with no rest
   A place with no trust

How could you know
Our family was ripped apart
At the whim of a crushing regime

Here I waste at Thu Duc
You at Con Son
Your youngest brother, abandoned
Waits alone

O God
   Why does such cruelty rule
   Casting me into prison
   Leaving my children alone and astray?

But no matter, our love will conquer!

At some point—we don't know exactly when—Thieu Thi Tao was transferred once more, this time to the Bien Hoa insane asylum. From there she managed to smuggle out a letter to Don Luce. On that day at Con Son she had not spoken directly to him—because she speaks English she addressed herself directly to the congressmen and to their aide, Tom Harkin. But Luce had stayed in touch with her mother. The letter:

Dear Nguyen Van Don Luce,

Nothing but your name give me affection. What a pity that I couldn't meet you on your coming to the tiger cages, but I've made acquaintance with you through my mother, your letters to her, and the newspapers. I still remember the gentleman who spoke with me. I don't know his name, but he seemed very nice. If you happen to meet him, please remember me kindly to him. [The gentleman was Tom Harkin, who was himself elected to Congress in 1974 as a representative from Iowa.]

I think that you are well informed about my conditions of living. Like more than a hundred of thousands of political prisoners in South Vietnam, I'm suffering a hell on earth. For six years in prison, I have lost health, knowledge, intelligence, memory. I'm ashamed to admit that you know Vietnamese better than I know English. Six years constantly seeking for affronting torments and repressions, seeking for the way to be able to live in peace, but not a minute serene!

And in the result, I've been sent to the Bien-Hoa lunatic asylum. Here I read you and write to you. It's really a great comfort for me, but a strain too. I can't concentrate for a long time.

I'm longing for hearing from you soon.

Cordially yours,

Thieu Thi Tao

That letter is sane if anything is sane. But it is nevertheless a letter about insanity.

Thieu Thi Tao is the age of my children, and a thousand years older. She has suffered paralysis. She has felt her mind slip away. Her sister contracted tuberculosis.

And the money that trained the men who tortured her, the

dollars that kept her in a cage, came from my country. They were American tax dollars. The brand name proudly printed on her shackles is Smith & Wesson. The cage she lived in was very likely made in America.

Thieu Thi Tao is one of thousands, tens of thousands, who are subjected to this brutality.

She is a political prisoner. A prisoner of politics. The politics of the United States of America, which supports this most corrupt and most cruel regime. There lies the real insanity.

Thieu Thi Tao modestly asks to be remembered kindly to her American friend. I ask that you remember her and that in your kindness you demand of your representatives in Congress an end to her confinement, an end of support for the government that has made her life a hell on earth, an end of our insanity.

—1974

I had a letter from Don Luce the other day (January 1997). He had new information about Thieu Thi Tao. His '97 letter reads: "She is now an agricultural scientist/botanist. She is married and has one daughter. She still has to wear a neck brace because of being hung from a hook as 'punishment' 25 years ago . . . The people who were in the cages have a club of former prisoners and meet regularly (and often challenge present policies) . . ."

Conversations in Moscow

As I live my talky, asking, and answering life in the United States, I often remember the First Amendment, how pleasant it's been to me and how useful to my country. I was taught to love it and wonder at its beauty by my parents, prisoners once of the Czar. And I do love it, though I also love literature, and it has made our literature one of the most lively and useless in the world. Of course, it's been good to write letters to the newspapers. Some are published. It *has* been pleasing to stand on the corner of Eighth Street and Sixth Avenue and hand out informational pamphlets, leaflets of protest, to assemble in rage a couple of times a year with tens of thousands of others.

The elected or appointed leaders of our country have often applauded our enactment of these freedoms. They were then able (with clear consciences) to undertake and sustain the awful wars we spoke and assembled against for ten years.

In October, as a delegate to the World Peace Congress from the War Resisters League, I visited the Soviet Union, where a different situation exists. Literature is taken very seriously. Poets and storytellers are dealt with as though their work had an important political life. But a Russian cannot distribute a dissenting leaflet to other Russians. (In fact, it's considered seditious.) And there is a concerned citizenry standing here and there, sometimes wearing a red armband, but often just going ahead with working life. Part of that life is the satisfaction of informing on neighbors.

Still, as an anarchist, a believer in no state, I have felt like a patriot in several. In this way, I considered myself a Russian patriot. In fact, if the entire World Peace Congress had been spoken in Russian and remained untranslated into the English Marxese of the daily bulletins, I could have been bought and sold a dozen times, because Russian is the conversation of my childhood. My nose somewhat stuffed by sentimental remembrance of those dead speakers, I stood in the Moscow hotel hearing Russian orders given and carried out in regard to rooms and luggage. Later I took a bus up Kalinin Prospekt, and one lady, looking like my mother, said of another lady, who looked like my aunt, "Listen to that one, she knows nothing; still, she teaches . . ." Then despite the hour, which was often suppertime, I wanted to walk around the streets of the city of Moscow and cry out (with exclamation points to explode each phrase), Oh, Mother Russia! Oh, country of my mother's and father's childhood! Oh, beloved land of my uncle Russya killed in 1904 while carrying the workers' flag! Oh, country my own of storytellers translated in my ear! of mystics and idealists who sharpened my English tongue. Three times a day in the dining room my bones nearly melted. "Please," I said, starting the days listening and answering, "one egg only, but coffee now." "Oh, of course, my darling, my little one, only wait."

Day and night I received this tender, somehow ironic address, full of diminutives, of words hardened by fierce consonants, from which the restrained vowel always managed to escape. This Moscow speech, like all urban speech, like New York speech, is extended by out-of-towners and foreign émigrés, then toughened to defend itself against transients and enemies.

I need to make some observations that have probably been made time and again and with more distinction by traveling reporters. It isn't that I don't pay attention, but I don't think the wide world is to be judged by America consuming or compared to its shopping crowds. I feel the witness's obligation to say: Yes, the streets of Moscow were roaring with people moving at top speed through mush and slush during morning, lunch, and evening rush hours. Yes, they were all warmly dressed in heavy coats and boots or galoshes, the children in magnificent fur-lapped hats. No, there were not a lot of red or blazing blue scarves, those colors together with greens and yellows and marigold orange were scrolled around the domes and turrets of the churches. Yes, GUM, the department store, was crowded with buyers, looking mostly for more hats and galoshes. Inside the hotel the young girls were not sizzling in Western high style, but did tend to rosiness of countenance, and yes, late in the Moscow evening, 11:00 or 12:00 p.m., we saw people walking about, returning, arm in arm, from visits to friends and family. And as happens in Chicago, New York, Santiago, San Francisco, and Rome, the cabs go flying by even though their green "free" light is lit.

Maris Cakars and I were the War Resisters League delegates to the World Peace Congress. Father Paul Mayer was one of many delegates from PCPJ (People's Coalition for Peace and Justice). He was a member of the preparatory committee, which had worked in Moscow in April organizing this enormous event. At a delegate meeting, the first or second day of the congress, though he was not present, he was elected co-chairman of the American delegation.

About this World Congress of Peace Forces, the press has been rather lazy; or perhaps it has edited itself too strictly. Most of its news stories were about the statement Paul Mayer read to the Human Rights Commission, which had been signed by a number of antiwar activists, including myself, and distributed by us to interested people. However, there *were* 3,500 *other* delegates. And many of those had suffered their country's oppression and were famous fighters against the colonial uses of their people. They traveled in exhaustion from commission to commission calling out their histories. I suppose journalists on foreign beats are familiar with the beauty and passions of the women and men of this world, but I am not. For me, they were astonishing to see. They came from Africa, Asia, continents, countries, and villages where occasion still allows golden magnificence or delicacy in dress and demeanor, instead of dour formality. Familiarity is no excuse for ignoring beauty.

On the last day of commission meetings, Paul Mayer read a statement signed by Noam Chomsky, Dave Dellinger, Daniel Berrigan, Paul Mayer, David McReynolds, Sidney Peck, and me. In it, the signers identify themselves as American dissenters. They establish that they are not cold warriors. They condemn the Soviet government for its persecution of dissidents, but call upon the dissidents themselves to join in protest against political murder in Chile and the continued imprisonment of hundreds of thousands in South Vietnam. I distributed this statement to fifty or sixty people who requested it (mostly Russians), but also to members of other delegations and the press.

We were corrected in a fairly sensible Russian tone by the next speaker and excoriated by several others (Asian, African, American, European). At supper that night I offered copies to the American delegates and explained our position. In this way, we found that many people shared our views but had not yet spoken. A steering committee meeting was called that night. Paul, who had been co-chairman of the delegation, was called a liar, an agent, a deceiver. They feared that it would be assumed that he spoke for the entire delegation, a legitimate fear—still, we met no one who assumed it after speaking to us and the steering committee. Paul was censured and resigned in order to maintain some unity. I have been told this is why people resign. In this case unity was not maintained. I was more contemptuously dealt with as a woman and a mere leaflet carrier. At all times the Russians were calmer than the Americans. For instance, the Russians never said we should be shot. A couple of American women said that I ought to be shot. Then they thought it over during the night. In the morning, they said I should not be shot but "something . . . something terrible should be done." It has been suggested to me that the Russians depended on some sort of strong American statement to prevent the burial of the Peace Congress by the American press.

What I've described so far is talk and paper, ideas and hope. As for direct action, the day before we left Moscow, Maris Cakars went to GUM, the lively, mobbed Macy's of Moscow, and deposited handfuls of leaflets (*The New York Times* ad for Soviet amnesty translated into Russian) on various strategic tables, counters . . . Finally he was seen, gathered up into energetic police arms, and taken to the police station across the street. He was, he said later, better treated than on certain similar American occasions.

I would have preferred to have been part of that action but felt a responsibility to work with Paul within the hopeful meaning of the congress and use whatever time could be saved from meetings to try to speak with at least a couple of Russian dissidents.

The First Visit

Paul Mayer had already talked to one of the most religious and conservative of dissident Russians, the novelist Vladimir Maximov, author of *Seven Days of Creation*—translated into German, not yet English. Paul Mayer is a Catholic priest and not as ashamed of saving souls as some other American radicals. He had been in Moscow in April as part of the congress preparatory committee and had gone to see Alexander Galich and Vladimir Maximov. He said later, "I couldn't dismiss these people; the mark of suffering was clearly on their faces, and the integrity so clear that when these awful things came out of their mouths I was perplexed, but I couldn't dismiss it."

According to Paul, Maximov believed that the Vietnamese and

Communism would have dominated the world if the United States had not bombed and smashed Vietnam. The United States, he said, had no choice. Maximov was Russian Orthodox. He told Paul there was a great spiritual awakening among Russians, who are now worshipping in tens of thousands in secret chapels. He said that social change and revolution have nothing to do with Christianity, that good works could not have a public life. It was Lent. Maximov was fasting. Paul Mayer was not. Maximov was angry and indignant with Paul. I understand they argued fiercely. However, since in the course of most wrestling, hugs occur, they ended as friends, and each expressed great longing to see one another again.

All of this had taken place at the Galichs' family dining table in April. Paul had exchanged medallions with Angelina Galich, received a medieval Russian medallion, and given her the cross Dan Berrigan had given him when his son Peter was born.

Therefore, Paul and I were welcomed in October with apples, sardines, tomatoes salted and unsalted, glasses of Georgian wine. There were immediate questions about diet and digestion from Angelina Galich, who called greetings to us from her bed, for she was quite ill.

Galich spoke to Paul briefly about Maximov, then took our statement from us. We had not yet read it to the Human Rights Commission. He liked the first words of solidarity and support. Then he became troubled. He was disturbed by the third paragraph, he said; it was not wrong, but he considered it an attack. He said they didn't know about Chile anyway. The Soviet press lied about them, the dissidents, why not also about Chile. There *was* a curtain of silence. Also, he didn't like the language—it was unjustified, but not incorrect.

There were fifteen or twenty minutes of uncomfortable discussion about words, sentences. Finally he said, "But you see, it was not Sakharov alone. Maximov and I at least were involved. We issued the statement together, you must put down our names. It all falls on him. Always because he's the famous one, he has to bear it all." We agreed at once and changed the sentence to read "or leading intellectuals such as Sakharov, Galich, and Maximov . . ."

Angelina called out from her bedroom and asked me to sit with her and a neighbor for a while and watch how, on television, the dancers of the Bolshoi were stunning the delegates of the World Peace Congress. She laughed and said, "Look what you're missing! Stuck with us!" I said, "Oh . . ." and hugged her. I was always short of vocabulary at the beginning of an evening and had to resort to gesture or affection. I did tell her that my parents came from Russia from the town of Uzovka, which became Stalino, which became Donetz. I announced this fact to nearly everyone I spoke to in Russia. It never interested them as much as it did me. The neighbor said, "That one, Angelina, wrote a book about the steelworkers of Donetz—for children." "Well!" I said. I thought of that town. In my head it is always a bloody Easter and my uncle is killed. My love of country, any country, is always being interrupted in its patriotic advance by terrible remembrance.

"What does your button say?" the neighbor asked. I answered in Russian baby talk, as though they were the foreigners: "We don't like Nixon. We don't want him to be President anymore. He's terrible." I had forgotten the word for scoundrel. "You don't like him? Why? We received all that wonderful bread from him. He wants to be friends. No?" Again and again we learned that the dissidents and the Soviet government people were all agreed (at least on October 25) that the American administration wasn't too bad.

When I joined Paul and Alexander Galich in the other room, I asked, "Is Angelina very sick?" "Sick," he said. "She isn't well at all. *I* am not well," he said. "My heart. I have no work."

The Second Visit

When we visited the second time, the house was so full of saucers and chairs and voices speaking and sighing in Russian that I was as though at home. Angelina said it, in case I hadn't noticed: "Here you and Paul are at home."

We were greeted by Alexander and Angelina Galich, Andrei and Yelena Sakharov. A little later Alexander and Nellie Voronel arrived, and then a young friend who spoke fine English. Voronel is a physicist; he wished to tell us about the fourteen Jews who had just been arrested, picked up on the occasion of the congress's opening. He showed us a petition asking for their release and explaining what had happened. Twelve others had signed their names. (Later on we brought it as requested to certain other delegates, including people from Amnesty International. We were able to report by phone the next day that they'd been released.)

We sat down at the table and saw at once the broad, fair Russian face of Andrei Sakharov, so mild, paying attention; the sharp, darker Semitic face of Yelena, distressed with whatever news she had, to make sure we would know and understand. It was hard to begin this conversation, because we had three languages, German, Russian, and English, and two kinds of voices: public, discursive voices and private voices—for friendly or infuriated remarks. Soon, however, we *were* talking about something.

"Tell me about Brazil, please," Sakharov asked. Paul began to tell about Brazil. Clearly, they intended to begin a sensible and fruitful conversation. I was not against it, but I understood Russian, so that my ear was constantly receiving Yelena's impassioned, agonized remarks or Angelina's protestations of pain and love, or Nellie would begin to translate into my right ear something my head had already sorted out—or Alexander Voronel, at a moment when collective breath was being taken, would call to us as though we were already far apart (and we might never meet again) a story of prison-camp horror or an argument he had been making to some invented American radical adversary in his mind.

At some point Paul and Galich decided to speak German, because Sakharov understands German. I foolishly deferred, as is my habit. Also, owning all those Russian words had made me feel rich and therefore generous. But I suffered. I lost exact language and several truths. I did understand Paul as he described the work of the United States in the training of Latin American police, the arrest and murder of labor leaders, the torture of priests, the destruction of whatever rights existed.

"Even of priests?" Voronel wondered. Paul tried to continue: the economic considerations of the United States were always foremost in Latin America.

"How many prisoners?" someone asked. "Here we have fifteen to twenty thousand."

We happened to have a *New York Times* clipping describing the U.S. training of 170 Latin American military and political leaders. They passed it around, reading it carefully. Nellie translated. Galich translated. They kept it.

I began to talk about Chile . . . the humanity of the Allende government, the twelve or fourteen daily newspapers on the streets of Santiago.

"They say only about a thousand were killed," Yelena said.

"Why did this happen?" asked Andrei. "How could it happen? Ask yourself this question."

"Why?" cried Yelena. "Why? Because they couldn't live under Socialism. Thank God for the United States."

"Maybe ten thousand," I said furiously, "were killed in Chile, ten thousand." This time I was angry because I had spent last December and January in Chile. Paul spoke quietly to Sakharov in German: "If we are to argue in arithmetical terms—I have a friend who says, Why bother with the Russians, what is ten or fifteen or twenty thousand when there are two hundred thousand prisoners in Saigon. Speak for them. Forget the Russians. But we don't think like that."

"What are we to believe," Galich said. "If the Soviet papers support it, or even if they don't attack it—they tell lies about *us*, after all."

Voronel said in Russian: "Those two [meaning Paul and me], they don't know what's going on here."

"Of course," said Yelena, "how could they understand."

Sakharov listened and drank his tea out of a saucer. Nellie Voronel whispered into my right ear, "You see, Andrei is a saint, look at his face, he isn't afraid for himself."

Then his good face was hidden, for Angelina and Yelena had leaned across him to speak of Mattvei, Yelena's new grandchild. Voronel said sadly, "It used to be the babies were named Mottel, now usually it's Mattvei."

"It's like that in the United States," I said.

"We must talk about one thing at a time, we must have one conversation at a time, please," said Paul. We looked at our new Russian watches, gifts of the Soviet Union.

Sakharov gently parted the two women who were speaking across his face and we saw him again. He tried to explain in broken German: "Our conditions here are such that you do not understand." Paul asked Galich to please read our statement aloud in Russian. Galich did this. What they seemed to hear most clearly was the sentence in which we reminded them of the sufferings of those in Santiago and Saigon and asked that they raise their voices for those distant victims. "You do not understand," they said again.

This saddened us. So we offered them the Russian translation of the *Times* ad, which had been prepared for Brezhnev's visit. It was signed by many American supporters and contained the names of Russian dissidents. They had never seen it. They each took a copy and began to read, speaking the names of the prisoners. "Here's Kuznetsov," Yelena said, "and Sylvia—that's his wife, they're twenty miles apart, they haven't seen each other in maybe three years."

Then they looked at the names of the signers. I showed them

the name of Ramsey Clark.* I tried to explain how terrible the language of Solzhenitsyn's article had been, how it had taken an entire page of *The New York Times* to slander the American left, praise the Indochina policy of the United States, and insult one of our good people (Ramsey Clark) to divide American dissenters from the Russian dissenters. "Wouldn't you be glad," I asked, "if a Russian prosecutor turned around and became your defender? Would that make him a silly butterfly, as Solzhenitsyn called Ramsey Clark?"

Except for Sakharov, who smiled with amusement, everyone laughed out loud at the idiocy of my suggestion. A Russian prosecutor turned around!! Another discussion disappeared before it could develop. Paul was in despair, but actually he had managed at different times to clarify the United States role in Latin America. We came at last to Jackson and the Jackson Amendment. Between us, in English, Russian, and German, we explained our fear that Senator Henry Jackson, a cold warrior, would return our country to the long years of the cold war from which we had just barely emerged. Another twenty years of ice would begin, even if Russia *should* begin to shift her domestic policies.

"What is he like, this Jackson?" Sakharov asked. "A popular senator?"

"Who wants to be President," Paul said.

"I hope he wins," said Yelena.

"But the workers must like him; after all, they elect him," said Voronel.

Paul described his constituency, the war industries of Washington. Of course the workers must have jobs. Jackson is powerful in keeping the industries there. "Ah, of course, they must have jobs." Voronel translated this for Sakharov. He nodded.

---

* Ramsey Clark was the federal prosecutor in the Benjamin Spock conspiracy trial only a few years before this conversation. He was the U.S. Attorney General.

We asked if it was dangerous for the three men or their families—the fact that we had used their names in the statement. Yelena said, "Yes, there is a danger. They will destroy him. They will get him yet."

"No no," said Sakharov. "It will have no effect on me. They must say it."

Nellie whispered, "A saint."

Then Yelena began to tell about the camps: they go for hundreds of kilometers, a straight line on either side of the railroad tracks. "They are allowed—you know, you can send them seeds, to plant flowers, but no vegetables. If a vegetable grows, they come and tear it up with their hands." Paul and I remembered that we had heard the same cruel story about the prisoners in the camps at Con Son in South Vietnam.

We said, "You see, you have no debate with us. We are not your opponents. You must not think of us this way." We were near tears, all of us. Everything was unfinished, but we had to return to the congress. We asked if we might repeat our conversations and use their names. They said, "Every word, every name."

Then we asked them to please speak about what we'd said and to let us know their thoughts. We would always be thinking about them. Andrei and Yelena came toward the door as we took our coats. "I am a physicist," he said. "I am not the best person. Why has it fallen on me?" We embraced and parted.

The Third Visit

We visited once more. By this time we loved Moscow, had missed most of it, had spoken at the congress, survived the anger of a little less than half the delegation, the approval of about one quarter, and the disinterest of the others. We had also talked to the Russians. We had talked to the Vietnamese we'd known for years so they might receive the statement and the explanation from us rather than the interminable rumor-cooking corridors of the Hotel Rossiya.

We wanted to speak to Alexander Galich before we left. We thought he had something to tell us, too.

This is what we knew about Alexander Galich: He had been born Alexander Ginsburg; he had been a playwright, script-writer, actor, songwriter, and balladeer. The *samizdat* are the underground literary communications of the Russians. Many of Galich's songs exist and are copied all over Russia, from *magnitizdat*—the underground tapes.

Galich was thrown out of the Writers Union, the Union of Cinematographers, and the Litfond in 1971. He had been born a Jew but had converted recently to the Russian Orthodox Church, as have several other artists and intellectuals. I cannot write about these conversions. My parents and grandparents have not passed on to me an unbiased or generous view of the Russian Church, and in order to keep history clear of compromising sentiments, when talking to my children, I have kept the old information intact, adding to it for mystery's sake the strict humanity of Dan and Phil Berrigan, Paul Mayer, Elizabeth McAllister, the sisters and brothers of the Catholic Resistance.

Angelina had prepared a grand dinner for us, but after she and I had indulged our common requirement for hugs, hand-holding, and kisses, she began to mumble angrily, "What am I doing here, I don't understand one word, why do I stay?" and she left us. The fact is, Galich *was* speaking English, which he does quite well, and I was, for once, taking notes speedily—as close to verbatim as my handwriting could accomplish.

The following remarks represent, I believe, a response from the Galich, Voronel, and Sakharov families. They are meant for all those who have cared about them and feared for them and been angered by them.

"It is for us very painful that we are published in this way in the West . . . We don't wish to speak with them necessarily, the ones who publish us. We also wish to speak with you. But we have so little opportunity to speak to the West, and no opportunity to speak here, that we must speak when we can. The first person who can write takes it. With you, we talk, we disagree, we agree."

Paul interrupted to say, "What about that article in *Der Spiegel* [a West German periodical, conservative]. Didn't it bother you that you were with this bunch that call themselves brothers? They're Fascists."

Galich continued: "Yes, we may hate them, but, Paul, we don't know, we don't know who our brothers are. You know we can't protect ourselves in the Western press. We have no rights. But every time I think now for half a year I know Paul, I say something, I wonder what he thinks, if he's reading it. Now I know Grace—has Grace read it? We have so few friends, real friends. We can't agree on every question. Say what you think about us, we are friends. We both believe in freedom, peace . . . We have lived and still live different lives."

In an effort to try to make us know their lives in terms of our own, he said, "I know the terrible McCarthy period, two, three years? Well, I was a prominent script and theater writer. Now I am ill. Bad heart. I don't tell you something my condition is worse than conditions of others. I must live now for 60, 65 rubles. I can write. But I cannot print a line, and my name is not mentioned. My old work will appear, but my name is not on it. What is better, the camp or to live like me? But for a writer, I don't know what is worse.

"Now, I can't tell you how much the names in the ad meant to us. And during Brezhnev's visit! What it meant to us! You see, it is like McCarthy without jobs, no possibility to live.

"Yesterday I was by my friend. He is leaving Russia, one of our best. So many people, writers, and poets in the '40s in Moscow, almost half think of emigrating, have handed in documents. No one wants to leave. But they have no possibility. Now there is a custom, a ritual, a few nights a week someone goes. Of course some people can go not at all. Hardest for scientists and old believers. Emigration today is easiest for Jews. About of every ten people who have made application, six will get it. With greatest pleasure they give passports . . . We have exceptions. Aronovich, one of our great conductors. Gabai killed himself.

"Another friend said to me, 'Why do you write about the Jews in Russia?'

"I said, 'We live in a strange time. Many of our friends leave their motherland. We are witnesses of this new exodus. How can we be silent?'

"He said, 'Yes, but please, others must do it, not you.'

"I said, 'Yes, you tell me I'm just a Russian poet, but why shouldn't I write about it? I'm a Jew.'

"My friend was a little drunk. He said, 'You Jews, you're the ones who made the Revolution. During the periods of 1937, you Jews were not in the last row. You played your role as judges, prosecutors. And now suddenly it's not your homeland. It's not here but there, and you get emigration permission. And what will happen to us Russians . . . We did all this together, and now while you leave, we have to stay.' "

A Small Adventure
The Hotel Rossiya is near St. Basil, the main domed church the czars liked to see from the Kremlin for reasons of beauty and security. It squats like a four-sided Pentagon on the looping Moscow River. Its entranceways, north, east, south, and west, are bound by hallways, which are crossed by hallways, marked with lounges, coffeehouses on several floors where hard-boiled eggs and chicken and apples are sold to midnight starvers. There are innumerable dining rooms of varying class and formality, in which about a thousand American computer salesmen may be eating borscht right now. It was interesting to walk round and round,

from entrance to entrance, past the gathering places of the Indians and Middle Eastern countries, where there were very few women; past the Africans, among whom there were many more.

We never had the time to do this for the plain pleasure of the walk, but on the first day we went looking for Jean Van Lierde, the Belgian delegate from War Resisters International. Another time we tried to find the inland lobby route to the foreigners' shop to buy presents for the folks at home. Our speediest walk occurred one 2:00 a.m., after an 11:00 p.m. meeting with Palestinians. Paul and I decided to find the North Vietnamese and talk to them, to show them the statement Paul had made and the names signed to it. After going up and down, round and round, through and back, sorry not to have a compass, there they were suddenly before us in some north hall, saying good night to one another. They were to leave Moscow at 4:00 a.m. There was Mr. Mai, with whom I had traveled for ten days in 1969 through the devastated villages of his country. (Vietnam is another country of which I am a patriot, not only because my left hand worked hard and long for their sweet lives and my heavily taxed right hand, in the years I paid taxes, laid out the cash to end those lives. But because of that trip with Mr. Mai, six Americans, and a dozen Vietnamese from Hanoi south to the Ben Hai River, I saw the work of my country's scientists and fliers, their brainy tantrums on the body of Vietnam.) "Ah," said Mr. Mai, looking at the signatures and, I think, sighing, "we see! There are the names of our friends." He took the mimeographed sheets and put them aside. "We will talk about this. Then we will let you know our views." He went on to say they were now rebuilding roads, hospitals, whole villages. "No more school under the earth," he said. "You must go home and tell our friends. There must not be war."

About three or four hours earlier we had stood in the winter wind on some wide boulevard trying to get a cab to get home in time for our usual late consultations and meetings. Our young friend and translator flung herself at a passing cab that had to stop for a light. The driver said, "And when am I supposed to get home?" "But what will they do?" she asked. "They're foreigners. Can they stand here all night?" "Girlie, please, I too have a family, am I never to see them?" She said, "Please, comrade, it's so cold and they're from the Congress of Peace Lovers." "Ach, peace lovers," he said. "Well, my dears, get in, let's go."

As we traveled along the broad boulevards of Moscow that night, we heard the maneuvering of iron and steel and caught glimpses of some rumbling tanks and enormous trucks. Paul and I thought the Mideast war had begun right there on Leningrad Prospekt. Then our cab was stopped, diverted, sent along a side street, stopped and diverted once more. We traveled through empty streets and squares. "The devil, there's no way to get there," said the driver. At the next stop point he explained to the policeman that he had to get to the other side of Red Square to the Hotel Rossiya, what was he to do with these people, foreigners. "Can't be done," said the authoritative citizen with the red armband. "Am I stuck with them, then, these peace lovers in the back?" "Oh, the congress, you should have said it. Go through. Say I said so."

And so we did, driving up to our entranceway over the ramps which held a couple of little twelfth-century churches in their arms, red brick and blue and white. We learned that the empty streets and the moving armament were only a preparation for the next day's celebration of the great October Revolution. All peace-loving nations celebrate in this fashion. So our anxieties rested.

More Conversation, Another Russian

The day before we left, my sense of the importance, or the propriety, of what is now called "full disclosure" to some official Russian became intense. There were a couple of these in charge of us, our comfort, our interpreter, our happiness, our views. It would not be right to leave, I thought, without speaking directly to Alexei N. Stepunin, Secretary General of the Institute of Soviet American Relations. I liked him anyway. He seemed at first something like the best of an old cop. That is, he was gray, handsome, he'd seen it all, bad behavior and no respect, suffered and absorbed corruption so that his hackles, fins, and hairs lay pretty flat when Americans did not sit at the tables assigned them, were brazen, rude. He was not surprised that some of us spent half the night dancing and the other half struggling like salmon upstream through the halls and stairwells of the Rossiya, past the rosy plump lady fuzz at the key desk, to private meetings in lounges and outdoor untapped balconies.

His office was actually two rooms, a bedroom and a sitting room. In the sitting room, four or five young men sat, our interpreters, smoking, gabbing happily in Russian, resting from that fierce all-day attentiveness which must be required for listening and responding to a foreign language, with the diverse accents and faddish idioms of our up-to-date country.

I showed him about half a dozen leaflets that had come our way, handed to us at the airport or delivered to us by different European delegates. Paul, Maris, and I had looked through them all, realized that we ourselves had to decide which was important and let the others be handled by the people who'd brought them.

We wanted to impress on him the fact that we had chosen one which supported the dissidents but did not ignore their political position.

Alexei Nikolaevich wondered *why* we had had to do that, say all that; he was surprised, particularly at Paul. He thought we understood that no one had said that the Soviet Union was a democracy. It was a dictatorship of the proletariat. They had no choice but to do what the proletariat wanted them to do. The proletariat did not want them to publish Solzhenitsyn; it was not interested in hearing from those second-rate poets with bourgeois longings. By this time, he looked more like one of my condescending but lovable uncles. I recognized his sentences as counters he *had* to use in an argument he *had* to make, but I didn't want to be diverted into one of those gabby rivers that feed the ocean of Marxist abstraction. Anyway, Paul, Maris, and I are also very much against bourgeois longings, though I suppose we have shared some of the comforts conferred on our ambitious American immigrant families.

We went dead ahead and said the point was this: We could not demand the freedom of the imprisoned Vietnamese, the Brazilians or Chileans or South Africans, without including in those demands freedom for the thousands of political prisoners in Russian camps.

Alexei sighed and said, "But, my dear, do you know the difference, how much better it is now than in Stalin times?"

We said, "Yes, of course, it must be much better, it was so terrible then, we believe it is better."

Paul and I nodded to each other—it certainly is better.

"Listen," he said, "we honor Sakharov; he has three Legion of Honor medals. He is our hero in physics, in science, but does that mean he knows something else? And, Grace, about Solzhenitsyn, he calls up on the phone and immediately he has a press conference with the whole foreign press. So . . . who else can speak with the whole West and they all stop to listen to him? Who? What is he complaining? He is giving interviews day and night." Alexei is disgusted with us, but he is used to Americans. They're his job.

We say that we have only a few minutes, we know he's busy, winding us all up in his books, reports, and meetings. We say we brought him all these because we wanted him to be clear about our position. We could not divide our concern, for Russian poets and generals in madhouses, Old Believers, and divergent Marxists in Mordavia camps, from our concern for political prisoners in all countries. "You have said that already," he said.

In the end I had to be true to my American creed, which is to leave them laughing, and to my Russian Jewish creed, which is to leave them in a little pain at least. "Alexei," I said, "Russia is powerful and rich like my country. It doesn't *have* to worry about free speech, free assembly, free *samizdat*, free underground papers. It can have all that, we do at home. We have had nearly half a million people at one time in Washington shouting protests into the windows of the White House and the Houses of Congress, and still our government does exactly what it likes. It has managed to bomb and torment the Vietnamese people for ten years. You too can have freedom of speech at home and continue to strong-arm Czechoslovakia. You can eventually have as many automobiles and street-corner meetings as we do, and you can export terror instead of containing it. It's a question of confidence. You have no confidence in your true strength, Alexei." Alexei looked at me with a wondering expression; then he threw his head back and laughed a first-class Russian basso laugh.

Well, after I said all this to Alexei Stepunin, I believed it; then I had to continue the thought. What pigs we Americans are! Not only do we consume one-third of the natural resources of the earth, but with all that fat ease, at least one-third of the natural freedoms of man. Then we leave to the rest of the world awful struggles for food, warmth, and shelter, along with oppression and tyranny, their certain companions.

The Last Russian

We were home. Exhausted by the hour, which may have been 8:00 or 9:00 p.m. New York time, and about 3:00 or 4:00 a.m. Moscow time. We threw ourselves, our luggage full of gifts, bulletins, position papers, and final commission reports into a cab. We began to talk with the cabdriver, who was friendly, easygoing, bearded. Well! What an astonishment! He was our final Russian, an émigré Jew from Ukraine, here ten years. He asked us, "How is Moscow? Beautiful? What do the people talk about?"

We asked him about his life here, and he said he missed Russia, his country; he missed the people, the language. He would love to go back and visit—not to live, of course—still, in many ways life over there *was* easier. The medical care; the children are taken care of—there's no question, you don't have to worry about every dollar. But here, he said, he could live a different life if he wanted, any kind of life, it was up to him; he liked that, now he was used to it.

We had come to West Eleventh Street, my street, and I couldn't speak to him anymore. It seemed certain, however, that we had fallen into his cab for a couple of reasons: the first, because Paul is a holy person whose life deserves an occasional selective revelation. The second, because I'm a storyteller; therefore, He probably moved in this unmysterious way (as He has many times) to offer to the beginning and middle of my experience an appropriate and moral end.

Postscript

I have just received the World Peace Council's report on the congress. In describing the work of Commission 12, it says *nothing* about the conscientious objection, the right to refuse to kill, capital punishment.

Vladimir Maximov is in Paris.

Alexander Galich had applied for permission to emigrate. He was certain he would receive it. He did not. He must be stunned by the government refusal. I see him at his desk, his hand on his heart. Inside that heart, anger and despair are probably making fatal trouble.

Yelena Sakharov has been called in by the KGB, at least half a dozen times since we left Moscow. She and her husband have been harassed at home, threatened in these interrogations, her children threatened—that is: all has continued as before.

Andrei Sakharov has published a long essay, *Why I Dissent*. In

it there are several paragraphs which are responsive, I believe, to
the letter we brought to Russia from American peace activists, to
our conversations in the Galich home, and to other communications the Russians have received from that large group on the
American left which supports the dissidents but insists on another
analysis of events, another look at who the wardens are in this
world and who the prisoners. The essay seems to separate his
views from the autocratic notions of Alexander Solzhenitsyn. He
says at one point: "A part of the Russian opposition intelligentsia
is beginning to manifest a paradoxical closeness to the secret
Party–state doctrine of nationalism." I have excerpted a couple
of paragraphs from the essay which address our concerns, the
subject matters Paul, Maris, and I carried to Moscow and forced
on the Russians—with the typical arrogance of safe persons:

> *I should like to talk about that part of the Western
> liberal intelligentsia (still a small part) which extends its
> activities to the socialist countries as well. These people
> look to the Soviet dissenters for a reciprocal, analogous
> international position with respect to other countries.
> But there are several important circumstances they do
> not take into account: the lack of information; the fact
> that a Soviet dissenter is not only unable to go to other
> countries but is deprived, within his own country, of the
> majority of sources of information; that the historical ex-
> perience of our country has weaned us away from exces-
> sive "leftism," so that we evaluate many facts differently
> from the "leftist" intelligentsia of the West; that we must
> avoid political pronouncements in the international
> arena, where we are so ignorant (after all, we do not
> engage in political activity in our own country); that we
> must avoid getting into the channel of Soviet propa-
> ganda, which so often deceives us.*

*We know that in the Western countries there are vig-
ilant and influential forces which protest (better and
more effectively than we do) against injustice and violence there. We do not justify injustice or violence, wherever they appear. We do not feel that there is necessarily
more of both in our country than in other countries. But
at the moment our strength cannot suffice for the whole
world. We ask that all this be taken into account, and
that we be forgiven the errors we sometimes make in the
dust kicked up by polemics.*

I read these words and they are absolutely true to the voice of
the writer, Andrei Sakharov, and to his character, which is modest, humane, and brave, just because it is the only decent way a
person can be on earth.

I have been lucky to know these people even for a few hours.
And to be at such appreciative ease. That Russian home in Moscow, seventy years after my father and mother ran for their lives,
was—in food, furniture, language, gesture—very like my own
home in the East Bronx. Still, there is a difference in the people.

The Russian dissidents who come to the United States nowadays are all called émigrés (by themselves, the media, the U.S.
government), a French word whose meaning includes the idea of
class. Those tens of thousands of others thrown into steerage,
stored and stacked in the tenements of Delancey Street and Rivington Street, were called immigrants, another class. Yet they,
too, came here for the shining pleasures of the First Amendment.
Under cover of that brightness, talking all the time, their children
have paid taxes for death and silence in other parts of the world.
The émigrés will have to know that.

—1974

Post-postscript
Time and the dissolution of the Soviet Union have in fact turned
the Russians who have come in great numbers to the United
States—and especially to Brooklyn—from émigrés into immi-
grants, like my parents.

—1976

Other People's Children

Our national grief at the thought of Vietnamese children who would be homeless after the American war seemed somehow more bearable during the war, when all our know-how was being used in making orphans. There did exist a history of homeless children and their wars, which could have been helpful, but we paid little attention to it. It was indeed offered to the country during the "babylift" last April, in public newspaper statements by social workers, historians, educators, religious leaders, and doctors, and in political street demonstrations on both coasts.

According to Joseph Reid of the Child Welfare League of America, there were 50,000 homeless children after the Nigerian–Biafran war. The United States (and other countries) thought these children should be offered for adoption. The Nigerians and Biafrans would not permit it. With the help of the International Union for Child Welfare in Geneva, all but twenty-seven of the children were reunited with family or village communities within two years.

Here is another lesson from history: my friend Karen DiGia was a displaced child in Germany after the Second World War. That is, she was lost in one direction, and her parents, if alive, were lost in another direction, far from home. Here, the Red Cross helped. It took a year and a half before Karen DiGia's living father was found and they were brought together. She was only one child among hundreds of thousands. Had she been adopted away into Italy or the United States or Japan in some well-meaning child-consumers project, her records filed and sealed, they would have never met; she would have become an orphan and he the father of a dead child.

Karen told me that the streets of German cities were full of pictures of children. "Have you seen this child, Anna Marie; she was wearing a blue smock; she wandered away from our camp . . ." Translated for Americans today, whose kind hearts and open purses intend to take Vietnamese children into the finality of adoption, there may well be pictures posted on the walls in Saigon or Danang: "Has anyone seen Phuoung, last seen in a blue smock; she let go of my hand for a minute . . ."

In Vietnam there is a saying: "If mother is lost, there is auntie; if father is lost, there is uncle." The parentless child becomes the child of the large household, the village, old aunts who may not even be blood relatives but who share the natural responsibility of all adults for all the young. This has already happened in North Vietnam, where there is only one "home" for orphans. This is happening now in South Vietnam—grown-up refugees and children in the tens of thousands are returning to their villages in what the Provisional Revolutionary Government called the "Campaign for the Return to the Homelands."

Well, how did the orphan airlift happen, then, considering these histories, these facts? I have to say it coldly. The war in Vietnam, which began in ignorance, self-congratulation, and the slaughter of innocents, ended in much the same way. The orphan airlift in April was a balloon of sentiment that raised some 2,600 Vietnamese children and floated them across 12,000 miles of sky. The groups most responsible for that sky of flying/dying babies were the following:

1. Adoption agencies, with contracts begun in professional decorum a year earlier. The agencies panicked when it appeared

that the war would end and the subject matter of their contracts, Vietnamese children, would disappear, absorbed into the life of their own country. These agencies, determined to meet those contracts, lost their businesslike cool and allowed themselves to be helped by . . .

2. World Airways. Anxious to add love of children to its reputation as one of the world's largest charter airlines, World Airways, in the person of Ed Daley, who owned 81 percent of its stock, leaped into the early-April headlines and news photographs as the first of the baby transporters (although the U.S. government stepped in immediately and halted future World Airways baby flights). World Airways stock rose from 4⅛ to 6½ in one week, Ed Daley held the babies in his arms, and the company applied to the Civil Aeronautics Board for a domestic license to fly coast-to-coast. *The New York Times* tells the story of a $300 million to $400 million fortune amassed during the war years, when, under a contract with the Defense Department, World Airways planes carried cargo while military planes often flew empty.

3. The adoption agencies were also helped by a cynical political decision by the Ford administration to use the children in order to dig military aid for Thieu out of Congress. The language by which the kindness of American families was mocked does exist: U.S. Ambassador to South Vietnam Graham Martin, according to *The New York Times*, told President Thieu's Deputy Prime Minister Phan Quang Dan, "The collective shipment abroad of these orphans should help swing public opinion to the advantage of the republic of Vietnam."

People who argued in favor of the airlift described the squalid, impoverished, unhealthy conditions of the orphan asylums in wartime Saigon, the possibilities of prejudice against mixed-blood children and handicapped children, and the superior opportunities in the United States in the years to come.

Actually, lovers of children have had every opportunity to help *all* the children of South Vietnam (but without direct ownership)—the 30,000 in orphan homes, the million or so who have lost one or both parents. Legislated aid could have gone from our own Congress to be distributed through international organizations like Medical Aid for Vietnam, the United Nations High Commission on Refugees, American Friends Service Committee, or the International Children's Fund. Private contributions can also be given to these organizations and earmarked for Vietnam. As of this writing, however, despite the fact that the Paris peace accords obligate the United States to provide postwar assistance to the country we devastated, no aid has ever been considered. The destruction of that small country in the last ten years cost Americans, at the government's lowest estimate, $150 billion. Lovers of children, we should be able to persuade Congress to offer one reconstructing billion for food, medicine, hospitals.

Still, it's the iron-hearted god of irony who points out that children who might be subjected to racial prejudice were being sent to the United States, the center of that pathology; that handicapped, war-mutilated children had been taken from a country where it would be the responsibility of family and community to keep them functioning in the ordinary life of the world. They were brought into a society which specializes in institutions, dumping grounds for the handicapped and the old, whose own Vietnam veterans are hidden in the recesses of Veterans Administration hospitals, whose black or handicapped orphans are unadoptable (and there may be as many as 100,000 of these children).

That same iron-hearted god of irony (who usually works in literature) spoke even louder, for we have the moral deafness of self-congratulators. A C5A, a plane that had at other times suffered structural problems (and was actually grounded for these problems in 1971), was stuffed with weapons, howitzers, sent to Vietnam, where it deposited the howitzers intact at the airport, then had its bare compartments filled with Vietnamese babies and older children "orphans," took off for the United States, and crashed in flames.

Years ago—1966 or 1967—people in the peace movement carried a poster of a well-dressed young man holding a cigarette against the arm of a child. On the poster a question was asked: *Would you burn a child?* In the next poster, the man applied the burning cigarette, and the answer was given: *When necessary.* The third poster showed a child burned and crippled by American napalm. There may be a fourth now, that plane crashing, the children burning, the war ending.

Who are these orphans?

Some *are* orphans, little persons who enter into a normal American procedure planned for the benefit of children, carrying the true papers of orphans. American parents had been waiting for them for a long time. Many are already being loved and cuddled behind the "adoption curtain," as Betty Jean Lifton, writer and author of *Twice Born: Memoirs of an Adopted Daughter*, has called it. Their records are sealed, their past no longer exists.

But some are not orphans at all.

When the first children were flown into San Francisco, they were kept briefly in the Presidio, an army base just outside the city. Two young Vietnamese women and a third who spoke excellent Vietnamese visited the Presidio to talk to the children. These women were Jane Barton, an AFSC worker who had lived and worked in hospitals in South Vietnam for three years; Muoi McConnell, who was a nurse in Danang; and Trang Tuoung Nhu, a Vietnamese woman born in Hue, who is Indochina coordinator of the International Children's Fund.

I talked with them and to Don Luce of Clergy and Laity Concerned and Doug Hostetter of the United Methodist office of the United Nations, both of whom had spent years with voluntary organizations in Vietnam and spoke Vietnamese and knew the city of Saigon. And I understood that the orphan asylums there were not necessarily full of orphans, but the streets often were.

Children were brought to these institutions during the war by parents who thought they would be safe. They were brought by women or men who were unable to care for their babies, and who believed they would have a better chance at a couple of meals a day in such a place. According to Judith Coburn, a journalist reporting in *The Village Voice*, they were also brought by Saigon bar girls who wanted their mixed-blood kids kept out of the hard life. Or there were children who, at the age of two, were deposited in orphanages by government people, having been taken away from their mothers, who were political prisoners. Any of these parents may have signed papers—papers that were supposed to prove the children's legal availability for adoption, papers that the poor in any country are often persuaded to sign in fear and despair for their kids. All these people might hope or expect to reclaim their kids at the end of the war.

Then there are the children who had not come from orphan asylums, who didn't know how they had been gathered up, or from where, to arrive at what place?—a child who'd survived the C5A crash but lost his mother's map and address; an eleven-year-old who later ran away from his foster parents in California, crying to go home to Vietnam; a boy who'd been in a refugee group from Danang and who had been separated from his mother; and the twenty-nine Cambodian children who arrived, mysteriously and without papers, on the East Coast of the United States. (The hard work of Congresswoman Elizabeth Holtzman [D-N.Y.] and her staff has kept these Cambodian children in foster care, safe from immediate adoption, while efforts are made to learn who they are and where they are from. The first thing learned was that twenty-one of the children had one living parent. The U.S. Immigration Service was forced by congressional pressure to send a letter to the foster parents advising them that the children's identity was being investigated and adoption would be delayed.)

A class-action suit has been brought in California by the Center for Constitutional Rights, asking that the adoption of *all* these children be held up, that they remain in foster care with their records open and their short lives unsealed while Vietnam reorders itself and time without war brings families forward to reclaim and renew their lives. At this writing, the case is in court. Witnesses are describing the confusion and exchange of children's names, not from unkindness, just from carelessness and pressure where rigor was particularly required. One woman, who had received a six-year-old Vietnamese girl for adoption, testified that the child was not an orphan and that she wanted to return to Vietnam. In addition, there should have been immediate photographing of each baby and child, in its own clothes, with its special characteristics—birthmarks and war wounds—described and recorded. In late June, a federal judge in San Francisco ordered the Immigration and Naturalization Service to determine within three months whether or not the 22,000 children are orphans.

I must say that I don't believe women could have invented the insane idea of transporting these children. I have not met one woman who isn't passionate on the subject—against or in favor —which is quite different from the cynicism and manic energy required for its invention and enaction. Many women truly believed that the American care and ownership of these babies would be the only way their lives would be saved. But most women were wild at the thought of the pain to those other mothers, the grief of the lost children. They felt it was a blow to *all* women, and to their natural political rights. It was a shock to see that world still functioning madly, the world in which the father, the husband, the man-owned state can make legal inventions and take the mother's child.

The Vietnamese have protested again and again, calmly at first, in the way they have of trying to explain to innocent or ignorant people their methods of caring for children, their view of family life, the extended family, the natural responsibility of community.

Then in anger, Dan Ba Thi, Provisional Revolutionary Government ambassador to the peace talks, said: "This is an outrageous attack on our sovereignty; the 1954 Geneva Convention forbids this kind of kidnapping. We demand the return of our Vietnamese children." And on May 19, 1975, Pham Van Ba, PRG ambassador in Paris, wired the U.S. District Court in California: "We demand that U.S. government return to South Vietnam children illegally removed by Americans. We will assist placement of these children in their family or foster homes."

These children are, after all, the "young shoots" of Vietnam. Surely all the parents and grandparents, the "aunties" who have suffered and fought for thirty years in horror and continuous loss of dear family, under French oppression and the napalm and bombs of the United States, who have seen the murder of their living earth—surely they will demand to be reunited in years of peace with the hopeful children. They must believe passionately that those small survivors are not to be deprived of the fruits of so many years of revolutionary and patriotic struggle.

A M s. reader's response:
I am appalled by the misinformation and lopsided reporting in "Other People's Children" by Grace Paley (September 1975).

I worked on the staff of the agency with the longest and largest ongoing adoption program in South Vietnam, and observed first-hand the orphanages and halfway houses of Saigon. As the mother of four Vietnamese children, I feel that Grace Paley has failed to perceive the essence and philosophy of intercountry adoptions . . .

The vast majority of Vietnamese orphans who have been adopted are illegitimate and totally abandoned—with no relatives waiting to retrieve them at war's end. The death rate for abandoned infants and young children was often as high as 80 percent.

Of those who stayed in the orphanages and survived, many were badly undernourished and neglected.

Starvation and emotional deprivation tend to foster weak bodies and dull minds. Were these children to be the hope of the future of Vietnam—its political and social leaders, its professors?

Paley quickly dismisses the racially mixed and handicapped children. Somehow her "iron-hearted god of irony" points out that these children would be better off left in an orphanage. Would she leave in an orphanage an abandoned, undernourished, Vietnamese/black infant who had nerve damage in his arms and hands from lead poisoning, as well as severe permanent damage to the retinas of his eyes? If he survived, perhaps he could look forward to being a blind street boy in Saigon. He is my son.

Would she leave an abandoned, six-pound, three-month-old Montagnard girl who had severe diarrhea, dehydration, badly infected ears, scabies, pneumonia, and cytomegalo (a virus which often causes debilitating birth defects or mental retardation)? She, who had been marked by death, is my daughter.

Would she leave an abandoned, sick Vietnamese/Cambodian asthmatic boy? He is my son.

Would she leave a nine-year-old boy whose entire family was killed by American bombs? Perhaps he could have stayed a bit longer and been drafted into the military. Then he could have fought in the war (which one of us ever knew when the war would end?) and, if not killed, he could have added more scars to the ones that already cover his young body. He is my son.

These four children are unique and very special human beings—as are all children. Their stories, however, are not. The children could have come from Timbuktu. Does the name of the country matter when a child is starving, dying, or lonely? She or he is a member of the human family.

Finally, Paley states that she does not believe "women could have invented the insane idea of transporting these children," and that most women "felt it was a blow to *all* women, and to their natural political rights." The fact is that the decision to care for the orphans, nurse them, feed them, bury them, love them, process adoption papers for eight years, and, in the end, send them on the airlift, was made, on the whole, by women.

Most of these women were not attempting to save the children from Communism, offer them Christianity, salve their guilt about the war, steal babies from their mothers' arms, or deprive a country of its future generations. Their reverence for a single human life crossed national, cultural, racial, social, religious, political, and economic boundaries. These women gave the children a chance at life—the promise of a mother and father instead of no one; the warmth of a bed instead of hard wooden slats; the satisfaction of a full stomach instead of a swollen, empty belly; the advantage of essential medical care instead of the threat of death from the measles, chicken pox, starvation; the security of knowing one is loved and wanted instead of rejected and lonely, and on and on.

Many of these women risked and lost their lives in order to give life. My children and I are in their debt.

Suzanne Dosh
Lakewood, Colorado

Grace Paley replies:
I do admire Suzanne Dosh's extraordinary generosity—the lifelong reality of it—not a gift of money alone but years of responsibility and affection.

However, I made three points—none of which are really discussed or argued by Ms. Dosh:

1. The Orphan Airlift was a cynical political game played by the government in the hope that drama and sentiment would persuade Americans to give military aid to Saigon and continue the war.

2. Many children in that airlift were not orphans, but no official procedure was followed—for example, photographing for the future of inquiry or for identification. There are, right now in *this* country, four or five Vietnamese women trying to get their children back.

3. There are other solutions to the problem of homeless children after war. Jewish children in the Netherlands after World War II were returned to their families, and more recently, 27,000 Nigerian children (many orphans) remained Nigerian.

—1975

I have been harsh on the bomber pilots, and so might anyone who had traveled a couple of hundred miles across their insolent work: the hospitals, schools, villages, streams they made their own by destroying. I am not Vietnamese; I do not have to let go of these recollections in order to live in this world.

But I am, and was in '69, sadder than I seemed to be in my reports, about the pilots' long, long incarceration, their uncomfortable or tortured entrance into the world of human suffering.

I still believe the "orphan" airlifts were an outrageous political ploy. But I did not consider the fact of Vietnamese racism in the case of mixed-race children. There may be another word for it relating to family village centeredness, but there is no good word.

I still admire Mrs. Dosh, who responded to my article in Ms., *though we might find even wider differences today. Certainly life in the middle-class homes of our defeated United States has been easier than life in unrepaired, impoverished, victorious Vietnam. Decades of American embargo have seen to that. Still, at a poetry reading organized by the Joiner Center at the University of Massachusetts, Boston, I heard American vets and Vietnamese vets read stories and poems. Among them, a wonderful American poet, a young Vietnamese American, Christian Langworthy. I told him how fine his work was, then felt obliged to truthfully tell him how angry I'd been when he and others first came to the United States, as children, part of one of America's war games; how glad I was that he was here with another language tune in his head to give our English the jolts it has learned over the centuries to use so well.*

*III / More*

In "Demystified Zone," I sent Faith to Puerto Rico as a representative of her PTA, which had a number of Puerto Rican members. Faith had worked for me in many of the short stories in at least three books, and I thought she'd do well with journalistic responsibility. Although, as usual, her son Richard kept interrupting.

I probably ought to say more about "Some History on Karen Silkwood Drive." This short report appeared in the late seventies —1977, I think. The Clamshell Alliance had organized opposition to the building of two Seabrook nuclear plants. The '77 demonstration and civil disobedience involved at least 1,400 people, who occupied the Seabrook parking lot and were finally arrested after a rather pebbly night on the hard ground. We considered nuclear power a war against the future, and it has proven to be so. We considered it economically foolish, and it has become more so. The life of the nuclear plant is short, about forty years; the radiation waste will remain toxic for thousands of years. When we would ask, Well, what are you going to do with this stuff? the feeble answer usually given, with averted eyes, by the plant authorities was "Well, we'll surely find a solution in thirty-forty years." Native Americans tell us we are responsible for human life to the seventh generation.

We were successful in this way: only one of the two projected plants was built. About fifty planned for the rest of the country were never built. There were many groups with names like Clamshell, and their nationwide success was due to intense local organizing, the will to be civilly disobedient, and some pretty wise legal maneuvering.

"Cop Tales" is a small accumulation of experiences with the police.

In 1979 we organized the Women and Life on Earth Conference. This was the first of a particular series of transforming Northeastern feminist meetings, gatherings, demonstrations. About eight hundred women came to the University of Massachusetts to talk about ecology, education, patriarchy. Many of us heard, for the first time, the term "ecofeminism."

Within the next year and a half, groups of many of the same women met again in Hartford, New York, and Vermont, to think about the connections of ecology and patriarchy to militarism and racism, to see that our understanding of the connections among those social oppressions was indeed a feminist analysis. What came next, what naturally followed all that talking and talking, was action, finally: the Women's Pentagon Action in 1981. Surrounding the Pentagon was not the newest idea in the world. In 1967 antiwar protesters had planned to levitate the Pentagon. We women turned our imaginations in an earthier direction and created a two-thousand-woman theater of sorrow, rage, and defiance, surrounding the building, barring its entrances. There were tombstones for sorrow and huge furious puppets to accompany anger. We had decided against speeches and speechmakers of any kind, and there were none. There were many arrests.

Of course in order to bring all these women together there had to have been many meetings in New York and New England. A position or unity statement had to be written. The women who gathered to write it came from many different organizations, some *in stern opposition to one another. But luckily we had never asked for support from organizations, only from women.*

I would write that statement. It was an honor for me, and of course the women were also relieved that someone would do the job. Still, it took weeks, because with the honor came the obligation to read and reread it at meetings—by phone to people who could not get to meetings. New ideas were introduced, and lots of questions. It seems odd now, but although we spoke emphatically about misogyny, it was late, almost before printing time, when someone said, What about sexual preference—homophobia? And this in an organization that was at least 50 percent lesbian. The document we produced was not a consensual one, which is usually compromised by that perfectly honorable mediating process. It was exactly, at some length, what everybody believed and hoped. Me too. I've included it, since the writing was my responsibility.

As American missile bases were established in Europe and the United States, Women's Peace Camps were organized. The most famous, I guess, in England—at Greenham. There were others in Italy, in Germany. In the United States, Seneca was not the only one. But it's the one I've written about. It seems to me the most interesting, the most poignant, because it was the place in 1590 where the Iroquois women also begged the tribes "to cease their warfare" and our own great early suffragettes held the first Women's Rights Convention in 1848. An added note—why? for information and praise. The Women's Rights Convention was preceded by the Anti-Slavery Convention of American Women in New York City in 1837. They met, they said, "in fear and trembling."

"Pressing the Limits of Action" is an interview I had with Meredith Smith and Karen Kahn that was published in the Resist *Newsletter. I was one of the early members of Resist, which in its logo is usually followed by the words "Illegitimate Authority." Resist is alive and extremely well after thirty years of supporting grass-roots organizations for social change in cities, towns, and*

neighborhoods throughout the country. I am among the older members, and people like to ask me questions about movement history and my own experiences in the anti-war and feminist movements in the hope that I will be useful. On occasion I am.

"Of Poetry and Women and the World" was spoken at a conference on Writers in Our World, organized by Reginald Gibbons at Northwestern University. The writers disagreed with one another with a certain amount of vehemence, and because we were in the United States continued to talk to one another on this occasion, if not later.

I've placed the preface to A Dream Compels Us ("El Salvador") in this section because much of my time in the mid-eighties was used in trying to be helpful to the Central American people in their struggle to free themselves of decades of United States military intervention. This intervention, which in Guatemala began forcefully in 1954, has become quite famous in the last few months—that is, the spring of 1997—as more and more information appears in the press. It is greeted with shamed surprise, but the facts have actually been known for about forty years. During these years about 100,000 Guatemalans died. They were the reasons for our demonstrations and eyewitness visits to those countries.

Demystified Zone

Faith had just returned from Puerto Rico. She had attended a conference on The Bilingual Child and Public Education. She was an active worker in the PTA and had been sent by the local school board.

The neighborhood newspaper, always longing for community news, wanted to interview her. The young reporter made a couple of remarks, then asked a general question: "Mrs. Asbury, I understand you talked with many people and visited schools and clinics as part of the work of this conference. What did you think of Puerto Rico?"

Luckily she had been forming and re-forming some sentences on the plane. She was able to deliver them—awkward but whole. "I think: first, around 1900 we stole their language from the people. The U.S. commissioners decided the Puerto Ricans should be educated in English—just the way the French did with the Vietnamese. Then, around the time the schools and the children were freed finally into their native Spanish, our cities needed new cheap labor, and the people were stolen from their language. That's what I think."

"May I quote you?" he asked.

"Yes," said Faith, feeling like the great traveler. "Quote me."

In the evening, she persuaded her son Richard to accompany

her. They visited her parents, who lived in the Home for the Golden Ages, an institution full of small apartments for the intact and dormitories for those unable to care for themselves. She told her parents that she had been interviewed and would soon be quoted. Her mother went next door immediately to inform a neighbor.

"I hope you didn't make a fool of yourself," her father said nervously.

"She handles herself pretty well lately," said Richard. "Don't worry, Grandpa. I worry sometimes myself," he said courteously. His grandfather looked at him and nearly fainted with love. "He looks wonderful, this boy," he said. "I like his hair long."

"I do, too," said Faith's mother, returning with her friend Mrs. Harrison. "I told her you would be in the paper. She wanted to meet you."

"Oh, Ma, it's just a little neighborhood paper."

"All right, my dream," her mother said. "You took a trip. You went to a different place. Tell us something."

"Well, okay," said Faith. "First, it's very beautiful. Very green and mountainous and, you know, an island. They call it Daughter of the Sun and Sea. They can grow anything—oranges, bananas, beans, tomatoes, avocados—anything—people have chickens—but you know, I went into a supermarket and *the eggs are all stamped U.S.A.!*"

Mrs. Harrison said, "They're poor people, I suppose. We send them eggs? It's wonderful. That's the good old U.S. of A. for you."

"Wonderful . . ." said Richard. "Wonderful? Don't you people understand anything?"

"What a temper!" said his grandfather, full of admiration. "What Richard means, Mrs. Harrison: We don't *give* them. We *sell* them. They *got* to buy the eggs. They quit doing all that agriculture themselves."

"Sure, we even send them rice from California," said Faith, "—which they could also grow."

"They should do it if they can," said Mrs. Harrison. "But the tropics . . . people get very lackadaisical, I suppose."

"You suppose," said Richard. He stood up and looked at the door.

"Calm down," said Faith. "Let me explain it a little. You know, when I visited one of the junior highs, I went into the kitchen— first of all, I must say the school was beautiful—on a hill, a campus really. In the kitchen I met these women very familiar to me, Puerto Rican women, after all. I know them from the PTA. And it turned out that a few, more than a few, had been in the States, worked in New York, but it was too hard. On Rivington Street, as a matter of fact . . ."

"Oh! Rivington Street," said her mother. "Imagine that."

"You're supposed to be explaining something," said Richard.

"I don't happen to have your machine-gun style, Richard, so just shut up! Where was I? The women. The women were school kitchen aides and they had these enormous bags of rice from California on the table and they were taking all sorts of little bugs and worms out of the rice."

"You see," said Richard, who couldn't be quiet another minute, "you see, they not only squeeze the local people out with the cheap U.S.A. prices but they send them junk. They do that all over. That's what it means to be a colony, you get junk. You're poor. You gotta take it. Junky rice, inflammable clothes, you *could* grow oranges but can't afford it. It comes cheaper from three thousand miles away, even including the oil. You want to know a fact. Little Puerto Rico was our fifth biggest market. A fact."

"He's right," said Faith. "It's not such a surprising idea—it happens right here. People are poor but they think they're rich. They own a houseful of plastic and tin."

"And who needs it?" asked Mrs. Harrison, who still refused to argue. "Garbage! But the President just said they could become a state."

"A state! What's so great about becoming a state? They already have the honor of having more dead and wounded guys from the last war, percentagewise. And look at Maine—they're giving all the shoe business to Korea. Maine's a colony, Vermont's a colony. A state! Big deal. Thank you, U.S.A."

"He does have a wonderful temper," said Mrs. Harrison.

"*He* was once like that," said his grandmother, poking her husband in the ribs.

"And what about you? Once upon a time. *I* remember," he said, smiling. "Once, on the boardwalk, she socked a cop who grabbed our boy for some foolishness."

This finished everything for Richard. "He was *once* like that. You were *once*. No wonder the world's in this condition. *Once!*" he shouted, and tore out of the apartment as though "*Once*" were catching, a contagious disease which might afflict his revolutionary limbs forever and set the muscles of his face in an ineradicable smile.

—1980

Some History on Karen Silkwood Drive

"What the hell are we doing here?" asks an old friend, who was young in years not so long ago, when I was only slightly middle-aged. "For Christ's sake, we cut right through the fences at the Pentagon." We were in Seabrook, New Hampshire, sitting in a parking lot outside the site of a proposed nuclear plant along with 2,000 other protesters organized by the Clamshell Alliance.

"No! No!" says a young listener, full of the joy of common discipline.

"But look, it's a goddamn parking lot!"

"Things don't have to go the same," I say. I am very tearful. "We don't have to defend our lives by repeating them. Anyhow, the parking lot is the heart of America. You close down the parking lots and industry is wrecked. A decent car wouldn't have any place to go. Of course, those bubbling asphalt lots will be hard to occupy in summer."

The young listener says the simplest true fact. "Look, brother, it took a lot of work to get two thousand people here. If we were only two hundred, we wouldn't have gotten to this lot. We'd be outside the access road at the Stop & Shop, eating cheeseburgers."

"Not me," said a young woman. "I would never eat that stuff." She is carrying a four-day supply of healthy groceries and offers us her family granola.

I have my own kitchen concoction of grains, fruits, and nuts. "Yours is very good," I tell her, "but you use more nuts than I do. Try some of mine."

"How long are you staying here?"

"Well, no longer than Monday morning. We can't stay any longer," I apologize.

She puts her kind hand on mine. "Oh, don't feel bad. You've done your best. You can only do your best."

I know what my best is, and I have to admit to her that this is my second best. But: "How long are you staying, honey?"

"Oh," she says, "a week, anything, as long as I can."

"What if we're all arrested tomorrow morning?"

"Well, as soon as we get out, we'll return, we really will. Our affinity group is solidly committed to return."

Within the comfort of our affinity group, we place our sleeping bags on oak leaves over the sand and stone. We have named our street Karen Silkwood Drive, and our new tent city is called Seabrook. It's quite beautiful—the American-Russian moon shines on the green, blue, yellow, orange plastic and nylon tents.

Late in the morning (9 a.m.) my husband goes off to listen to the almost continuous parliament of spokespersons sent from each affinity group to bring views and initiatives to the Decision Making Body—the DMB. A new democratic process is being created.

"They never stop talking," someone says.

"Everyone has something to say," someone answers.

I decide to attend a Friends meeting on the northeast corner near the helicopter gate, the National Guardsmen, and now and then the dogs. We sit on the stony landfill, the dust blowing. I say to myself, Why, this must be just what Quang Tri looked like—the bulldozed, flattened, "pacified" countryside. I can't help those connections. They stand up among the thoughts in my head, again and again.

Anyway, I'm not very good at Friends meetings. My mind refuses to prevent my eyes from looking at the folks around me, and I'm often annoyed because I can't get the drift of the murmur of private witness. I did hear one young man near me say, "May Your intercession here today be the fruit of our action." I think this means "God helps those that help themselves," a proverb that sounds meaner than it is.

Finally a woman as gray as I am spoke up loud and clear. She intended to be heard. She told about the Westover Army Base witness during the Vietnam War. She had met a soldier later, she said, who told her it was the persistence and sagacity of the Quaker witness at Westover that had helped those draftees understand the war and turn in action against it.

The arrests begin at 3:30 and continue for thirteen hours. People are moved in buses and trucks. There is lots of time for argument—no, discussion—to go limp, to go rigid. In the end, many give up the luxury of individual torture for the security of arrest by affinity. So we are picked up and dumped into an army truck at 7:30. Twenty-seven of us remain sitting or organized into sardines, we sleep on the floor until morning. One of our clan stands talking to the state troopers and Guardsmen, some of whom haven't slept for forty-six hours. He talks and listens all night long, about the war, about Phu Bai, where he was stationed, about the Navy, the Marines, horses, actions, guard duty, guns. A man's life, I think. I had forgotten the old interests and disgusts.

In the morning, Steve, the Clamshell staff man, who is twenty years old, types out our first news release. He tapes it to a Frisbee, and David, his brother Clam, with a great swing flips it out over the army snow fence into the hands of the UPI photographer. The National Guardsmen watch, then bring us Cokes and orange soda.

I write this on the sixth day. Fourteen hundred people have remained in bail solidarity inside the detention centers of New Hampshire. There is no peaceful atom, and in our time war has been declared across the years against the future, which was once the holding place for hope.

One more story:

In another time, my friend and I vigiled every Saturday afternoon for eight years on Eighth Street in Manhattan. We offered information and support for resistance to war—legal and illegal, civilian and military. We were mostly mothers and fathers. The faces on our posters were American and Vietnamese. On our square in the middle of traffic, we were attacked for years with spit, curses, and scary driving tactics. Then, in the last two years, to our surprise people began to shout, "Right on! Stick with it!"

One day an old lady stopped me as I was giving out leaflets. I loved her at once, because she reminded me of my own mother and several aunts, who seemed in their construction to have only good posture to offer in the fight against gravity.

"They're wonderful boys," she said.

"Oh yes," I said.

"We have to do everything we can for them," she said.

"We do," I said.

"Because what's going on, what they're trying to do to them, is terrible, especially to the Vietnamese people, how they suffer, without end," she said.

"Yes," I said.

"So you have to keep it up, the support. The boys sit in jail, I know what it's like. They don't want to kill people, they give up everything, they're brave, they're the hope."

I remembered my job. "Can you join us? To stand with our big sign over there, or give out leaflets in case you hate to stand?"

"No, no, I can't do it right now. Sometime maybe."

"Could you give me your name? We're a local group."

"Yes, certainly," she said. "My name is Sobell, I'm Morton Sobell's mother."

I said, "Oh, Morton Sobell. Oh . . ."

Then, without a thought, we fell into each other's arms and began to cry, because her son was still at that time hopelessly in jail and had been there for years, all through his young manhood. And the sons and daughters of my friends were caught in a time of war that would use them painfully, no matter what their decisions.

Then we were embarrassed. We kissed each other, we nodded, we laughed at ourselves, we said "Enough!" She crossed the street, and I continued to give out leaflets.

—1977

Cop Tales

At the Wall Street Action last October, the police were on one side of the sawhorses. We were on the other. We were blocking Wall Street workers. The police were blocking us. One of them was very interested in solar housing. Our solar expert explained the science and economics of it all. Another cop from Long Island worried a lot about the Shoreham nuclear power plant. "Can't do anything about it," he said. "They'll build it. I hate it. I live there. What am I going to do?"

That could be a key to the police, I thought. They have no hope. Cynical. They're mad at us because we have a little hope in the midst of our informed worries.

Then he said, looking at the Bread and Puppet Theater's stilt dancers, "Look at that, what's going on here? People running around in the street dancing. They're going every which way. It ain't organized." We started to tell him how important the dancers were. "No, no, that's okay," he said. "The antiwar demonstrations were like this at first, mixed up, but they got themselves together. You'll get yourself together, too. In a couple years you'll know how to do it better."

Earlier, about 6 a.m., two cops wearing blue hardhats passed. One of them looked behind him. "Here come the horses," he said.

"Let's get the hell out of here!" And they moved at top casual walking speed in the opposite direction.

Also at 6 a.m., but about fifteen years ago, we would walk up and down before the Whitehall Street Induction Center wearing signs that said I SUPPORT DRAFT REFUSAL. It wouldn't take more than a couple of hours for the system to gather up its young victims, stuff them into wagons, and start them off on their terrible journey. At 9:30 on one of those mornings, about twenty women sat down all across the street to prevent the death wagons from moving. They sat for about thirty minutes. Then a plainclothesman approached an older gray-haired woman: "Missus, you don't want to get arrested." "I have to," she said. "My grandson's in Vietnam." Gently they removed her. Then with billy clubs, a dozen uniformed men moved up and down that line of young women, dragging them away, by their arms, their hair, beating them, I remember (and Norma Becker* remembers), mostly in the breast.

Last May at the rainy Armed Forces Day Parade, attended by officers, their wives, and Us, some of Us were arrested by a couple of Cops for Christ. At the desk, as they took our names, smiling, they gave us "Cops for Christ" leaflets. We gave "Disarm for Human Life" leaflets.

Another year, one of the first really large antidraft actions—also at the Induction Center at dawn. We were to surround the building. The famous people, or *Notables*, as the Vietnamese used to say, sat down to bar the front entrance. That's where the TV cameras were. Our group of regulars went around to the back of the center and sat down. Between us and the supply entrance stood a solid line of huge horses and their solemn police riders. We sat cross-legged, speaking softly as the day brightened. Sometimes someone would joke and someone else would immediately

---

* Chair of the War Resisters League.

say, Be serious. Off to one side, a captain watched us and the cavalry. Suddenly the horses reared, charged us as we sat, smashing us with their great bodies, scattering our supporting onlookers. People were knocked down, ran this way and that, but the horses were everywhere, rearing—until at a signal from the captain, which I saw, they stopped, settled down, and trotted away. That evening the papers and TV reported that a couple of thousand had demonstrated. Hundreds had been peacefully arrested.

At Wall Street, too: A gentleman with a Wall Street attaché case tried to get through our line. The police, who were in the middle of a discussion about Arabian oil, said, "Why not try down there, mister. You can get through down there." The gentleman said he wanted to get through right here and right now, and began to knee through our line. The cop on the other side of the sawhorse said, "You heard us. Down there, mister. How about it?" The gentleman said, "Damnit, what are you here for?" He began to move away, calling back in fury, "What the hell are you cops here for anyway?" "Just role-playing," the cop called in reply.

There were several cheerful police at the Trident nuclear submarine demonstration last year. One officer cheerily called out to the Trident holiday visitors to be careful as they trod the heads of the demonstrators blocking the roadway. "They're doing what they believe in." He asked us to step back, but not more than six inches. He told a joke. He said he hated war, always had. Some young state troopers arrived—more help was needed. They were tall and grouchy. A black youngster, about twelve, anxious to see what was going on, pushed against the line. One of the state troopers leaned forward and smacked the child hard on the side of the head. "Get back, you little bastard," he said. I reached out to get the attention of the cheery cop, who wore a piece of hier- archical gold on his jacket. "Officer," I said, "you ought to get that trooper out of here, he's dangerous." He looked at me, his face went icy cold. "Lady, be careful," he said. "I just saw you try to strike that officer."

Not too long ago, I saw Finnegan, the plainclothes Red Squad boss. I hadn't seen him in a long time. "Say, Finnegan," I said, "all these years you've been working at one thing and I've been working at the opposite, but look at us. Nothing's prevented either of us from getting gray." He almost answered, but a lot of speedy computations occurred in his brain and he couldn't. It's the business of the armed forces and the armored face to maintain distance at all times.

—1980

For two years we have gathered at the Pentagon because we fear
for our lives. We still fear for the life of this planet, our earth,
and the life of the children who are our human future.

We are women who come in most part from the northeastern
region of our United States. We are city women who know the
wreckage and fear of city streets; we are country women who
grieve the loss of the small farm and have lived on the poisoned
earth. We are young and older, we are married, single, lesbian.
We live in different kinds of households, in groups, families, alone;
some are single parents.

We work at a variety of jobs. We are students–teachers–factory
workers–office workers–lawyers–farmers–doctors–builders–wait-
resses–weavers–poets–engineers–homeworkers–electricians–artists–blacksmiths. We are all daughters and sisters.

We came to mourn and rage and defy the Pentagon because it
is the workplace of the imperial power which threatens us all.
Every day while we work, study, love, the colonels and generals
who are planning our annihilation walk calmly in and out the
doors of its five sides. They have accumulated over 30,000 nuclear
bombs at the rate of three to six bombs every day.

They are determined to produce the billion-dollar MX missile.

They are creating a technology called Stealth—the invisible, un-perceivable arsenal. They have revived the cruel old killer, nerve gas. They have proclaimed Directive 59, which asks for "small nuclear wars, prolonged but limited." The Soviet Union works hard to keep up with United States initiatives. We can destroy each other's cities, towns, schools, children many times over. The United States has sent "advisors," money, and arms to El Salvador and Guatemala to enable those juntas to massacre their own people.

The very same men, the same legislative committees that offer trillions of dollars to the Pentagon, have brutally cut day care, children's lunches, battered-women's shelters. The same men have concocted the Family Protection Act, which will mandate the strictly patriarchal family and thrust federal authority into the lives we live in our own homes. They are preventing the passage of ERA's simple statement and supporting the Human Life Amendment, which will deprive all women of choice and many women of life itself.

In this environment of contempt and violence, racism, woman hating, and the old European habit of Jew hatred—called anti-Semitism—all find their old roots and grow.

We are in the hands of men whose power and wealth have separated them from the reality of daily life and from the imagination. We are right to be afraid.

At the same time, our cities are in ruins, bankrupt; they suffer the devastation of war. Hospitals are closed, our schools deprived of books and teachers. Our black and Latino youth are without decent work. They will be forced, drafted to become the cannon fodder for the very power that oppresses them. Whatever help the poor receive is cut or withdrawn to feed the Pentagon, which needs about $500 million a day for its murderous health. It extracted $157 billion last year from our own tax money, $1,800 from a family of four.

With this wealth our scientists have been corrupted; over 40 percent work in government and corporate laboratories that refine the methods for destroying or deforming life.

The lands of the Native American people have been turned to radioactive rubble in order to enlarge the nuclear warehouse. The uranium of South Africa, necessary to the nuclear enterprise, enriches the white minority and encourages the vicious system of racist oppression and war.

The President has just decided to produce the neutron bomb, which kills people but leaves property (buildings like this one) intact.

There is fear among the people, and that fear, created by the industrial militarists, is used as an excuse to accelerate the arms race. "We will protect you," they say, but we have never been so endangered, so close to the end of human time.

We women are gathering because life on the precipice is intolerable.

We want to know what anger in these men, what fear that can only be satisfied by destruction, what coldness of heart and ambition drives their days.

We want to know because we do not want that dominance which is exploitative and murderous in international relations, and so dangerous to women and children at home—we do not want that sickness transferred by the violent society through the fathers to the sons.

What is it that we women need for our ordinary lives, that we want for ourselves and also for our sisters in new nations and old colonies who suffer the white man's exploitation and too often the oppression of their own countrymen?

We want enough good food, decent housing, communities with clean air and water, good care for our children while we work. We want work that is useful to a sensible society. There is a modest technology to minimize drudgery and restore joy to labor. We are determined to use skills and knowledge from which we have been excluded—like plumbing or engineering or physics or composing. We intend to form women's groups or unions that will demand safe workplaces, free of sexual harassment, equal pay for work of comparable value. We respect the work women have done in caring for the young, their own and others, in maintaining a physical and spiritual shelter against the greedy and militaristic society. In our old age we expect our experience, our skills, to be honored and used.

We want health care which respects and understands our bodies. Physically challenged sisters must have access to gatherings, actions, happy events, work.

We want an education for children which tells the true story of our women's lives, which describes the earth as our home to be cherished, to be fed as well as harvested.

We want to be free from violence in our streets and in our houses. One in every three of us will be raped in her lifetime. The pervasive social power of the masculine ideal and the greed of the pornographer have come together to steal our freedom, so that whole neighborhoods and the life of the evening and night have been taken from us. For too many women, the dark country road and the city alley have concealed the rapist. We want the night returned, the light of the moon, special in the cycle of our female lives, the stars and the gaiety of the city streets.

We want the right to have or not to have children—we do not want gangs of politicians and medical men to say we must be sterilized for the country's good. We know that this technique is the racist's method for controlling populations. Nor do we want to be prevented from having an abortion when we need one. We think this freedom should be available to poor women, as it always has been to the rich. We want to be free to love whomever we choose. We will live with women or with men or we will live alone. We will not allow the oppression of lesbians. One sex or one sexual preference must not dominate another.

We do not want to be drafted into the Army. We do not want our young brothers drafted. We want *them* equal with *us*.

We want to see the pathology of racism ended in our time. It has been the imperial arrogance of white male power that has separated us from the suffering and wisdom of our sisters in Asia, Africa, South America, and in our own country.

To some women racism has offered privilege and convenience. These women often fail to see that they themselves have lived under the unnatural authority and violence of men in government, at work, at home. Privilege does not increase knowledge or spirit or understanding. There can be no peace while one race dominates another, one people, one nation, one sex despises another.

We must not forget that tens of thousands of American women live much of their lives in cages, away from family, lovers, all the growing years of their children. Most of them were born at the intersection of oppressions: people of color, female, poor. Women on the outside have been taught to fear those sisters. We refuse that separation. We need each other's knowledge and anger in our common struggle against the builders of jails and bombs.

We want the uranium left in the earth, and the earth given back to the people who tilled it. We want a system of energy which is renewable, which does not take resources out of the earth without returning them. We want those systems to belong to the people and their communities, not to the giant corporations which invariably turn knowledge into weaponry. We want the sham of Atoms for Peace ended, all nuclear plants decommissioned, and the construction of new plants stopped. That is another war against the people and the child to be born in fifty years.

We want an end to the arms race. No more bombs. No more amazing inventions for death.

We understand all is connectedness. The earth nourishes us as we with our bodies will eventually feed it. Through us, our mothers connected the human past to the human future. We know the life and work of animals and plants in seeding, reseeding, and in fact simply inhabiting this planet. Their exploitation and the organized destruction of never-to-be-seen-again species threatens and sorrows us.

With that sense, that ecological right, we oppose the financial connections between the Pentagon and the multinational corporations and banks that the Pentagon serves.

Those connections are made of gold and oil.

We are made of blood and bone, we are made of the sweet and finite resource, water.

We will not allow these violent games to continue. If we are here in our stubborn thousands today, we will certainly return in the hundreds of thousands in the months and years to come.

We know there is a healthy, sensible, loving way to live and we intend to live that way in our neighborhoods and our farms in these United States, and among our sisters and brothers in all the countries of the world.

—1982

The Seneca Stories: Tales from the Women's Peace Encampment

My friends and I came to the Seneca Women's Peace Encampment from Vermont. No matter what else we saw in the five days of work/action/arrest/talk, we felt the wide eventful sky above us, a blazing place from which sudden thunderstorms attacked. We had driven south out of the Green Mountains, out of the hills where cows pasture on narrow spiraling terraces down to great flat fields of corn, long, barely sloping acres of soybeans. So much horizon!

We came into a careful, conservative New York area that had once experienced extraordinary history. In the 1590s, the women of the Iroquois nation had met in Seneca to ask the tribes to cease their warfare. In 1848, the first Women's Rights Convention met in Seneca Falls. During the 1850s Harriet Tubman led slaves north through this country. Her safe house still stands. The towns and countryside of Seneca County seemed to be a geography of American Herstory, where women of color and women of less color once lived powerfully and rebelliously, offering their female leadership in a dream of peace and justice for women—and men, too. In fact, the planned encampment was named just that, the Women's Encampment for a Future of Peace and Justice.

There were many greeters when we passed the Amish farm and

made a sharp right into the encampment. Women poked their heads into the windows of our car to assure us of a welcome, to tell us where to park, where the "Non-Registration" booth was, to tell any men in the car that they would be welcome in the large area around the house and garden but beyond the barn the women wanted privacy and safety. We bumped our car over the terrible corrugations that had once been the earth of a farmer's cornfield. We learned that we were expected to put three hours of work into camp maintenance every day. We contributed seven dollars. We found out quickly that the condition of the soil beyond the parking in the tenting fields was also pretty poor. Corn uses the land up, and it was a hope often expressed that this land could be renewed, returned to the fertility of the green farms of the county.

Because of friends from New York and New England who had camped earlier we knew: Seneca was Stories. The story of the flag; the story of the TV camera crew; the story of the woman who climbed the army depot tower and painted out the words MISSION FIRST—leaving the words PEOPLE ALWAYS; the story of the astrologers who advised the protesters on what day and what hour to do civil disobedience; the story of the men who apologized, the women who joined us; the story of the woman who wore a shirt saying *Nuke the Bitches Till They Glow,* who was moved a tiny bit, so she removed the words *Till They Glow,* reserving further action for deeper thought; the story of boardwalks and ramps lovingly built to keep us all from twisting our ankles, and all that work—the plumbing and electrical work—done by women; the story of rumor, invention, and absolute factual truth in the lovely combinations that become myth.

Here are some of the stories I lived in or alongside of—and a couple of stories told me so often that I've begun to think I was a part of those stories, too.

On Saturday, July 30, 1983, about one hundred women left

Seneca Falls to walk twelve miles to the encampment. They carried large cutouts of Susan B. Anthony, Elizabeth Cady Stanton, Harriet Tubman, Sojourner Truth, and other women their walk honored. They intended to show the connections between the everyday killing oppression of women and the battering of our world in man-made war. They walked peacefully through uninhabited miles of field and scrub and small towns lined with American flags. When they came into Waterloo, they saw a huge sign stretched between two houses. It greeted them: NUKE THEM TILL THEY GLOW. THEN SHOOT THEM IN THE DARK.

They turned the corner to cross the Waterloo bridge and were met by several hundred Waterloo citizens, nearly all holding little and large flags, nearly all screaming foul cries and words they hoped would insult the women: "Commies," "Lezzies," "Kill them," "Nuke them." Many carried flagpoles with pointed tips, and their enraged screams and jabbing terrified our women, who, after brief discussion, decided to sit down. (This is often done in confrontations to show that violence is not intended and also to give the sitters a chance to talk quietly about what to do next.) The sheriff, an elected official who had known all about the walk weeks earlier, had no way to control the infuriated crowd that consisted of his neighbors, who were, after all, voters. He offered a detour, which made sense to some women. But for the women sitting under the barrage of hatred, it seemed foolish to turn their backs. Besides, they felt somewhat stubborn about upholding their right to walk through an American town without vicious abuse. They thought that right was worth a good deal. Many women tried courageously to look into the eyes of the men and women barring their way . . . to somehow change the confrontation into a meeting. Finally, and ironically, the quiet women were arrested for disorderly conduct, while the screamers were allowed to go. One by one, the women were dragged off to become the fifty-four Jane Does who spent five days in the only jail big enough to hold them all—the Interlaken High School.

Among the women arrested was one prominent Waterloo citizen who was horrified by the behavior of the townspeople. Her daughter was one of the first to come to the encampment the next day to inform us that many of her neighbors were ashamed, that the hard screaming knot didn't represent them, though it would be seen again and again—at the Seneca Depot truck gate, at the Interlaken High School, where thirteen brave vigilers who were keeping a watch at night were surrounded by huge trailer trucks, assuring darkness, invisibility, and terror. Here, too, the flags were used to poke and jab at the circle of women.

The green lawn outside the Interlaken High School was a place where lots of play happened, too. In the daylight we pantomimed the August 1 march for our Jane Does watching from distant windows. We played out the fence-climbing arrests, we sang to them and, in fact, sang so well that day by day, the taunters became quieter. If we shouted, they shouted. But when we sang, they listened. I listened myself. We were singing beautifully. And we were saddened for the opposition, which tried a couple of songs, worked on "Jingle Bells," but foundered on "America the Beautiful," which we joyfully took up.

A story: one of the vigilers at the Interlaken High School prison was approached by a man who told her he'd been one of the people at the Waterloo bridge. He hadn't screamed, he said, just waved his flag. He asked what the whole thing was about, for godsakes. She explained the reason for the camp, the historical purpose of the walk. "Oh," he said, "I thought you were all sitting down in the road because the VFW wasn't letting any women be part of *their* parade. And I agreed with them. That's why I was mad."

Two days after the August 1 march, I was a greeter at the camp entrance. A big car turned in. Father and son. The father leaned out the window and said, "We came to say we're sorry about everything. That's all." The son spoke through the far window. "We wanted to ask you women how you do it. Those people were really rotten to you. I heard them. They insult you and they call you names and you're so calm. My father and me—we honor you. We don't understand, but we honor you."

Two young women came up out of darkness to join us in our night circle at Interlaken High School. Someone tells me they own or work in a restaurant near the depot. They sit with us as we go around the circle trying to see who will go home and who will sit the night out with a good chance of arrest. The two young women sit with us for about an hour, listening to us listen to one another, then proudly and deliberately walk past their neighbors on the way down to their car. The words "Traitor, traitor" follow them in a halfhearted way.

A great deal has been written about that hostility at Waterloo, as though a country that refuses to pass something as simple as the Equal Rights Amendment would not have pockets of vicious misogyny, as though a nation with tens of thousands of nuclear bombs, army bases, weapons factories in the midst of unemployment would not be able to raise a furious patriarchal horde.

From that rage of flags that seemed so pervasive in the towns of Seneca County we must go back to the days before the camp's opening. A Waterloo man came to the already exhausted, worried organizers and maintainers of the camp and said, "Take this flag and place it at the camp entrance, or else we will tell the world, the media, the town, how you refused the American flag." The women met to discuss this—as we were all to meet time and time again in large and small circles. There was so much strong feeling on either side that a committee of fifteen was charged with resolving the problem: five women in strong opposition, five women in determined support, and five easygoing intermediate mediators. After seven hours under the only shade tree in that part of the camp, it was suggested that women could make their own flags. And many flags *were* made, not national flags, but painted and embroidered banners with pictures and sayings about our lives— also a couple of handsome handmade American flags—and all these were hung on lines in the front yard of the camp, along the road. However, the flag of the provoker was not accepted. As a result, the flag entrepreneurs of Seneca County did an incredible business, as anyone driving through the red-white-and-blue towns will tell.

In the Nicastro Restaurant a couple of miles up the road, the encampment leaflet and vision statement are tacked to the wall right next to two awards to Mr. and Mrs. Nicastro: Parents of the Year. In their guest book we have all written our thanks for the decency of this family to all the women who drank coffee and ate fine celebratory dinners after jail. They allowed their place to be used during the summer for meetings between the campers and the community.

On August 1, about 2,500 women marched from the nearby Sampson State Park to the depot. It was a long, hot walk, stalled by the sheriff every twenty-five feet or so; he was waiting for state troopers. He feared another confrontation. The angry opposition had already entrenched itself and its flags at the truck gate. But this time a band of very brave Waterloo citizens stood with their children not too far away, holding signs that said they'd fight for our rights whether they agreed with us or not.

Once at the gate, women came forward to transform the military steel mesh into an embroidery of banners, dolls, children's photographs, quilts, christening dresses, lovers' photos. Then they stepped back, and the women who planned the civil disobedience came forward. Immediately women began to climb over the high fence. I thought it was rather ridiculous, but as I and my Vermont affinity group of six women looked and looked, it became more interesting. It was the riskiness of the fence. I thought, This may be the last fence I'll be able to climb in this life (I'm sixty and I see a fence shortage ahead), so I joined the others and we climbed that fence that looked to us women—young or old—a lot like the school fence that encircled girlhood, the one that the boys climbed adventurously over again and again. We were carted off by young soldiers—many of them black and Hispanic—all of them perplexed, most of them quite kind. There was a physical delight in the climbing act, but I knew and still believe that the serious act was to sit, as many women did, in little circles through the drenching night and blazing day on the hot cement in front of the truck gate with the dwindling but still enraged "Nuke Them Till They Glow" group screaming "Lesbian bitches" from their flag-enfolded cars.

To this gate the curious citizens of Waterloo or Romulus or Geneva came. Folks who'd read of this excitement brought their children and their coolers to watch silently, and sometimes speak, asking the hard questions again: "What about the Russians?" or "We have to make a living, don't we?"; and sometimes to say sadly, "Did you really burn a flag and then urinate on it?" No. No. No.

So we *had* troubled them. And we asked: Wouldn't it have been wonderful if hundreds, thousands of Germans had sat down before the gates of the Krupp gas-oven plants and troubled the contented hearts and minds of the good German people? They might have also asked those first two questions.

On Wednesday, August 3, people gathered at the fairgrounds in Waterloo outside the big corrugated-metal building in which the trial would be conducted. Lots of visible media—meaning TV. Our Jane Does had continued their resistance: they were carried into "court," then back out into the yard as the judge tried to conduct one trial after another. They demanded a common trial and dismissal of unjust charges. We, their supporters, were removed from the building. Singing again. Finally the senselessness of individual trials became clear. Three women were allowed to speak for the group. Then the judge dismissed the case and ordered the charges dropped. He, like the sheriff, was an elected official but saw the wind blowing in a different direction. Outside in the terrible heat, I walked among the men and women, the cameras, the stalwart youths standing like statues holding enormous flags on thick flagpoles. And found a group of Waterloo women with cardboard signs. WE SUPPORT YOUR RIGHT TO WALK THROUGH OUR TOWN. THE CONSTITUTION SHELTERS YOU. Our Seneca sisters were hugging them, thanking them for their bravery. "Oh," said one of the women, surprised and embarrassed, "we didn't think we'd be so important as all that." "You're the most important of all to us," we answered.

There were so many other events that ought to be written about, and I know will be. But briefly . . . the busloads of women who came all the way from Minnesota . . . the women from Greenham Common in England, and Comiso in Italy, and from the Netherlands and Germany who worked so hard to share their experiences with us . . . the religious women who asked if they could pray in the depot chapel, were given permission, then asked to leave when the pacific nature of the prayers was understood . . . the walk to Harriet Tubman's house . . . the civil disobedience actions of Labor Day, when women chose to dig a hole under the fence instead of climbing over it.

One of the most important events, and I do think of it as an event in itself, was the local news that the Seneca encampment became. That news coverage is part of the news I brought home. The combination of stubbornness that is nonviolent action, the peculiar, arduous, delicate process of our constantly public meetings set against the opposition's vituperative rage illuminated the issues. What we talked and acted about was Peace and Justice, and the way we went about it spoke to the word "Future."

One more story: I am waiting to use the phone. There are two phones. I am pretty annoyed with the long, gabby calls of the people on the line in front of me, until I'm finally close enough to hear a couple. One woman is giving information about her entire affinity group to a contact person . . . Someone's dog has to be picked up . . . A mother must be called . . . A job has to be put off. The woman on the other phone is young and in tears. She's saying, "Mom. Ma, please, it's my world they're gonna blow up." Then some silence. Then: "Ma, please, I have to do it. It's not terrible to get arrested. I'm all right, Ma, please listen, you got married and had us and everything and a house, but they still kept making nuclear bombs." More tears. "Listen, listen please, Ma."

I wanted to take the phone from her and say, "Ma, don't worry, your kid's okay. She's great. Don't you see she's one of the young women who will save my granddaughter's life?"

—1983

" Pressing the Limits of Action "

When did you first get involved in civil disobedience actions? Can you tell us some stories about early actions that you were involved in and then how you got involved in the peace movement?

If you consider the important actions of the civil-rights movement I don't think I've done so much. There aren't a lot of experiences that seem striking or interesting, but it does seem that my general disposition has been disobedient, civil or otherwise, though years ago we did have some kinds of local success. We were adamant about keeping the buses out of the park [Washington Square]. We were adamant about not letting the park be cut into for real-estate interests. One of the things I learned was stubbornness. And I've thought more and more that that's the real meaning of nonviolent civil disobedience—to be utterly and absolutely stubborn.

Another example—although no one was arrested—they would not allow any music in the same park, which is hard to believe right now. But they wouldn't allow any guitars or singing, flutes or oboes, anything. And we finally simply sat down together in the fountain circle with the children and we just sat and played guitars and recorders and fiddles. The police came from another

* An interview with Grace Paley by Meredith Smith and Karen Kahn.

precinct; they didn't dare send the sixth. They went after us, knocking people around a little, but we were stubborn. Then we won. Now it's so noisy you can hardly stand it. It seems if you have these early successes, no matter how small, they seem to form hopeful expectations.

Also, there was one action that seemed to wake us up in New York, and probably Boston, too. That was around the civil defense shelter drills. Dorothy Day was the only person in New York who, for a couple of years, refused publicly to take shelter. Then one year there were fifteen women and men. Then we were hundreds who stood in the open of City Hall park. Those actions were simple, because the drills were idiotic. Disobedience began to occur everywhere. People were arrested. The drills ended.

I don't think the thing for me has been civil disobedience so much as the importance of *not* asking permission. For instance, we had kids in our public school who had trouble reading or writing. A few of us just got together and said we'd better go ahead and help out. We suspected that the principal wouldn't want us around. So we simply went into the school and scattered ourselves among the teachers and began to work with the kids. It's true that three months later we were kicked out, but we got a lot done, and methods and forms were created so parents could come back and be useful. People will say to this day, "How did you women do that? Who did you talk to?" We didn't talk to anyone. We just did it. So I can't say that was civil disobedience. It was just an effort to make change by making change. We talk a lot about living in a free and democratic country but we're always asking permission to do very simple things.

Another fact, I came out of a socialist background as a kid and my meeting with pacifists was an extraordinary experience. I met people in the American Friends and the War Resisters League, people like that, totally unfamiliar to me. I had a normal Socialist childhood.

What's a normal Socialist childhood?

Well, you know, on May Day you wear a red tie. I was a Falcon (Communist children were Pioneers). Then you sometimes took a course in Marxism when you were twelve or thirteen, something like that. I always worked as a kid in the student unions and in groups like that. The idea of nonviolence or pacifism may have been abroad in the land, but it was not abroad in my head at all. It never entered my mind. In those years—I'm talking about the forties—political positions shifted and changed and you really couldn't hold your course in them because so much depended on what the Soviet Union said or did and whether you were for or against it. On either side you were often steered by that.

So my meeting in the early sixties, very early, maybe even '59, with what I later discovered were Friends, was a real breakthrough. The whole idea, the simple sentence "Speak truth to power" really shook me. Meanwhile, I was writing more and more [stories] and thinking about the truth of art and the truth of politics and going further—*Act* truth to power. Circumvention and manipulation in the movements of my youth had begun to disgust me—that was one of the reasons I got into so much local work—I had really just had it with the grown-up men and the big picture without quite realizing it.

The first action I took that could be described in formal terms as civil disobedience was during the Armed Forces Day Parade in the sixties. Somebody said, "You want to do that with us?" And I said, "Oh sure." So we sat down in front of the parade, sat down and threw flowers at the tanks, etc. And the good thing about that is that I got six days in jail. I've never spent more than that at any one time. I learned a lot. I learned that it was interesting. I mean, when you're in jail, it's not as if you're no place. You're in another place. You're SOMEPLACE. It is not as if you're not among people. You're among women and they're interesting, not frightening. Whoever they are, the people, the prisoners, those women can educate you.

And the whole experience is one that, well, you are suddenly in an American colony. You can think of that vast prison population that way. You have to go into it from time to time. This is how the colonized live. Prison is not a metaphor.

How does your commitment to nonviolence affect the kind of political work that you do?

Well, first of all, I think most people are nonviolent. I think there's an awful lot of junk written about the naturalness of competition and revenge—survivalism. Which is not to say there aren't certain cultures where people go out and kill each other and kill each other back. But for me, when I say nonviolence, it only means I will be nonviolent as long as I possibly can. I can't think that armed struggle is the only way to change the world or the neighborhood. And it's just words. I know this view will anger people—even some who are dear to me—but most of the people in the United States who use the term so frequently have no idea of what killing and war and death are. They have no feeling for the suffering. "Armed struggle" is two words in a pamphlet, repeated many times in a book. So you can see I hate the cheap use of that term. Still, nonviolence does *not* mean personal safety. *Pacifism is not passive-ism.* If it means that, it's useless. So I will try with others to make change in this world as stubbornly as I possibly can without inflicting pain or death but without dodging conflict confrontation—even initiating it—as at Greenham, Seneca, Livermore, Griffiss, all the wonderful Ploughshares actions at draft boards.

All of this is related of course to what I said about not asking permission to move through my time in this world. It relates also closely to the idea, the Quaker idea again, that there is a light in every human being and that light has to be addressed first before anything else. And that doesn't mean that I don't get angry. I've elbowed a few cops in my time for getting too close for my comfort or, in certain cases, my children's. But it does mean that your first approach to another human being is with the assumption that that woman or man is human and you can at least begin to talk—approach without hatred.

Then you say, "How do you feel about the Nicaraguans—El Salvador?" Well, first I don't judge them. I don't judge other people, other nations that our government and their own have pressed beyond bearing. In the second place, how can I judge them in the position they're in when I myself, without such experience of oppression, have lived with all the abstractions of war in my own head. As a little girl growing up—as any little girl growing up in my generation—we really looked to that little-boy image of energy no matter how lively we were ourselves. People assume it's a natural progression—the only forward. It took me a long time to think in other ways. Our histories are written in chapters of war and violence. Where are the long histories of nonviolent lives and actions? In fact, we here in the United States have infinite possibilities for nonviolent actions. There are people who talk a lot about armed struggle and there are many passive-ists who say they can't possibly withhold taxes, they'd get in trouble with the IRS.

How did you become a feminist?

It's a long process. It begins in childhood, doesn't it? I've always had a lot of girl friends—women friends and always circles of friends. I've never been far from the lives of women. But I liked men a lot, too. I think it was called boy crazy once. During the Second World War, I lived in army camps for a couple of years with my husband. In those days all the boys I knew were in the Pacific or Europe. At war. I still have a lot of feeling for soldiers. At Seneca—the Women's Peace Encampment—I saw those kids and they meant something to me. We don't think about those young fellows enough. But your question: After my kids were a couple of years old, I began to write stories that were really mostly about women's lives. That was because I was pained by the peculiar life of the women my age—in their twenties and thirties, a lot of them with kids and a lot of them alone already, objects of considerable contempt but kind of tough, ironic, becoming angry. I didn't think of myself as a feminist writing those stories, but I would say I'd begun to educate myself without knowing it. I was learning from myself, among others.

And then when, in response to nuclear testing and the Vietnam War, the Greenwich Village Peace Center was formed, we tried to form a women's task force. But Women's Strike for Peace had gathered itself together within that year and they seemed to fill peace-women's needs for more autonomous action. I was more interested in local work then, and in fact, many of us in the Peace Center came out of PTAs, park work, tenants' organizations—we had lived in the community's life. There were very strong women at the center and we didn't suffer too much the experiences you've probably heard about from women who worked in mixed (men and women) antiwar groups. Also, we were on home turf, not at meetings far away. Still, I had enough discontent to join an early consciousness-raising group. And I thought of myself more and more as a feminist. But when several women left Resist in the early seventies, I didn't do that, I didn't think we should all leave. At the time I thought we should (we women) have gotten together and decided in some common way who should remain, who should go. It seemed important for feminists to continue to work inside groups like Resist that were offering support and funding to women. The war was still going on, there were also resistance groups that had to be supported—in and out of the Army. (Maybe that was the central committee of my youth still talking.)

It was in early consciousness-raising groups that I began to think of myself as a feminist and also see that I had been one for some years in argument and concern. But it was really later that I decided that was the way I wanted to work. I had to go through some years of the anti-nuke movement first, really, before I decided I wanted to work in autonomous women's groups.

What was it about your experiences in the anti-nuke movement that led you to make that decision?

The split over the Seabrook actions. Both sides infuriated me. That's wrong, there were at least three positions, when Clamshell on a moment and a half's notice decided not to do the planned CD at Seabrook, and then the other side's bossy male leadership wanted to take over the place (naturally disgusted but with the same macho thoughtless muscle-making). These were, by the way, mostly Boston people (I was working and living in Vermont at the time). So I'd begun to say words like that—rural, urban— and also to see the differences.

When you said you had to go through the whole anti-nuke movement, did you see that as being separate from the feminist movement? Did you see them as being two different things?

Well, of course they were. There were some women's affinity groups. In Vermont and New Hampshire, we were part of a general coalition (Upper Valley Energy Coalition) that became so big we had to decentralize, geographically and ideologically, into affinity groups. Bob and I worked with an affinity group that is still in pretty strong business, and also I was associated with the women's affinity group—WAND—which produced an important little book, *Handbook for Women on the Nuclear Mentality* (I was not involved in its production).

What is your definition of feminism?

Any definition has got to use the word "patriarchy." If you're a feminist it means that you've noticed that male ownership of the direction of female lives has been the order of the day for a few thousand years, and it isn't natural. That it's an unnatural way of organizing life on this earth. Feminism's not about ranking priorities and oppressions, but it's about demanding changes on an even vaster scale—placing the lives of women as close to the center as class and race have been for most radicals and of course exposing the connections.

New York Women's Pentagon Action is having a public meeting with El Salvadoran women about "What does a revolution have to be for women to be liberated?" We've been talking informally with them for several weeks. They are feminists—that is, they're not simply a support group for male organizations. And talking to them you begin to see how hard it is. It means—for them—that you are responsible for your country's freedom, women, men, children. It means—for them—the hard act of *not* accepting the authority of men every step of the way. It means keeping the quarrel going, not relinquishing it at all, and still working and fighting alongside the men, because the woman-consciousness must be woven into the means if it is to be the fabric of the revolutionary end. They know the experience of Algerian women who were returned to the veil. They have no intention of repeating it.

Can you talk about some of the divisions in the feminist movement—racism, for example. Why is the women's movement practically all white?

The feminist movement is not all white. There are large groups within the movement that are. But the big wide movement? No. There are very many women of color who are feminists. They're organizing without white wisdom or presence. They don't need white women to organize for them. We live in different situations. It seems there must be ways for us all to work together finally. And I think we're coming to that. But before working together, you clarify, you empower yourselves, you establish trust and love, then you're strong enough. It's a process. The process is a powerful feminist statement.

They do suffer some divisions similar to white feminists, but even more painful. Some groups say, "Well, we can't be liberated until our brothers are also liberated." And they say, "Our brothers are really very oppressed and treated with contempt." But then there's another group that says, "Yes, that's true, but they're oppressors themselves and we don't want to live like that. It's they, our brothers, who should be making common cause with us." I've talked to Latinas and black women who feel that way. So it's a matter of time and white attention to problems of racism, before we all come closer together. Of course it's something I long for, and since I'm an optimist I see it coming.

Other divisions are between women who think the issues of violence and war are not feminist issues. They are exactly that. Isn't the violence against women and the violence of our insane interventions and nuclear buildups part of the same upbringing of boys—warriors in the playground, at home, on the job, at war? Another division: between heterosexual women and lesbians, an awful, painful division. Some of it is due to plain well-known homophobia, a historical sickness. I work in a group, the Women's Pentagon Action, that includes a high percentage of lesbians. Great numbers of lesbians are putting their time, their energy into antimilitarist work—they're important in almost any antiwar or antimilitarist or antiracist action that's happened in the last couple of years. Not to see that power and its usefulness to the world is a willful blindness.

But we were just talking about civil disobedience. Some people think it's an elite act because some of us have privileges of white skin or maybe jobs we won't lose the minute we are arrested. Well, it's true that people of color are treated worse in prison than white women. They are. (Of course, the great civil-disobedience movements—King, Gandhi—were not exactly white.) When white women (or men) use the argument—therefore *nobody* should do it—I don't understand them. It seems to me that privilege is obligation, that if it's easier to go to jail, so to speak, or more possible, then direct actions that may lead to arrest are exactly what we ought to undertake when that is what's called for.

It's sort of like having democratic rights and not using them. It's a totally different subject but people will always come to you when you're giving out leaflets and say, "You wouldn't be able to do that in Russia." So therefore you shouldn't do it here? Well, of course you have an obligation to push the privileges of democracy, to push and extend them everywhere. And people who can should do so. We also have to be willing to divide up the work without feeling that some folks are being snotty about it or braver. They're not braver. For instance, when my children were babies, I was a lot more cautious. We must investigate, imagine, press the limits of nonviolent action.

Some of this will probably seem naïve to some people. It's a naïveté it's taken me a lot of time and thinking to get to.

—1984

" Of Poetry and Women and the World "

Our panel has a kind of odd definition, and I think the three of us have taken it to mean whatever we want to talk about. And since what I want to talk about partly follows the last panel, it may be a very good way of working our way into other subjects.

I have to begin by saying that as far as I know, and even listening to all the people talking earlier, I have to say that war is man-made. It's made by men. It's their thing, it's their world, and they're terribly injured in it. They suffer terribly in it, but it's made by men. How do they come to live this way? It took me years to understand this. Because when I was a little girl, I was a boy—like a lot of little girls who like to get into things and want to be where the action is, which is up the corner someplace, where the boys are. And I understand this very well, because that was what really interested me. I could hardly wait to continue being a boy so that I could go to war and do all the other exciting boys' things. And it took my own life, really, for me to begin to change my mind somehow—after a number of years of actually living during the Second World War. I lived a lot in Army camps. And I liked living in those Army camps; I liked them because it was very exciting, and it seemed to be where it was all at, and there were a lot of boys there, one of which, one of the boys, was my husband. The other boys were just gravy, so to speak.

But as time went on in my own life, and as I began to read and think and live inside my own life, and began to work as a writer, I stopped being a boy. At some certain point, I stopped being one, I stopped liking being one, I stopped wanting to be one. I began to think there would be nothing worse in this world than being one. I thought it was a terrible life, a hard life, and a life which would ask of me behavior, feelings, passions, and excitements that I didn't want and that I didn't care about at all. Meanwhile, at the same time, what had happened was that I had begun to live among women. Well, of course I had always lived among women. All people, all girls, live among women, all girls of my time and culture live among mothers, sisters, and aunts— and lots of them too. So I had always lived among them, but I hadn't really thought about it that much. Instead, I had said, "Well, there they are and their boring lives, sitting around the table while the men are playing cards in the other room and yelling at one another. That's pretty exciting, right?" And it wasn't really until I began to live among women, which wasn't until I had children, that I began to look at that life and began to be curious about it.

Now, that brings us to writing: how we come to writing and how we come to think about it. When I came to think as a writer, it was because I had begun to live among women. Now, the great thing is that I didn't know them, I didn't know who they were. Which I should have known, since I had all these aunts, right? But I didn't know them, and that, I think, is really where lots of literature comes from. It really comes, not from knowing so much, but from not knowing. It comes from what you're curious about. It comes from what obsesses you. It comes from what you want to know. (A lot of war literature comes from that, too, you know—the feeling that Robert Stone had, that "this is it." The reason that he felt like this is that it *hadn't been it* at all. So he wondered—but more of that later.) So I wondered about these lives, and these are the lives that interested me.

And when I began to write about them, I saw immediately, since my reading and thinking in my early thirties followed a period of very masculine literature, that I was writing stuff that was trivial, stupid, boring, domestic, and not interesting. However, it began to appear that that was all I could do, and I said, "Okay, this is my limitation, this is my profound interest, this life of women, and this is what I really have to do. I can't help myself. Everybody's going to say that it's trivial, it isn't worth anything, it's boring, you know. Nobody's hitting anybody very much [but later on, I had a few people hitting each other]. And what else can I do?"

I tell that story only for other writers who are young or maybe just young in writing. To tell them that no matter what you feel about what you're doing, if that is really what you're looking for, if that is really what you're trying to understand, if that is really what you're stupid about, if that's what you're dumb about and you're trying to understand it, stay with it, no matter what, and you'll at least live your own truth or be hung for it.

We've talked about whether art is about morality or— I don't even understand some of those words, anyway. But I do understand words like "justice," which are simpler. And one of the things that art is about, for me, is justice. Now, that isn't a matter of opinion, really. That isn't to say, "I'm going to show these people right or wrong" or whatever. But what art is about—and this is what justice is about, although you'll have your own interpretations—is the illumination of what isn't known, the lighting up of what is under a rock, of what has been hidden. And I think people feel like that who are beginning to write. I was just speaking to somebody who's a native American, who was saying that what he's doing is picking up this rock at the mouth of a cave, out there in the desert, picking it up and saying, "I've got to light this up, and add what I find to the weight and life of human experience." That's what justice is about, and that's what art is about, that kind of justice and that kind of experience.

As for me, I didn't say, "Well, I'm going to pick up this rock and see if there are any women under it." I didn't think about it that way. But what I thought to myself was: Am I tired of some of these books that I'm reading! Some of them are nice, and some of them are exciting, but really, I've read about this stuff already. And who's this guy Henry Miller? You know, big deal. He's not talking to me. My life's not going to get a lot sexier on account of him. His is, no question about it. Maybe.

So, luckily, I began to understand it. It was just luck or pride or something like that. Or just not being able to accept slurs at myself or my people, women, Jews, or whatever. Even in Shakespeare, it always hurt my feelings. So I didn't really know that that's what I was going to do, but that's what I set out to do, and I did it, and I said, Yes, those lives are what I want to add to the balance of human experience.

We were accused of having been doomstruck the other day. And in a way we should be, why shouldn't we be? Things are rotten. I'm sixty-one and three-quarters years old, and I've seen terrible times during the Depression, and I do think the life of the people was worse during the McCarthy period. I just want to throw that in extra. That is to say, the everyday life, the fearful life, of Americans was harder in that time than this. But the objective facts of world events right now are worse than at any other time. And we all know that, we can't deny it, and it's also true that it's very hard to look in the faces of our children, and terrifying to look in the faces of our grandchildren. And I cannot look at my granddaughter's face, really, without sort of shading my eyes a little bit and saying, "Well, listen, Grandma's not going to let that happen." But we have to face it, and they have to face it, just as we had to face what was much less frightening.

If I talk about going to the life of women and being interested in that, and pursuing it, and writing about it all the time and not thinking about whether it was interesting or not, and finding by luck—I like to say by luck, you know, it's polite somehow—finding by luck that it was interesting and useful to people, I also need to talk a little bit about what the imagination is. The word "imagination," as we're given it from childhood on, is really about imagining fantasy. We say, "Oh, that kid has some imagination, you know. Some smart kid; that kid imagined all these devils and goblins, and so forth." But the truth is that—"the truth," you know what I mean: when I say the truth, I mean *some* of the truth—the fact is, the possibility is that what we need right now is to imagine the real. That is where our leaders are falling down and where we ourselves have to be able to imagine the lives of other people. So men—who get very pissed at me sometimes, even though I really like some of them a lot—men have got to imagine the lives of women, of all kinds of women. Of their daughters, of their own daughters, and of the lives that their daughters lead. White people have to imagine the reality, not the invention but the reality, of the lives of people of color. Imagine it, imagine that reality, and understand it. We have to imagine what is happening in Central America today, in Lebanon and South Africa. We have to really think about it and imagine it and call it to mind, not simply refer to it all the time. What happens is that when you keep just referring to things, you lose them entirely. But if you think in terms of the life of the people, you really have to keep imagining. You have to think of the reality of what is happening down there, and you have to imagine it. When somebody said to Robert Stone, "Isn't there a difference between the life of Pinochet and of you, sir?" you have to imagine that life, and if you begin to imagine it, you know that there's a damn lot of difference between those two lives. There's a lot of difference between my life, there's a lot of difference between my ideas, between my feelings, between what thrills, what excites me, what nauseates me, what disgusts me, what repels me, and what many, many male children and men grown-ups have been taught to be excited and thrilled and adrenalined by. And it begins in the very beginning. It begins in the sandbox, if you want to put it that way. It begins right down there, at the very beginning of childhood. And I'm happy, for my part, to see among my children and their children changes beginning to happen, and also among a lot of young men—that's one of the things that's most encouraging to me: to think that some of these young guys have been listening, and imagining the lives of their daughters in a new way, and thinking about it, and wanting something different for them. That is what some of imagining is about.

So those are the things I've been thinking about a lot as a writer, both solitary in the world and at my desk. I just want to read you one little piece, and that's how I'll conclude. I probably left something out, but you can't say everything. We're really talking about society and artists, and this was in relation to the question of what was the responsibility of the writer, if there was any. And I thought, Every human being has lots of responsibility, and therefore the poet and the artist also has responsibility, why not? But this is the responsibility of society.

It is the responsibility of society to let the poet be a poet
It is the responsibility of the poet to be a woman
It is the responsibility of the poets to stand on street corners
giving out poems and beautifully written leaflets
also leaflets they can hardly bear to look at
because of the screaming rhetoric
It is the responsibility of the poet to be lazy, to hang out
and prophesy
It is the responsibility of the poet not to pay war taxes
It is the responsibility of the poet to go in and out of ivory
towers and two-room apartments on Avenue C
and buckwheat fields and Army camps
It is the responsibility of the male poet to be a woman
It is the responsibility of the female poet to be a woman

It is the poet's responsibility to speak truth to power, as the
     Quakers say
It is the poet's responsibility to learn the truth from the powerless
It is the responsibility of the poet to say many times: There is no
     freedom without justice and this means economic
     justice and love justice
It is the responsibility of the poet to sing this in all the original
     and traditional tunes of singing and telling poems
It is the responsibility of the poet to listen to gossip and pass it
     on in the way storytellers decant the story of life
There is no freedom without fear and bravery. There is no freedom
     unless earth and air and water continue and children
     also continue
It is the responsibility of the poet to be a woman, to keep an eye
     on this world and cry out like Cassandra, but be
     listened to this time.

—1986

" El Salvador "

I wondered what possible contribution I could make to this rich book of facts, this book of women whose lives have been a longing and a struggle for a revolution that would transform their entire country and include women's lives in that transformation. (This has not always happened in revolutions.)

We were actually on our way to Nicaragua, but stopped in El Salvador. We owed this—the next three days—to our own U.S. government, which did not permit Nica Air to fly from the United States to Nicaragua. Still, the planes of my rich country seem to almost line the skies of the planet—unless some other earth-and-heaven–owning nation says, "Not over us! Not just yet!"

In the course of those packed, well-organized days we saw the streets of San Salvador guarded against its own citizens by soldiers dressed in heavy weaponry. We traveled to barbed-wire camps, dusty, full of displaced villagers. We learned from the idealistic and endangered Catholic and Lutheran caretakers that the barbed wire was not so much to keep the peasants in as to prevent the death squads from easily snatching a hounded mountain villager or a guerrilla's cousin for questioning and torture.

We saw orphanages where an energetic priest tiptoed around visiting U.S. congressmen. He hoped they would have contacts with philanthropists who might help pay for the cottage camps so that little children could have books to learn from and prostheses to walk with. (Just a few miles from this camp, this orphanage, on the very same road, four nuns had been killed, removed from the dangerous occupations of active compassion and prayer by busy killers.) Walking among these children whose parents were murdered or imprisoned or in exile, I couldn't help but think of Vietnam, where first our government created orphans, then decided to adopt, nurture, and finally educate them, away from the life and history of their people.

We were able to visit Ilopango prison—the women's prison—a little while after the fasting, the strikes, the struggles described in *A Dream Compels Us*. And found, ironically, a somewhat freer environment than we had observed in San Salvador. Young women greeted us, black-tammed commandantes who had been captured in the mountains. A chorus sang the "Internationale" to us. A theater group made a play. We met several young women who, having been fruitlessly interrogated, were shot in the leg to ensure immobility, then raped and arrested. In Ilopango prison there were many small children—some the babies of love, some of rape. For the legless young women, sixteen, seventeen years old, there was only one pair of crutches, which meant that only one woman could get around at a time, making for a kind of sad listlessness in the others. We called the MADRE* office in New York (we were members of a tour organized by MADRE), and they announced this need on the WBAI radio station. Within a couple of days the office was jammed with crutches, and within two weeks a group from NACLA† had brought the crutches down

---

* MADRE is a New York–based nonprofit organization dedicated to developing political and material support for the women of Nicaragua and El Salvador.
† The North American Congress on Latin America (NACLA) publishes the bimonthly *Report on the Americas* and sponsors research on political, economic, and social developments in Latin America and the Caribbean.

to Ilopango. A small shiny pebble in a dirty field of torment, hypocrisy, murder.

Back in San Salvador we visited the Mothers of the Disappeared. Their office had been raided and nearly destroyed a couple of days earlier. The women greeted us generously, as though they didn't know that it was our U.S. tax money that was being used to increase and deepen their sorrow. (They knew a great deal.) They had placed two huge photograph albums on the table, which we looked at. We could hardly turn the pages, as it would be an act of abandonment of the murdered son or daughter photographed on that page—usually a teacher or health worker, the same dangerous professions attacked by the Contras in Nicaragua.

In San Salvador I

Come   look   they said
here are the photograph albums
these are our children.

We are called the Mothers of the Disappeared
we are also the mothers of those who were seen once more
and then photographed   sometimes parts of them
could not be found

a breast   an eye   an arm is missing
sometimes a whole stomach
that is why we are called   the Mothers
of the Disappeared   although we have these large
heavy photograph albums full of beautiful
torn faces

In San Salvador II

Then one woman spoke   About my son
she said   I want to tell you   This
is what happened

I heard a cry   Mother
Mother   keep the door closed   a scream
the high voice of my son   his scream
jumped into my belly   his voice
boiled there and boiled until hot water
ran down my thigh

The following week I waited
by the fire making tortilla   I heard What?
the voice of my second son   Mother quickly
turn your back to the door   turn your back
to the window

And one day of the third week
my third son called me   Oh Mother please
hurry up   hold out your apron   they are
stealing my eyes

And then in the fourth week   my
fourth son   No

No   It was morning   he stood
in the doorway   he was taken right
there   before my eyes the parts of
the body of my son were tormented   are
you listening?   do you understand
this story?   there was only one

> *child   one boy   like Mary I had*
> *only one son*

I have written these few remembrances of a country my country won't leave alone because the faces of the people I saw in those short days do not leave me. I see it clearly right now. The teachers of ANDES—the teachers' union—demonstrating on the steps of the great cathedral, where hundreds, mourning Oscar Romero's murder, had been shot only a couple of years earlier. They held banners and called for decent wages, and an end to disappearances. On those historic steps they seemed naked to the rage of the death squads. I could see how brave they were because their faces were pale and their eyes, searching the quiet crowd, were afraid. Still, they stood there, shouted the demands, and would not be moved.

—1989

IV / A Few Reflections on Teaching and Writing

"The Value of Not Understanding Everything" is probably one of the first talks I ever made—mid-sixties or earlier. I must have thought that a march of blunt sentences would set the right authoritative sound. But I see in rereading it that though I was a woman addressing women, I used the pronoun "he" all but once. Well . . . that's the way it was. It's that persistent "he" that now seems strange and artificial.

"Some Notes on Teaching" was originally written for a collection by Jonathan Baumbach on that subject and reprinted in Points, a periodical published by the Teachers & Writers Collaborative. I have just looked at it after many years. I was glad to see Paul Goodman's poem (why are his poems and short stories not known?)—as good as, well, anyone's. I would, of course, make some changes in the books and writers I suggested. I do stand by the ones I mentioned in this article.

In the last fifteen years I've been asked to write a number of prefaces (sometimes called forewords or introductions). I agreed to do so if I loved the writer, the subject, or wished I'd written the book myself, in which case I'd feel sad or ashamed not to accept the request.

I studied Christa Wolf's essays in The Author's Dimension, read and reread them before I began to write that introduction. I'd been

to visit her a couple of times and admired the novels Christa T.,
Models of Childhood, Cassandra, *and later* Accident. *I believed
that the attacks on her from the West German critics had more to
do with her interest in writing about women; the East German
bureaucrats didn't like that interest too much, either. She didn't
think that was the problem. I did.*

Norman Fruchter's excellent novel Coat upon a Stick *was re-
published by the Jewish Publications Society. I had read it in its
first publication years earlier and loved thinking and writing about
it. It's wonderful when a fine piece of work is given another chance.
The fact is, I admired Fruchter in 1969. We were in North Vietnam. We traveled with others for about three weeks. He was one of
the filmmakers. He now works with children, education, the poor.*

*In the case of Clarice Lispector, I accepted the word of transla-
tors and Portuguese speakers that she did truly bring a new sound
to Brazilian literature. I was interested in the fact that her parents
were Russian Jewish immigrants in Brazil, and the sounds of those
two early languages, Russian and Jewish, in her ear on the way
to Portuguese were the same that sang to me in childhood on my
way to English.*

*I had been aware for years that Antonina Nicolaevna Pirozh-
kova's seven years with Isaac Babel were important and had been
translated. Anne Frydman, the translator and my friend, was full
of this project and loved the journals. Then she was able to bring
them to the attention of Steerforth Press.*

*At the end of this section I've put some shorter pieces in praise
of writers—and people—I admire.*

*Writing an introductory paragraph or two means I can keep
talking about Don Barthelme, for instance, my neighbor, a great
writer, friend. We shared a street, West Eleventh—looking in my
case north, in his, south. He saw directly into the elementary school,
the teachers, the children. It domesticated him, which he needed.
He used that improvement to talk about the whole city.*

Not too long ago I was teaching an afternoon workshop at Man-

hattan Community College. There were GED students, English as a Second Language students, and some hoping-to-get-into-college-next-semester students. I'm expected in some of these classes to read a story of my own which they have already read, which I do, and there are always lots of good questions. This time I thought I'd try something else. So I read them Don's story about Hokie Mokie the jazz saxophonist. They loved it, they wanted to know who the guy was who wrote it—was he a musician, could he come and read them another of his stories?—or would I? No, he can't come, I said, he's dead. A beautiful writer and understander, inventor in the English language, a funny guy, a moralist, younger than I— and gone—he would be glad to know you loved his story. But this is the great thing: there are his books and they're still talking. You can't shut them up.

Barbara Deming was my teacher before I knew her, and she's my teacher now. I learned about nonviolence from three people: Bayard Rustin in one brilliant two-hour talk in 1961 in our brand-new Greenwich Village Peace Center—my politics and the politics of my friend Mary Gandall were turned around for life. I never heard him speak again, though for a year or two I saw him often. Then A. J. Muste at the War Resisters League, not so much by his speech as by his way of listening to the young men who were about to decide whether to go to prison or to war. And then Barbara Deming.

I think it was the May Day demonstration of 1973. Barbara and I were among about fifteen hundred people who were arrested pro-testing the continuing, seemingly endless war. We were, in our group, the first to step into the street to stop the Washington traffic as it moved, continuing, we believed, the business of war. Thanks to the decision of a dozen enraged drivers not to kill us for some reason, we were simply arrested. Then gathered into police buses and distributed here and there. We were dropped off in an old football field (why old?), where a number of young people, declared anarchists, proved the virtue of undominated organizing by digging a latrine at once and creating a tarpaulin shelter with some tarps lying around the field. It began to rain. God's little rain. Then it stopped and became quite cold.

There were several hundred people who began, for warmth, to huddle in the edges of the shelter or lean into one another. Many of my students were there and naturally had forgotten their sweaters or by now lost them. To keep warm, Barbara and I walked arm in arm and talked and talked. Meanwhile, concerned helicopters flew over us and probably radioed information to other responsible means of transportation, which soon brought members of Congress into our football field. They seemed to worry most about the young people and the old people. At that time Barbara and I were somewhere in between and did not attract attention.

Then our own tough New York congresswoman Bella Abzug appeared and came to speak to us. She wanted to know if we were okay, had there been any trouble? No, we were fine, just talking one of our first long personal talks.

But it was getting cold. She gave us a rather long look. Barbara and I had had political differences with Bella—better to say differences about strategy or belief in electoral processes, and we were equally firm in our different views of civil disobedience as an appropriate, realistic response to the continuing war in Vietnam.

Well, she gave us, the mud, and the rain a grinning look and said, "I guess you're where you want to be and I'm where I want to be."

I've often told this story and learned with some amusement that she has, too.

I've included Claire Lalone, my husband's mother, and my conversation with her. There's a painting of her in what I call our middle room (to get to any other room you have to walk through it). A young handsome woman of the 1920s, a French Canadian working-class girl who had a hard time and assumed she was supposed to. Who can forget her generosity, her lack of bitterness, her pleasure when, dying, she imagined the transformed lives of younger women?

The difference between writers and critics is that in order to function in their trade, writers must live in the world, and critics, to survive in the world, must live in literature.

That's why writers in their own work need have nothing to do with criticism, no matter on what level.

In fact, since seminars and discussions move forward a lot more cheerily if a couple of bald statements are made, I'll make one: You can lunge off into an interesting and true career as a writer even if you've read nothing but the Holy Bible and the New York *Daily News*, but that is an absolute minimum (read them slowly).

Literary criticism always ought to be of great interest to the historian, the moralist, the philosopher, which is sometimes me. Also to the reader—me again—the critic comes as a journalist. If it happens to be the right decade, he may even bring great news.

As a reader, I liked reading Wright Morris's *The Territory Ahead*. But if I—the writer—should pay too much attention to him, I would have to think an awful lot about the Mississippi River. I'd have to get my mind off New York. I always think of New York. I often think of Chicago, San Francisco. Once in a while Atlanta. But I never think about the Mississippi, except to notice that its big, muddy foot is in New Orleans, from whence all New York singing comes. Documentaries aside, my notions of music came by plane.

As far as the artist is concerned, all the critic can ever do is make him or break him. He can slip him into new schools, waterlog him in old ones. He can discover him, ignore him, rediscover him . . .

Apart from having to leave the country in despair and live in exile forever—or as in milder situations, never having lunch uptown again—nothing too terrible can happen to the writer's work. Because what the writer is interested in is life, life as he is *nearly* living it, something which takes place here or abroad, in Nebraska or New York or Capri. Some people have to live first and write later, like Proust. More writers are like Yeats, who was always being tempted from his craft of verse, but not seriously enough to cut down on production.

Now, one of the reasons writers are so much more interested in life than others who just go on living all the time is that what the writer doesn't understand the first thing about is just what he acts like such a specialist about—and that is life. And the reason he writes is to explain it all to himself, and the less he understands to begin with, the more he probably writes. And he takes his ununderstanding, whatever it is—the face of wealth, the collapse of his father's pride, the misuses of love, hopeless poverty—he simply never gets over it. He's like an idealist who marries nearly the same woman over and over. He tries to write with different names and faces, using different professions and labors, other forms to travel the shortest distance to the way things really are.

In other words, the poor writer—presumably in an intellectual profession—really oughtn't to know what he's talking about.

When people in school take their first writing classes, it is sometimes suggested to them that they write about their own experience. Put down what you see. Put down what you know. Perhaps describe a visit you have just had with a friend.

Well, I would suggest something different. I would say, Don't knock yourself out. You know perfectly well what happened when your friend Helen visited last Friday. This is great practice for a journalist and proper practice for a journalist. As for an inventing writer, I would say something like this:

Now, what are some of the things you don't understand at all? You've probably taken all these psych courses, and you know pretty well what is happening between your mother and yourself, your father and your brother. Someone in your family has surely been analyzed, so you've had several earfuls as well as a lot of nasty remarks at dinner. Okay—don't write about that, because now you understand it all. That's what certain lessons in psychology and analytical writing effect—you have the impression that you know and understand because you own the rules of human behavior, and that is really as bad as knowing and understanding.

You might try your father and mother for a starter. You've seen them so closely that they ought to be absolutely mysterious. What's kept them together these thirty years? Or why is your father's second wife no better than his first?

If, before you sit down with paper and pencil to deal with them, it all comes suddenly clear and you find yourself mumbling, Of course, he's a sadist and she's a masochist, and you think you have the answer—*drop the subject.*

If, in casting about for suitable areas of ignorance, you fail because you understand yourself (and too well), your school friends, as well as the global balance of terror, and you can also see your last Saturday-night date blistery in the hot light of truth—but you still love books and the idea of writing—you might make a first-class critic.

What I'm saying is that in areas in which you are very smart you might try writing history or criticism, and then you can know and tell how all the mystery of America flows out from under Huck Finn's raft; where you are kind of dumb, write a story or a novel, depending on the depth and breadth of your dumbness. Some people can do both. Edmund Wilson, for instance—but he's so much more smart than dumb that he has written very little fiction.

When you have invented all the facts to make a story and get somehow to the truth of the mystery and you can't dig up another question—change the subject.

Let me give you a very personal example: I have published a small book of short stories. They are on several themes, at least half of them Jewish. One of the reasons for that is that I was an outsider in our particular neighborhood—at least I thought I was—I took long rides on Saturday, the Sabbath. My family spoke Russian, but the street spoke Yiddish. There were families of experience I was cut off from. You know, it seemed to me that an entire world was whispering in the other room. In order to get to the core of it all, I used all those sibilant clues. I made fiction.

As often happens when you write something else, a couple of magazines asked to hear from me. They wanted a certain kind of story—which I'd already done—

But the truth of the matter is, I have probably shot my Jewish bolt, and I had better recognize that fact and remember it. It's taken me a long time, but I have finally begun to understand that part of my life. I am inside it. I could write an article, I imagine, on life in the thirties and forties in Jewish New York, but the tension and the mystery and the question are gone. Except to deceive my readers and myself, in honor I could never make fiction of that life again. The writer is not some kind of phony historian who runs around answering everyone's questions with made-up characters tying up loose ends. She is nothing but a questioner.

Luckily for my craft—for my love of writing—I have come up against a number of other inexplicable social arrangements. There are things about men and women and their relations to each other, also the way in which they relate to the almost immediate destruction of the world, that I can't figure out. And nothing in critical or historical literature will abate my ignorance a tittle or a jot. I will have to do it all by myself, marshal the evidence. In the end, probably all I'll have to show is more mystery—a certain juggled translation from life, that foreign tongue, into fiction, the jargon of man.

—mid-1960s

A woman invented fire and called it
                    the wheel
Was it because the sun is round
        I saw the round sun bleeding to sky
And fire rolls across the field
        from forest to treetop
It leaps like a bike with a wild boy riding it

Oh   she said
                    see the orange wheel of heat
light   that turned me from the
        window of my mother's home
to home in the evening

Here are about fifteen things I might say in the course of a term.
To freshmen or seniors. To two people or a class of twenty. Every
year the order is a little different, because the students' work is
different and I am in another part of my life. I do not elaborate
on plans or reasons, because I need to stay as ignorant in the art
of teaching as I want them to remain in the art of literature. The
assignments I give are usually assignments I've given myself,
problems that have defeated me, investigations I'm still pursuing.

1. Literature has something to do with language. There's probably a natural grammar at the tip of your tongue. You may not believe it, but if you say what's on your mind in the language that comes to you from your parents and your street and friends, you'll probably say something beautiful. Still, if you weren't a tough, recalcitrant kid, that language may have been destroyed by the tongues of schoolteachers who were ashamed of interesting homes, inflection, and language and left them all for correct usage.

2. A first assignment: To be repeated whenever necessary, by me or the class. Write a story, a first-person narrative in the voice of someone with whom you're in conflict. Someone who disturbs you, worries you, someone you don't understand. Use a situation you don't understand.

3. No personal journals, please, for about a year. Why? Boring to me. When you find only yourself interesting, you're boring. When I find only myself interesting, I'm a conceited bore. When I'm interested in you, I'm interesting.

4. This year, I want to *tell* stories. I ask my father, now that he's old and not so busy, to tell me stories, so I can learn how. I try to remember my grandmother's stories, the faces of her dead children. A first assignment for *this* year: Tell a story in class, something that your grandmother told you about a life that preceded yours. That will remind us of our home language. Another story: At Christmas time or Passover supper, extract a story from the oldest persons told them by the oldest person they remember. That will remind us of history. Also—because of time shortage and advanced age, neither your father nor your grandmother will bother to tell unimportant stories.

5. It's possible to write about anything in the world, but the slightest story ought to contain the facts of money and blood in order to be interesting to adults. That is, everybody continues on this earth by courtesy of certain economic arrangements; people are rich or poor, make a living or don't have to, are useful to

systems or superfluous. And blood—the way people live as families or outside families or in the creation of family, sisters, sons, fathers, the bloody ties. Trivial work ignores these two FACTS and is never comic or tragic.

May you do trivial work?

WELL

6. You don't even *have* to be a writer. Read the poem "With Argus" by Paul Goodman. It'll save you a lot of time. It ends:

> *The shipwright looked at me*
> *with mild eyes.*
> *"What's the matter friend?*
> *You need a New Ship*
> *from the ground up, with art,*
> *a lot of work,*
> *and using the experience you*
> *have—"*
> *"I'm tired!" I told him in*
> *exasperation,*
> *"I can't afford it!"*
> *   "No one asks you, either,"*
> *he patiently replied, "to venture*
> *forth.*
> *Whither? why? maybe just forget it."*
> *And he turned on his heel and left*
> *me—here.*

7. Luckily for art, life is difficult, hard to understand, useless, and mysterious. Luckily for artists, they don't require art to do a good day's work. But critics and teachers do. A book, a story, should be smarter than its author. It is the critic or the teacher in you or me who cleverly outwits the characters with the power of prior knowledge of meetings and ends.

Stay open and ignorant.

(For me, the problem: How to keep a class of smart kids—
who are on top of Medieval German and Phenomenology—dumb?
Probably too late and impossible.)

Something to read: Cocteau's journals.

8. Sometimes I begin the year by saying: This is a definition
of fiction. Stesichorus was blinded for mentioning that Helen had
gone off to Troy with Paris. He wrote the following poem and his
sight was restored:

> *Helen, that story is not true*
> *You never sailed in the benched ships*
> *You never went to the city of Troy.*

9. Two good books to read:

> *A Life Full of Holes*, Charhadi
> *I Work Like a Gardener*, Joan Miró

10. What is the difference between a short story and a novel?
The amount of space and time any decade can allow a subject
and a group of characters. All this clear only in retrospect.

Therefore: Be risky.

11. A student says, Why do you keep saying a work of art?
You're right. It's a bad habit. I mean to say a work of truth.

12. What does it mean To Tell the Truth?

It means—for me—to remove all lies. *A Life Full of Holes* was
said truthfully at once from the beginning.* Therefore, we know
it can be done. But I am, like most of you, a middle-class person
of articulate origins. Like you I was considered verbal and tal-
ented, and then improved upon by interested persons. These are
some of the lies that have to be removed:

---

* Really?

a. The lie of injustice to characters.

b. The lie of writing to an editor's taste, or a teacher's.

c. The lie of writing to your best friend's taste.

d. The lie of the approximate word.

e. The lie of unnecessary adjectives.

f. The lie of the brilliant sentence you love the most.

13. Don't go through life without reading the autobiographies of Emma Goldman

Prince Kropotkin

Malcolm X

14. Two peculiar and successful assignments. Invent a person —that is, name the characteristics and we will write about him or her. Last year it was a forty-year-old divorced policeman with two children.

An assignment called the List Assignment. Because inside the natural form of day beginning and ending, supper with the family, an evening at the draft board, there are the facts of noise, conflict, echo. In other years, the most imaginative, inventive work has happened in these factual accounts.

For me, too.

15. The stories of Isaac Babel and the conversation with him reported by Konstantin Paustovsky in *Years of Hope*. Also, Paustovsky's *The Story of a Life*, a collection of stories incorrectly called autobiography.

Read the poem "The Circus Animals' Desertion" by William Butler Yeats.

Students are missing from these notes. They do most of the talking in class. They read their own work aloud in their own voices and discuss and disagree with one another. I do interrupt, interject any one of the preceding remarks or one of a dozen others, simply bossing my way into the discussion from time to time, because, after all, it's my shop. To enlarge on these, I would need to keep a journal of conversations and events. This would be against my literary principles and pedagogical habits—all of which are subject to change.

Therefore: I can only describe the fifteen points I've made by telling you that they are really notes for beginners, or for people like myself who must begin again and again in order to get anywhere at all.

—1970

" " *One Day I Made Up a Story*

One day I made up a story. I imagined a wild old woman leaning on her elbows at her open window, next door to the schoolyard, making a speech to the street. She shouted: Listen. Stop! I must tell you that smart, greedy madmen intend to destroy this beautifully made planet. Listen! The coming murder of our children by these men has got to become a terror and a sorrow to you, and starting right this minute, it had better interfere with any daily pleasure.

Then the old woman shut the window. She played the piano for a while. Then she opened the window and shouted again: Stop! Listen!

That same day, I read about a laboratory in California called Livermore in which young men with extraordinary brains are using their imaginative dreamy minds to refine our present gross methods for disintegrating a body a tree a house a pebble.

Outside that laboratory, as we all know, there is earth fire water air. These are the essential garments of the people, Chief Seattle said, of the tribes of animals, of all growing creatures, as well as the blades of grass, their grainy seeds that feed us all. For the young men inside the laboratory (whose intelligence and ambition really shine in their newspaper faces), earth fire water air seem to be discrete problems to be interestingly solved.

Later that day I was part of a television panel that was as full of facts as laboratories are full of brilliant young men. Our side and the opposers kept tossing huge mouthfuls of nuclear numbers at one another. How many warheads, how many missiles, what kind; their quality was evaluated before each impassioned throw of words. In this language, the sorrow of the people and the suffering of this poisoned earth were not included, were not imagined.

Imagined! Imagination! That's one of the gifts hundreds of generations of women and men working eating loving have given us. Why has it been used to break the world apart into smaller and smaller pieces? It couldn't have been easy to do, because we —animals, bugs, trees—are connected to one another by streams of spit, water, necessity. The hard hug of sunlight holds us all. And we are attached to this earth by the fact of gravity as well as the invention of love. So the connectors have always been there.

I myself can't imagine the lives of those young men or the lives of the corporate bosses of our economy, whose patriarchal dream is exhausting our mountains and rivers, scratching the sleeping elements like uranium out of the Navajo lands into wide-awake, terrifying energy.

I can't imagine their lives, but I see they are the disconnectors. They have fed us despair. Still, at the edge of that despair there is a kind of determined light which has been called hope. Hope is not an ephemeral thing. It's a reality created out of our long human history of birth and rebirth, in which bravery, mutual aid, stubborn struggle, and imagination have been powerful enough to shift the awesome downward trajectories of war and oppression.

And this is where we are now. The old woman cries warning to the street full of schoolchildren and grown-ups. We look up. We listen. We take the children by the hand and help them cross the dangerous streets. Then as life goes on we show them the earth under the asphalt, the surprise of water-eating grass and water-saving cactus, and all the colors and threads of this world the disconnectors have been laboriously snipping. Why do we do this? To keep our girls and boys from becoming smart, greedy madmen obviously. And this is one of the ways we may be able to start again and again, until the amazing year or decade or century in which, at home in our only world, we finally stay started.

—1985

Imagining the Present

I was trying to remember exactly how we started Teachers & Writers Collaborative. It was in 1965 or 1966 I think. I felt kind of shy with all those people: Anne Sexton, Muriel Rukeyser, Denise Levertov, Mitch Goodman, Tinka Topping, and Paul Lauter, and Florence Howe, who later created, with others, the Feminist Press. There were a lot of things happening around that time. We had learned about money becoming available from "up there," you know, from that bad old state that people are always talking about these days, and that the money was for the children of our city, for literature and literacy. And as it turned out, the ideas that were discussed in our early meetings were being talked about all over the country, so that wherever you go now, you'll find poets in the schools, and you'll find different organizations bringing them to elementary schools, high schools, and community centers. The results were far-reaching.

Not long ago I gave a talk at the Associated Writing Programs. The AWP is not as much about children as about extremely grown-ups, specifically people teaching writing in the colleges. It has become a profession, with a whole bunch of degrees that one has to have. But even that—the idea that writing could be taught! How extraordinary! The idea of teaching writing seems very peculiar to some people. Anytime I speak in public, someone will get up and say, "You can't teach writing." What they mean is that you can teach grammar and spelling, but you can't teach writing. They're under the impression that you can teach math —the same people!—whereas writing is language, something you've been doing all your life, since you were a little tiny kid, right? So the idea of teaching writing: what does it mean, finally?

For some people it meant that as a teacher you had to make great writers: either a student becomes a great writer or what's the point in teaching writing? Whereas the person who believes that you can teach math never thinks about whether or not the idea is to make a great mathematician. Nor does the history teacher believe that it is essential, in order to be an honorable teacher of history, to produce a great or famous historian. In a way, they are right about what they're doing: they want to produce women and men who love history, or math, or chemistry, and would understand what they (the teachers) are doing, and love and maybe understand the world a little bit better. Our idea was that children—by writing, by putting down words, by reading, by beginning to love literature, by the inventiveness of listening to one another—could begin to understand the world better and begin to make a better world for themselves. That always seemed to me such a natural idea that I've never understood why it took so much aggressiveness and so much time to get it started.

At one of our early meetings, we were walking along the beach, and Muriel, Anne, and Denise were reading poems to each other in the evening, which made it very beautiful and memorable for us. And then we found out that we had to write a grant! We had to figure out how to write a proposal to ask for the money. We sat there and wrote it, but one of our big arguments was about how to write it. Someone had already informed us that there was a whole grant-writing language. It was new at that time, but it was "interesting." But we argued among ourselves, saying, "We're trying to get money for this Teachers & Writers program, and we're writers, so let's just *write* it!" Finally, as we came to the end of it, there were a couple of people, more experienced in this kind of writing, who looked at it and said, "You can't do it this way. You have to use a certain kind of form for it." But we felt extremely brave, saying, "No, we're not going to end that way, we're going to end this with a noble statement as writers."

Now I want to say just a few things about the imagination. I've looked at a lot of other speeches about writing and the imagination, and I'm all for it. I'm not against the imagination, so I don't want you to think that. But I read somewhere that Isaac Babel said that his main problem was that he had no imagination. And I thought about that a lot, because if you read him, you know that what he's trying to say—except for a few pieces, such as "The Sin of Jesus"—is very close to his life, the terrifying life that he led in the Cossack Red Army during, I guess, 1920, '21, '22. And so I tried to figure out exactly what he meant. I guess what he really didn't understand was the amount of imagination it had taken for him to understand what had happened, what was real. There were people in his unit who, if they had tried to tell him what was going on in this particular hut or pogrom-suffering village, couldn't have. Yet he was able to use what he *did* know about life and poverty and war to stretch toward what he *didn't* know about the Cossack Red Army. So I think about that as the *fact* of the imagination.

That leads me to think of the headline that Jordan Davis held up when he introduced me: MCNAMARA ADMITS HE MADE A MISTAKE.* Well, McNamara finally developed an imagination is all I can say. Of course what he *may* have imagined is what was going to happen to him in the next world if he didn't admit it. Something like George Wallace the other day at Selma, who also said

---

* It turns out that—according to his tapes—Lyndon Baines Johnson in 1964 also thought the war might not be a good or workable idea.

he had been wrong. But the idea of McNamara's living through that time, allowing some of us to spend either our youth or the prime of our lives fighting in or against that war, and trying to help our neighbors imagine what was happening in Vietnam, while he and a few others were up there thinking, You know, it's possible we're not right, it's possible we shouldn't have gone in there, maybe we made a mistake, and then not speaking another word about it for the next thirty years!

At that time, hints came to us that there was dissension in the administrations, and that the children of a lot of those people, being young and healthy, had some idea that this was a terrible business that their parents were involved in. I mean, it's bad enough being the child of any parent: you suspect how wrong your parents are from the beginning. You *think* they're wrong, but you don't *know* they're wrong. But these young people *knew* their parents were wrong, and had to live with that. What I'm trying to say is: Where is the imagination in that? What do we need our imaginations for?

First of all, we need our imaginations to understand what is happening to other people around us, to try to understand the lives of others. I know there's a certain political view that you mustn't write about anyone except yourself, your own exact people. Of course it's very hard for anyone to know who their exact people are, anyway. But that's limiting. The idea of writing from the head or from the view or the experience of other people, of another people, of another life, or even of just the people across the street or next door, is probably one of the most important acts of the imagination that you can try and that can be useful to the world.

Certainly one of the things that haven't been sufficiently imagined yet, apart from the deaths of 60,000 Americans, is the terrible suffering that the Vietnamese people have been subjected to all these years. From the very beginning of the war, and then after the war, when everyone—the left with joy, the right with bitter rage—ran around saying that the poor little Vietnamese had beaten the Americans. Well, they never did. We—the United States, that is—beat them. And we continued to embargo them and keep them in terrible poverty, with unexploded bombs going off under their children for all these years. So, not to be able to imagine the suffering that we imposed directly on them, and for our 1996 congresspeople not to be able to imagine the suffering that they're going to impose on the poor people of this country —it's hard for me to believe that they can't imagine it. Unfortunately, I think they do. They simply don't care. Another subject.

So I'm talking about the imagination in another way. We're living in a very lucky time, in some respects, in this country. As far as literature is concerned, we're really fortunate, and I think that Teachers & Writers and poets-in-the-schools programs and the other organizations that have been involved in basic literacy work have had something to do with it. We're living in a time when the different peoples in this country are being heard from, for the first time. I'm happy to have lived into this period when we hear the voices of Native Americans—twenty or twenty-five years ago you didn't even know they were writing, apart from token publication. That was the general condition of American literature at that time. The voices of African-American men and women, the voices of women of all colors, Asian women, Asian men, all these people—*this is our country*—and we're living at a time when we can hear the voices of all these people. So whenever I hear complaints about what's going on in literature in this country—those people without imagination talk that way—I want to remind them: When before now did this happen? Then they will say with that denigrating tone, "multiculturalism." Or "diversity." Or "political correctness." They use those words to try to shut all of us up. This is what the imagination means to me: to know that this multiplicity of voices is a wonderful fact and that we're lucky, especially the young people, to be living here at this time. My imagination tells me that if we let this present political climate defeat us, my children and my grandchildren will be in terrible trouble.

I will probably think of other things to say to you when I'm asleep, but it won't bother me so much because I'll know you're all asleep, too! But I would like to thank all of you. I think you've overrated me somewhat, but if there's ever a time in your life when you like to be overrated, it's when you're old. I thank you for doing it, and I thank all the young people and children who are here to-night, who have been writing poems and plays. They honor us with their presence. The child, you know, is the reason for life. Thank you, all.

—1996

Is the problem of education really a problem of schooling? Isn't there a class meaning in the assumption that a perfect school will produce the extraordinary person?

For many years I've been something of a pain in the neck to my friends whose kids are in private schools or alternative free schools. I must admit I'm obsessed with the notion that the children of radicals belong in the public elementary-school system. There, they and their parents and teachers can take part in the great social struggle for sensible education for *all* the children. The school is the event: the school and its citizens are the education.

It's true—that isn't what's usually meant by "radical education," but it is at least a more truthful way to educate radicals.

The public school served the industrial needs of a society which required workers who could read and write; it socialized their souls into an American value system. But it also amazed the immigrant with the possibilities of language, science, literature, history.

Private "progressive" schools came from a rising class of families with the loving wish to reform the rigid classrooms of their childhood and with enough money to do so. They hoped their children would be more creative, more fulfilled than they—a continuation of their own high reforming intelligence—just as Catholic-school parents educate for a continuation of the Catholic household and upper-class schools for upper-classness—the sense of owning the world which precedes actual grown-up inheritance.

Even when the local public school was fairly good, the class decision was to extract its children from among the others. In some cases, this turned the local school into a ghetto. In other cases, an array of exclusive schools was established. (We wrote lots of angry articles about that kind of thing when it happened in the South.)

The results were particularly noticeable in my own neighborhood. While there were once half a dozen public elementary schools, there are now two. There are five or six exclusive schools and as many Catholic schools. The public schools are not only fairly good but offer choice—that is, in one, children work in open classrooms and broader age groups; the other is more conventional and some neighbors prefer it.

These two schools exist in all their interesting difference as a result of passionate (and continuing) struggle around the ideas of education, teacher responsibility, and neighborhood control. Some of my radical friends, whose children attend exclusive schools, had strong opinions and great longing to take part in these struggles as they have in more furious ones—like busing. "Who's that guy? When'd he get into the act?" neighbors have asked. Who will listen to people who have abandoned the people?

One last remark: There *are* examples of alternative or "free" schools that made sense—the First Street School (on the Lower East Side of New York), for instance, where Mabel and George Dennison and Susan Goodman persevered for a couple of years. The lives of *those* children required the most "private," the most attentive of schools.

Some of the energy of the Free School Movement was in that useful direction. The pressure of that movement persuaded some Boards of Education and State and National Arts Councils to fund non-authoritarian educators who were able to teach in public schools one or two days a week.

But very often the rhetoric of that movement served as an excuse for loving parents to withdraw their child from the community—abandoning the local school. What was just ordinary self-concern and ambition in the middle class was, my puritan nature suggests, a serious mistake for the radical parent.

—1977

Christa Wolf

About ten or twelve years ago I visited my friend Marianne Frisch in West Berlin. I asked her if I could somehow meet the writer Christa Wolf. Yes, they were friends, Marianne said, and took me by way of Checkpoint Charlie through the Wall past the taciturn, well, hostile guards into that other country, the German Democratic Republic.

Christa Wolf is the second writer I've ever sought out; the first was W. H. Auden, in New York in 1939, the year, maybe the day, that ten-year-old Christa stood watching the SS march through her town, bayonets pointing toward Poland. She remembers that day, sharp as a wood carving, and tells about it in one of these essays.

Why did I want to see her? I had read *The Quest for Christa T.* and *Patterns of Childhood*. I thought we would talk for hours, this pacifist feminist who would never describe herself like that. What interested me was the woman, the writer who had a passionate commitment to literature and believed at the same time that she had to have a working relationship with society—and a responsibility as well. She seemed to be exactly the writer I wanted to know—not too many like her, though some are dear to me anyway.

And so we came to her apartment in East Berlin on Friedrichstrasse, trolleys rumbling by. I wanted to cry out, Don't give up the trolley for the bus; your cars are bad enough. But of course my German was only a failed street Yiddish of about twenty words and her English had just begun. Still we became friends. For me, a lucky mystery.

When you read these transcribed talks, essays, interviews, you'll be reading Christa Wolf's political and literary history in the country which, after Allied shaping, became, in 1949, the German Democratic Republic, the special concern of the U.S.S.R. Berlin, itself divided, was stuck in the GDR's chest. Eventually the Wall was built, graffiti on one side, soldiers with guns on the other.

Between 1949 and 1959, Christa Wolf studied German literature in Leipzig and Jena, married Gerhard Wolf, a critic and poet, had two daughters, worked in a factory in industrial Halle, hoping to become the worker-artist the First Bitterfeld Conference wanted her (and all other artists) to become. This is described at the end of her talk at the Second Bitterfeld Conference. She worked for the GDR Writers' Union and edited *Neue Deutsche Literatur* and several contemporary anthologies.

Then what? How does a person, a young woman, learn enough, live enough, read and listen enough to finally become one of the most important European writers, to break through the walls of her own early understanding and narrow education in "the snares of theory," as she writes? Of course she was by nature thoughtful, interested, loved her native language and its speakers. She also hated not to be truthful, not to know what had really happened.

It's a vital fact that she was a citizen of a small country, its history fractured right at the decisive years of her entrance into young womanhood. She was needed—an experience most American writers don't have too often. The country was poor but lively with direction, socialist direction, newness happening all around her among the ruins, idealism, and a way to turn away from a shameful national past. In a review of Fred Wander's book *The*

Seventh Well, she says, "After the war, we had to learn to live under the eyes of nations that shuddered at our name."

At the Second Bitterfeld Conference in 1966, she began her talk by discussing at some length the values of art in a socialist art-valuing society. She described the envy of West German youth at the breadth of the GDR literary themes. Having put participants at a certain smug ease, she offered a couple of harsh stories of repressive narrow-mindedness in the GDR, one about a writer sent to talk to a work-crew leader, in which the true facts of the worker's life censor him out of the story; the second about a schoolboy who notices the deadly imposition of stereotypes and falsifications in his textbooks. She urged her audience to be more self-critical, the writers to be less fearful.

She must have been thinking of her next book, *The Quest for Christa T.*, which was published in 1968. It's about a young woman who cannot, will not, live the rhythm of that society (and dies young). It's an exploration for Christa Wolf, through Christa T., of what it means to say, to be "I," "the difficulty of saying 'I.' " In "Interview with Myself," she asks: Will others be interested? She's not sure, but trusts that her whole life and experience, which grow out of an intense concern for the development of her society, will evoke problems and questions in *her* that are important to others. "My questions are what structure the book—not events." The book did provoke discussion, criticism, and censorship.

Another question she asks herself: "So, while working on this book, you have found out how you ought to write in the future?" She answers: "On the contrary. I have tried out one road, which I cannot take a second time . . . I have discovered that one must try at all costs to break out of the ring of what we know or think we know about ourselves, and go beyond it."

This "Interview with Myself" is only one example of Wolf's need to demystify the artist and her work. In essays and interviews over the years, she offers explications and meditations that may be useful to herself and her readers. Doing so probably frees her to make her novels as complex as they need to be and still feel she has included the reader. I like her solution. I think it's right to say whenever possible, and if asked: This is the way I journeyed into the unknown individual soul, bumping into history, society, and *myself* at every turn.

Patterns of Childhood was published in 1976. It is another fictional autobiographical journey, this time to the near, unspoken, hardly-to-be-borne German past, in which the child who saw, who knew, is hidden. The adult who pushed her aside, forgot and suppressed her, now must find and know her. Wolf called this kind of labor "subjective authenticity," in which "authenticity" makes the word "truthfulness" look like a barely scratched surface. How hard that must have been to write, how much harder life itself became.

In that year, Wolf Biermann, a popular singer and composer, was allowed to travel to an engagement in West Berlin. He was not allowed to return. Wolf wrote: "1976 was a caesura in cultural policy development in our country, outwardly indicated by Wolf Biermann's expatriation . . . A group of authors became aware that their direct collaboration, the kind they themselves could answer for and thought was right, was no longer needed. We are socialists, after all. We lived as socialists in the GDR because that's where we wanted to be involved. To be utterly cast back on literature brought about a crisis for the individual, an existential crisis." It must have been a political crisis, too. As one of the signers of a protest letter to the government, Wolf was dismissed from the executive board of the Berlin section of the Writers' Union. In a 1983 interview, she agreed with me that she had been stopped by that experience and the repression that followed. In another place she wrote: "It was the origin for me among others of working with the material of such lives as Günderrode's and Kleist's."

These conflicts, this falling back on literature, became *No Place on Earth,* which I think of as a play of mourning for the Romantic writers of the early nineteenth century—Günderrode, Kleist, Büchner—who were sentenced to suicide and madness. "They wrote hymns to their country," Anna Seghers said, "against the walls of whose society they beat their heads." *No Place on Earth* is the wonderfully invented work in which the characters speak their own words from their letters and poems. The silencing of Biermann's expatriation had given Wolf the gift of new form.

There are several essays on Karoline von Günderrode and Bettina von Arnim in *The Author's Dimension.* Wolf examines their lives and work almost as if they could be our teachers, if only we would pay attention to their personal pain in the historic moment. But it is the hard-squeezed lives of Günderrode in the early nineteenth century and Ingeborg Bachmann in the twentieth that lie heaviest on Christa Wolf's good mind.

Heaviest . . . As much as she cared about her contemporaries and her elders like Anna Seghers or Bertolt Brecht, it was the weight of Ingeborg Bachmann's work, its difficulty and mystery, its social consciousness trapped with no way to turn but death, that influenced her most. It made her think back to the other Germans a hundred and fifty, two hundred years earlier, walled in their particular German geography and culture; it made her decide not to die—or leave the GDR, her country, its walls. She and Gerhard would remain. She would struggle on her own terms and answer through work, her literary work, since she and others were prevented from speaking on radio or television and from political reporting.

When she presented the Kleist Prize to Thomas Brasch in 1987, she remembered how she had failed to persuade him to remain in the GDR in 1976. She said: "Contradiction is too cozy a word for the permanent friction forced on writers of the modern era . . . Brasch stands between two systems of value both of which confront him with false alternative values."

Wolf's fear of coming holocausts to bury all holocausts, a

fear normal to any European who had lived through one or two twentieth-century world wars, culminated in the important work *Cassandra*, accompanied by four essays, accounts of reading and travel with Gerhard Wolf to Athens and Crete, methodology, and history. There is a determination to go back in time, to get under it all, that place, that time, ancient Greece, which offered to literature forever, by way of great Homer's song, war and a trivialization of ordinary life and, of course, female life.

I think that one of the aspects of Wolf's work that bothers—I mean enrages—the male critics of West Germany, apart from her disinterest in Hemingway, is her criticism of male hierarchical modes, her disinterest in the hero. "As long as there are victors," there's not too much hope for the world. The only hero is the anti-heroine Cassandra, who sees how decent Aeneas will finally, going forth, only re-create the same patriarchal system. "We have no chance against a time that needs heroes." Cassandra sees her death before her, and all the other deaths. She can't do much, but she can *see*. That is her task on earth, to see, to teach seeing, to tell.

I have not talked about *Accident*, a book I admire. It's about Chernobyl, a brother's brain operation, a woman's ordinary anxious day, "the significance of daily structure," which Christa Wolf says she learned, little by little, by living in the country for half of each year. It's a short book that moves gracefully from newscast to the garden vegetables, to the children on the phone, to the hospital operating room.

And then *What Remains*: a collection of older stories, including a novella describing Wolf's surveillance by the East German secret police a number of years ago. This story infuriated West German critics, who thought she should have published it much earlier. It was a jumping-off point for a scapegoating attack on Christa Wolf which held her responsible for all GDR corruption, bureaucratic crime, and political repression. This campaign chose to disregard Wolf's work which, in fiction and talk and interview, dealt with the life of the individual in a stultifying society, the pathetic condition of education, which, she pointed out, prepared young people for a life of dependent thinking, the untold stories of German literary history, as well as German difficulties in facing the Nazi past and the complicity of those still alive—her own generation.

The last part of this collection includes some short pieces, a report on a reading in Mecklenburg, "We Don't Know How . . . to think directly, to tell, we never learned in school." I'd like to quote from another essay, "Momentary Interruption":

> November 4, 1989, in Alexander Square in East Berlin was the moment when artists, intellectuals, and other groups in our society came together . . . That moment was by no means just a fortunate accident, as amazed Western reporters interpreted it. It was the . . . climax of a long process in which literary and theater people, peace groups, and other groups had been coming together under the aegis of the Church, to meet and share talk . . . and drew encouragement for action. For years we addressed certain tasks in what we intended as our opposition literature: to name the conflicts which for a long time were expressed nowhere else, and thus to generate or strengthen a critical attitude in readers; to encourage them to resist lies, hypocrisy . . . to keep alive our language and the other traditions of German literature and history from which attempts were made to cut us off . . .

This talk was given at the University of Hildesheim when Wolf received an honorary doctorate in January 1990. In it there is also the sad sentence: "Our uprising appears to have come years too late."

Yes. As the young people ran laughing through Hungary into

the West and the Wall corridors were opened and the Wall taken down, crumb by stony crumb, and the German election approached, and the currency changed, it was clear that an autonomous free democratic socialist East German nation would not be born. Certainly, when the cry "We are the people" changed to "We are one people," the heady hopeful weeks in East Berlin and Leipzig, the long candlelight vigils, talk, argument, dissent, and planning ended. Freedom, unemployment, and colonization of East Germany began. As Christa Wolf writes:

> [The] politicians, economic managers, and party officials need a fatherland to carry on their enterprises. There is no motherland in sight, no more than before.

—1992

Coat upon a Stick

Coat upon a Stick is about an old man, a Jew living and praying in one of the last synagogues of the Lower East Side. His old body suffers pain; his soul, a thin little prayer-soaked soul, is starved by deceit and fear. It is terrified of memory. Throughout the day of this book he is actually unable *not* to steal, cheat, or proudly outwit any adversary he may meet—at the newspaper stand or the supermarket. But these are only the little, ten-cent crimes of late, bitter poverty. (With the same furtiveness—as though ashamed—he secretly gives away his only coat to a friend in a wheelchair.) When young, he betrayed a young woman, robbed the man who helped him get to the United States from Russia, deceived his co-workers, chiseled his customers. He has never forgiven his son, Carl, who grew up with a burden of Orthodoxy too heavy for the second-generation boy. Carl has a sensible son of his own, about to be bar mitzvahed. He tries to visit from time to guilty time, to make peace with his father's insulted love. The old man's rage against Carl for leaving home, the secure house of Jewish law, is a terrible sound in this book, an unforgiving cry torn out of the old man's throat again and again.

The other old men—and the rabbi, in his cynical, hopeless way—are not much better, only a couple of dollars richer. Then, out of this narrow mean world that Norman Fruchter has shown us with relentless unsentimentality, Zitomer, one of their own, suddenly rises out of the congregation, ablaze with revelation. This community, he shouts, does not live by the Ten Commandments. They probably don't even know them. Do they understand that the commandments were given to Moses to guide the moral life of the people of Israel for the next thousands and thousands of years—to define them among barbarians—that the commandments are the basic law written by God's own hand in stone? He interrupts the services, stops to harangue the men at work in their stores, even in front of customers. Though the prophets are not mentioned too often, Zitomer's voice is the scream of Amos, or maybe Micah crying out against landlords and profiteers. Zitomer's name carries in its Russian parts the four possible meanings: "Jew," "to live," "peace," and "world." This may be accidental, but I hear it.

And so the central dialogues of the book are created. The Law of Moses and the prophets' dreams are set in opposition to the laws and strictures of the priests. Still we may wonder, the book wonders—was it the moral law or was it the priests' laws that gathered the Jews up into a net, a net that kept most of them from falling into Rome, Christianity? There were knots whichever way they turned. During the hundreds of years of European Jew hatred, that net must have seemed to be the very fabric of God's love. The people turned inward, turned their backs to the oppressor, and became fistfuls of men and women in a great dispersion, a people who for almost two millennia created communities that did not engage in aggressive war.

I said dialogues. And there *are* dialogues. This is a very Jewish, constantly talking work. It believes that what happens inside a person's head is dialogue, not stream of consciousness or third-person reporting. Free association is just right for psychology, but these Jews are made of history and they talk in long, hard sentences, especially to themselves. They *are* the tradition of argument and discussion learned in yeshivas and shuls. In the midst of ritual obedience they somehow keep the adversarial conversation going with themselves, each other, or with the God who has always been pressed to answer questions, to be responsive. What *were* the final plans for Sodom? Should Israel or should Israel not have a king? The prophets themselves often felt unequal to their moral tasks, which occasionally included too much traveling. Why me? asked Jonah, and went in the opposite direction.

But somewhere in Jewish consciousness, sour and sad, is God's recorded answer to Moses. After so much work and talk on the mountain, Moses longed only to see His face at least once. The answer: "No man shall see me and live." But finally God gives in a little (as usual). He offers ". . . while my glory passes by . . . thou shalt see my back parts but my face shall not be seen." Thinking of that small impoverished congregation in *Coat upon a Stick*, I remembered that passage. Of course He may have said to Himself, "This is probably not the first Jewish joke, but it's a good one and should last this disobedient, argumentative people a couple of thousand years at least."

Coat upon a Stick seems to happen on the famous Lower East Side, where once-dense populations of immigrants ate, slept, peddled, worked in small shops, picketed bosses, organized unions, made poems for newspapers. A world, in other words. That population has disappeared into the suburbs, the massive tenements of the Upper West Side. The community is abandoned. Here and there blacks poorer than those remnants of Jews appear, house cleaners of slums or customers in the pathetic Jewish shops.

But where are the women in this book? A couple of landladies, a grumpy wife. There are no women in the synagogue's balcony, no old wives behind the mechitsa. The patriarchal law of the synagogue, the separation of the sexes, has turned to iron. Finally no women come at all, to the daily stitching and restitching of the law.

Also, where is Germany? The putrefaction of the Holocaust which has touched our Western bodies, slaughter and slaughtered.

Where is its taint? This book was written in the earliest sixties. The Holocaust, it's true, had not yet become that last call by aging survivors whose stories their children manage to tear from them even when they don't can't won't talk. Tell us, tell us, the young beg. What was it like to be a Jew in those days in that place? Tell us before you die so we, the third and fourth generations, can be Jews again. The work of research and publication was not yet complete. Perhaps it—the word "Holocaust"—had not yet become its own definition. Still, Carl, the son, is a TV repairman, a job that was born in the post–World War II world, and he travels to his father's decimated community from the working-class suburbs of Queens.

The absence of the Holocaust, like the absence of women, works to throw the shul and its congregation up up into the timeless air where true magic happens. True magic is always direct, which reminds me of the way in which Fruchter brings the figures of the old man's past to haunt him. "Haunt" is probably the wrong word, for they come not as dreams out of mist but by true magic. As a meaty rabbit leaps out of a real hat, the wife of the cheated friend (both long dead) visits, sits at his table, drinks tea, jumps youthfully to his kitchen counter, and refuses to leave until he screams, Go! Go! These scenes, together with the long internal conversations, give the book a certain rudeness, a forthright clarity.

Near the end, the old man visits Zitomer and his talking friends in their converted storefront. They, too, are old Jews—union organizers, Communists, bringing unfortunate memory of worker betrayal to the old man. They are no doubt prophets, too, who play chess and offer one another little illuminations of truth and utopian prophecies.

But somehow the old man wants to know: Has he been a good Jew? How *is* one to be a good Jew, a good person? Surely one can be both at the same time. The argument between the prophets and the priests isn't resolved. For those of us who came after or out of the generation that accepted the Enlightenment, who want to remain Jews in the Diaspora, it's important to know that these questions are still asked—probably more now than when Fruchter's book was written.

I last saw Norman Fruchter at a meeting of Brooklyn Parents for Peace, called to inform neighbors of the dangers of allowing nuclear naval carriers into New York Harbor. He came late because he's a member of the local school board.

The first time I met Norman Fruchter we were in North Vietnam. It was '69. We were traveling the length of North Vietnam on a dirt road called National Highway 1. He, with a couple of others, was making a film about this journey, the lives of the Vietnamese people and the life of the devastated earth under American bombing. This is what impressed me: brains, anger, wit, kindness.

This extraordinary book had already been written, though I didn't know it at the time. If I *had* read it, I would have seen Fruchter more clearly—a kind of American-born Zitomer, a Jew that is, who, by definition, had a traditional obligation to be one of the creators of a just world.

The amazing final fact is that, having read *Coat upon a Stick* twice, I find myself talking to it. And every now and then, because it is a work that cannot do without dialogue, it answers me.

—1987

Language: On Clarice Lispector

Clarice Lispector spent the first two months of her life in the town of Chechelnik in Ukraine. This is a small, short fact. The interesting question, unanswered in the places I've looked for it, is: At what age did she enter the Portuguese language? And how much Russian did she bring with her? Any Yiddish? Sometimes I think this is what her work is about . . . one language trying to make itself at home in another. Sometimes there's hospitality, sometimes a quarrel.

Why did they go to Brazil, anyway? an American immigrant Jew provincially asks. Well, a South African cousin answers, since Jews are often not wanted in their old homes, they travel to distant, newer, more innocent places. My mother's best friend emigrated to Argentina. There was a letter from Buenos Aires once. But not again.

Unless Clarice Lispector's parents were linguists with an early knowledge of Portuguese, they must have spoken Russian, as my parents did most of my childhood. It must have been that meeting of Russian and Portuguese that produced the tone, rhythms that even in translation (probably difficult) are so surprising and right.

It's not unusual for writers to be the children of foreigners. There's something about the two languages engaging one another in the child's ears that makes her want to write things down. She will want to say sentences over and over again, probably in the host or dominant tongue. There will also be a certain amount of syntactical confusion which, if not driven out of her head by heavy schooling, will free the writer to stand a sentence on its chauvinistic national head when necessary. She will then smile. There are not so many smiles in Lispector's work, but they happen in the sudden illumination of a risky sentence. You feel that even the characters are glad.

Once you have stood a sentence on its head or elbow, the people who live in those sentences seem to become states of literary mind—they seem almost absurd, but not in a cold or mean way. (There isn't a mean bone in the body of Lispector's work.) But there is sadness, aloneness (which is a little different than loneliness). Some of the characters try desperately to get out of the stories. Others retreat into their own fictions—seem to be waiting and relieved by Lispector's last embracing sentence.

Lispector was lucky to have begun to think about all these lives (men's lives as well as women's) in the early years of the women's movement, that is, at a time when she found herself working among the scrabbly low tides of that movement in the ignorance which is often essential to later understanding. That historical fact is what has kept her language crooked and clean.

In this collection there are many solitary middle-class Brazilian women, urban, heavily European. There are a couple of black cooks, nannies. I thought at one point in my reading that there was some longing for Europe, the Old World, but decided I was wrong. It was simply longing.

It seems important to say something about geography. First Lispector's. She lived for an infant's moment in Russia. Then in Brazil in Recife, then in Rio de Janeiro; then with her diplomat husband in Europe and the United States; then her last eighteen years in Brazil.

Brazil is a huge country. Its population is African black, Indian brown and golden, European white. There are landless peasants.

There are the Indian people, whole villages and tribes driven out of their forest homes by development. There is the vast ancient forest which, breathing, produces so great a percentage of the world's oxygen, which, breathing, we absolutely require. There is the destruction of that forest continuing at such a rate that a sensible breathing world might be terrified. Imagine living in, being a citizen of, a country in which the world's air is made. Imagine the woman, the urban woman, writing not about that world but in it. She had to find a new way to tell. Luckily it was at the tip of her foreign tongue.

—1989

Isaac Babel

When I read Antonina Nikolaevna Pirozhkova's memoir of daily life with Isaac Babel I realized that I'd known very little about him. Only his death was famous. And of course until fairly recently most of us had that wrong, too. But I did know his work, though not until the early sixties, when the Meridian edition first appeared.

One must begin by telling those who still don't know those stories that they are unusual in a particular way. That is, any one of them, those in *Red Cavalry* and *Tales of Odessa*, as well as those extracted only in the last few years from bureaus and closets of old Russian friends, can be read again and again. I don't mean every five or ten years. I mean in one evening a story you read just six months ago can be read a couple of times—and not because the story is a difficult one. There's so much plain nutrition in it, the absolute accuracy and astonishment in the language, the breadth of the body and the height of the soul. You *do* feel yourself healthier, spiritually speaking, if also sadder—or happier, depending on the story.

Where did those sentences, that language, come from? Babel's head in childhood was buried in Hebrew, in talmudic studies. His adolescent head was European, full of French. Russian was an everyday matter, clear and crisp, the vowels in an armor of consonants. His grandmother spoke Ukrainian. When he was ten he came to Odessa. It was like every tough city, full of smart talkers; you could listen to that city all day and begin again the next. Some kind of lucky composting had begun.

It was in Odessa, on his way to becoming a real Russian, that the story "Awakening" was made. He was supposed to be taking violin lessons, which would help him become a man like Jascha Heifetz. He would then play for the Queen of England. Somehow he began to never reach his music school but wandered, walking in Odessa, down to the docks. He found, or was found by, a good man, the kind who appears in a child's wandering time to say, "Go this way, not that!"—forcefully. He taught the boy the names of flowers and asked, "Well, what is it you lack? A feeling for nature. What's that tree?" The boy didn't know. "That bird? That bush?" Then he said, "And you dare to call yourself a writer?" (The boy had been daring.) He would never be a writer, a *Russian* writer, without knowing the natural world. "What were your parents thinking of?" But those days were also among his first meetings with the "others"—the wild free Russian boys, diving, swimming, clambering on the boats, the ships in Odessa harbor. He is finally taught to swim. At last he can join them.

Years later, still longing, like most young Jewish revolutionaries (like my own parents) to become a real Russian, he has a harder time with the "others." The Revolution has happened. The civil war is unending. Liutov (the name he gives the narrator of the Red Cavalry stories) is assigned to the Cossacks of Savitsky's VI Division. He is billeted with half a dozen other Cossacks who look at the "specs" (eyeglasses) on his nose, are disgusted, and want to look no further. The quartermaster who has delivered him says, "Nuisance with specs . . . but you go and mess up a lady, and a good lady too, and you'll have the boys patting you on the back." There are no women around but the landlady. He's hungry. He sees the goose, takes hold of it, places his heavy boot on its neck, cracks its head, presents it to the landlady. "Cook it!" "Hey you," one of the Cossacks calls out almost immediately, "sit down and feed with us." He's asked to read them the news. Out of *Pravda* he proudly reads Lenin's speech and is happy to "spy out the secret curve of Lenin's straight line." They slept then, all with their legs intermingled. "In my dreams I saw women. But my heart, stained with bloodshed, grated and brimmed over."

Loneliness, differentness, hunger enabled him to brutally kill the goose. But he was unable to go much further. In the case of Dolgushov ("The Death of Dolgushov"), he could not bring himself to end Dolgushov's agony, though the Cossack's belly was pouring his intestines out of its wide wound and Dolgushov begs him to "waste a cartridge" on him. He cannot do it, and he hears words of contempt from the comrade, Afonka, who has pity for Dolgushov and helps him to leave this life.

And later, in "Going into Battle," caught with an unloaded pistol, he asks "for the simplest of proficiencies, the ability to kill my fellow man."

In a story from *Red Cavalry*, "Sandy the Christ" (so named for his noticeable mildness) hears his stepfather in his mother's bed. He calls out to stop him, to remind his stepfather that he is "tainted." He begs him to consider his mother's fine white skin, her innocence, then trades them for permission from this man to become the village herdsman. I have read that story many times, and as I come to the last paragraphs, my heart still beats faster. Of course it isn't the story line alone, which is certainly interesting. It must be the way of telling.

How did he come to that?

When he was quite young he loved French literature, particularly Flaubert and Maupassant. In fact, according to information in *You Must Know Everything*, he wrote his first stories in French. Then he began to think about how to write about war:

he came upon *Authentic Stories of the Great War* by the French writer Captain Gaston Vidal. He admired the stories, the facts of the stories. But he had just come back from fighting on the Romanian front and was soon to become Liutov, the war correspondent, the writer, the storyteller for the Red Cavalry, Budenny's First Cavalry. He began to translate the stories, and in one long moment (all his writing moments were extremely long) he created a language, a style, his brand-new sentences. In *You Must Know Everything* there is an excellent example. By reducing a tendentious twelve-line paragraph from one of those stories to three lines, he produced clarity, presentness, tension, and a model of how always, though with great difficulty, to proceed.

Here is Babel talking about his method of working with Konstantin Paustovsky in his book *Years of Hope*:

> If you use enough elbow grease even the coarsest wood gets to look like ivory. That's what we have to do with words and with our Russian language. Warm it and polish it with your hand till it glows like a jewel . . .
>
> The first version of a story is terrible. All in bits and pieces tied together with boring "like passages" as dry as old rope. You have the first version of "Lyubka" there, you can see for yourself. It yaps at you. It's clumsy, helpless, toothless. That's where the real work begins. I go over each sentence time and time again. I start by cutting out all the words I can do without. Words are very sly. The rubbishy ones go into hiding . . . After that I type the story and let it lie for two or three days. Then I check it again sentence by sentence . . . I shorten the sentences and break up the paragraphs.

In the end there were twenty-two versions of "Lyubka the Cossack," a wild story full of smugglers, infants, an old man, contraband, brothels, sailors, traveling salesmen, prostitutes, a baby howling to be nursed. A short story!

To make matters clearer he wrote a story about the French writer he loved. It's called "Guy de Maupassant." In it the art of translation, the game of love, and the punctuation of sentences are of equal lively value. After years of love for this master he said one day, startled with the knowledge, "You know Maupassant—he has no heart."

In the course of Babel's long conversation with Paustovsky he said, "I've got no imagination. All I've got is the longing for it." What could he have done with more imagination? He was a Jew, his childhood spent in the provincial ghetto of a provincial town. Only fifteen years later he became the great chronicler of the Red Cavalry at war, their energy, fidelity, their violent natures. He wrote about a life of physical movement almost totally opposite his own sedentary youth and culture. He had the imagination to be just. It took all his strength, all his longing.

Babel would probably be called a minimalist today, but there's hardly a maximalist or mediumist who can tell a story, engage and shape a character with so much of the light and darkness of history, with grief *and* humor. The fact is, there's a larger, more varied population in Babel's four, five hundred pages of stories than in any three novels of most writers. A bald statement, to be proven another time.

Red Cavalry is about men and what they expect of one another in the way of honor, physical courage, love of horses, abuse of women and Jews. It's about a young man, a Russian, too, but to them a foreigner, who is falling in love with their bravery and suffering. At the same time, he is trying to give us the facts of the case. When women appear, it's because of what men need to do *to* them as the men demand food and sex. The women are usually pregnant, which makes very little difference in the men's demands. The young man Babel doesn't shirk *his* honorable duty, which is to tell the story whole, as beautifully, that is as truthfully, as he can.

In the Odessa stories and others, some of which were written later, the women are able to . . . well, fly. Lyubka (called the Cossack, a Jewish woman) is wild and irascible, "a monstrous mother," and is in many ways more interesting than Benya Krik (the King). And this literary and historical and unbrutalized entrance of women allows for all kinds of humor and imagery ("Meanwhile misfortune lurked under the window like a pauper at daybreak"). Which must have been a relief, because Babel liked to laugh.

"The Jewess" is a profound figure, forced with strong familial love out of her place and time by her son—into his. This story, had Babel had the time the times did not allow, might have become a novel.

Claudia in "Oil" is the head of the Oil Syndicate. She's a modern woman. We know her, her closeness to women friends, her great sense of humor, her political interest and brains. Was she a woman like Antonina Pirozhkova, an engineer who had a great deal to do with the building of the Moscow subway as well as assorted tunnels and bridges? In any case, it's good to have met these women. They must still be there, old and tough—I would like to meet them again.

But some stories, I must admit, you simply can't read more than once every couple of years, because in reading them, sorrow grips you so. An example would be the first story of *Red Cavalry*, "Crossing Over to Poland." Perhaps I feel this because it is so close to my parents' story of their own town's drowning in the 1905 manufactured waves of pogroms. The murder of my seventeen-year-old uncle Russya in that pogrom; the picture given to me many times of my grandmother, alone, bringing the wagon to his place of slaughter to lift his body, take him home. Within a few months she sent my young father and mother away with their Russian language to become Americans. There are only a few others, also wonderful, where the air of his normal hopefulness cannot raise the story out of heartsick sadness.

I see I have been a bit solemn, even in describing "Awakening," a story made famous by its humor—the large size of the violin cases, the small boys carrying them, the international hopes of the fathers, the narrow streets of the ghettos. Why is it that with the best intentions in the world, disparate size is comical except to the people involved, the unrequited lover of the disinterested and beautiful woman is a joke, at least until someone says, What's so funny about that? Heifetz and Zimbalist and Gabrilowitsch *did* come from Odessa. That's where they studied the violin. Any loving parent would think, My son is also smart, maybe even gifted. Why do you laugh?

There is a kind of subgenre (in which I have been implicated) called short shorts, which probably couldn't have happened without Babel's work. But what is missed much of the time is the density of that work. They are not pieces of life. They are each one *all* of life. Each one, even the shortest, is the story of a story.

Among other intentions, I think Babel hoped to tell two kinds of stories—the first about lives absolutely unlike his own, in order to understand, or at least know and maybe even become like the "others."

But a second need was to say, Look, that life is like mine. I am after all like him and he like me. What a relief! This happened from time to time. Here are two examples: In "The Story of the Horse," Klebnikov, the commander of the first squadron, has been deprived of his white stallion by Savitsky, the divisional commander. He writes a letter of resignation from the Communist Party, beginning: "The Communist Party was founded, as I understand it, for joy and sound justice without limit, and it ought to consider small fry also. Now I will come to the question of the white stallion . . ." And Babel ends: "He was a quiet fellow whose character was rather like mine. He was the only man in the squadron to possess a samovar . . . We used to drink scalding tea together. We were shaken by the same passions. Both of us looked on the world as a meadow in May—a meadow traversed by women and horses."

And at the end of "Sandy the Christ," after the son has made his bargain with his stepfather, Babel writes: "It was only recently that I got to know Sandy the Christ, and shifted my little trunk over to his cart. Since then we have often met the dawn and seen the sun set together. And whenever the capricious chance of war has brought us together, we have sat down of an evening on the bench outside a hut, or made tea in the woods in a sooty kettle, or slept side by side in the new-mown fields, the hungry horses tied to his foot or mine."

In the matter of his small production (for some reason I feel this must be answered), apart from what I've said about the weight of its quality against the weight of the paper used by most writers, he had other journalistic and literary responsibilities.

He had to support his wife and child in France—they refused to return, wisely. He traveled with Pirozhkova on writing assignments to mining districts and to collectives—kolkhozes, where beet production was impressive, and to smaller fields where the agricultural leaders had turned to seed production for the whole region. (A few years later, he would learn that many of the working organizers of these successful projects had been arrested, maybe executed.) He also worked on many filmscripts, once with Eisenstein, who was his good friend. He worked as a writer. That was his work.

We know that great boxes of his manuscripts were carted off by the NKVD. Among them, Pirozhkova is sure (and I am, too), was his book to be called "New Stories." Did "they" fear these stories? He held them up for the usual scrutiny—one day or one year too long. We really don't know about his production. We do know that we wish we had a lot more of his stories.

Babel and Pirozhkova could not have been blind to events. Early in 1918, Babel must have heard Gorky's warning: "Lenin, Trotsky, and their supporters have already been poisoned by the corruptive virus of power."

But they could not understand the confessions made again and again by people they admired. (Nor can anyone to this day quite take in the totality.) Pirozhkova, in her forthright way, asked why they didn't just stand up for what they believed if they disagreed with the directions taken. But Babel understood something. The Party—maybe they didn't want to see the Party go down. They had not yet included torture in their calculations; at least Babel said nothing about this to his wife. Still, he must have understood that someone in charge did not love him. There were problems with the publication of stories. He and Pasternak were not included among the Russian writers invited to the important cultural conference in Paris (the Congress for the Defense of Culture and Peace). Only after the French delegation furiously demanded their attendance were they allowed to appear. And again later, when Soviet prizes were given out to scientists and cultural figures, Babel and Pasternak were not honored.

After Gorky died in 1936, Babel said to Pirozhkova, "*Now* they won't let me live."

Still, almost to the end, until the moment of his arrest, he was considered influential. The wives and children of people arrested came to him asking that he intervene. He would try, but always returned grim-faced, not wanting to speak about it. He did not like to worry his wife. But he continued to offer care, and in more than one case shelter, to women whose husbands were in prison or had been executed. Many of his friends considered this unwise. When he was finally arrested, very few people called Antonina Pirozhkova or visited her again. Ilya Ehrenburg became the comforting exception.

Babel's grandmother had admonished: "You Must Know Everything." He did try. And eventually he knew a great deal. He knew war. He knew work. He knew love. He gave long classical reading lists to Pirozhkova. He didn't like literary talk. He didn't want to discuss his work.

Sad for her and sad for us. Maybe, among his other thoughts, he hoped to protect her, a powerful and responsible working woman important in the construction of the new Soviet infrastructure. Was he also trying to save her from the destructive forces of disillusion? When Lion Feuchtwanger visited, she asked Babel what they'd talked about. "He spoke of his impressions of the U.S.S.R. and of Stalin," he said. "He told me many bitter truths." Then Babel said no more.

For the most part, I have tried to say something in these few pages about what I feel for Babel's work. It was the work of a man who, like the Gedali character from *Red Cavalry*, longed for the joy-giving Revolution, thought he would wait as long as he could. He thought he could put his own joyful spirit out like an oar in history's river and deflect the Revolution's iron boat by acting in a straightforward way for others. He thought laughter and jokes might work. In fact, Pirozhkova learned that one of his arresters had been asked by the interrogator in charge, "Did he try to make a joke?"

Reading Pirozhkova's memoir, I feel I have come to know something of the man, to see Babel and his work in some common brilliant light of the hopeful Revolution, unending love of *the* people as well as people, darkened at the edges by fate, the busy encroachment of evil. But Antonina Pirozhkova will tell you the whole story. Though she lived only seven years inside it, hardly an hour escaped her loving attention, and then her memory. He is, as she was determined, restored to us—a great writer, a good man.

—1996

I have trouble writing about Don because I have refused his death. So far as the rememberer in me is determined, he's still in Texas. I was afraid he'd get stuck there, what with the working presence of so much family and his responsibilities at the University of Houston. This is not a joke. It's called denial and is somehow tangled up with anger. One of the results of his presumed death is the bookstore problem. If *Sixty Stories* is in, then you can't find *Forty Stories*. This may be because of the famous crisis in shelf space, the press of time, the longing of readers to rest for a couple of years in simple sensational material, easier language. And what of *The King*, that last dreamed history of war and love and language—all that generosity and gallantry.

Still, proving him alive, there are brilliant young people laboriously imitating him. Why shouldn't they? Young people listen, or ought to, as they begin their work, for some breathtaking voice that will help them open their own throats. At first, of course, it may sound like a lot of coughing. In any event, that imitation is really not possible. Don's imagination had spent some time living alongside the arts of painting, architecture, philosophy, music. Then he added a journalistic interest in the day—I mean the immediate morning-to-night American day. His language, invented along a syntactical line between Texas and New York. The fact is, he could have been only clever, and he *was* clever, but his intelligence ran harder and deeper than his wit.

He was in his life and work a citizen. That means he paid attention to and argued the life of his street, his city (New York or Houston), his country. He never played a game of literary personalities. If he organized an event, a reading—as he did, for instance, at the 1986 PEN Conference, he stood back, had others present their work. He wasn't the least bit modest, he was anxious, he was courteous.

He was always worried in the very act of hilarious opposition. There was sadness in our lightest conversations, across that literature of his. We laugh, but the poem in the prose is dark.

If you were a female person, it's perfectly true that he'd often meet you with a sort of attentive bossiness, which is the Southern male's ingrained behavior with women. It was really an awful pain in the neck. A regional problem and serious.

He was, according to students, an extraordinary teacher, rigorous, picky, not mean—but a teaser. Sometimes. "What did he really mean by that?" a student whispered to me once when I visited his class. "You can write anything you want but you may not mention the weather," he told his classes at City College in New York and at the University of Houston. The weather, the very geography of platitude. Still, he knew about those easy clichés. He knew their ancient usefulness and perseverance. He grabbed them, gave them a good half turn to laugh a social truth into a sentence—he was certainly a sentence maker.

He was my neighbor and a true friend. *This* kind of friend. One day in 1973 he crossed the street to talk to me on my stoop. "Grace," he said, "you now have enough stories for a book." (My last book had been published in 1959.) "Are you sure? I kind of doubt it," I said. "No, you do—go on upstairs and see what you can find in your files—I know I'm right." I spent a week or so extracting stories from folders. He looked at my list at dinner at his house. "You're missing at least two more," he said. "You've got to find them now. I'll wait here."

Many others have stories about that kindness to colleagues. We had a sad political parting, which lasted about a year after the 1986 New York International PEN Conference. He considered his position long-term, overriding that year's key speaker. He thought me disloyal and was angry. I was never angry at him, partly because political opposition is more natural to me, but mostly because I never didn't love his fine tragic heart and brilliant work. He smoked and drank in the manner of American writers (his only untransformed cliché) and died of the cancerous sorrow of these addictions. His very breath which made those perfect sentences tormented then broken.

—1990

Thinking about Barbara Deming

At the Friends' Meeting House a couple of weeks after Barbara Deming died, we gathered to remember her for one another, to take some comfort and establish her continuity in our bones.

Later our friend Blue gave me two little wool hats assigned to me by Barbara as she worked those last weeks at dying. That work included the distribution of the things of her life, how to be accurate and fair in the giving, how not to omit anyone of that beloved and wide-webbed community. I imagine that when she came to my name she thought, Grace needs wool hats up there in the North where the body's warmth flies up and through the thinning hair of her head. Besides, I noticed that she likes little wool hats.

"This too," Blue said, and gave me an envelope. In it were shards and stones gathered from the rubble of Vietnamese towns in '67 or '68. On the envelope, these shaky letters were written: "endless love." Nothing personal there, not "*with* endless love." The words were written waveringly, with a dying hand, on paper that covered bits and pieces of our common remembrance and understanding of another people's great suffering. I thought Barbara was saying, Send those words out, out out into the airy rubbly meaty mortal fact of the world, endless love, the dangerous transforming spirit.

Prison Notes is the story of two walks undertaken to help change the world without killing it. Barbara Deming was an important member of both. Twenty years of her brave life lie between them. Both walks were about connectedness, though the first began as a peace walk in 1964—from Quebec to Guantanamo, the American army base in Cuba. In Georgia, it became impossible to demonstrate for peace without addressing the right of all citizens, black and white, to walk together down any street in any city of this country. Before the events in Albany, Georgia, had ended— the jailing, the fasts, the beatings—the peace movement and the civil-rights movement had come to know themselves deeply related, although there are still people in both movements who do not understand this flesh-and-blood connection.

The second walk, in 1983, began in the city of Seneca, New York. The walk, organized by the Seneca Women's Peace Encampment, continued through upstate towns in order to reach the huge missile base in Romulus. Its purpose was, in fact, to connect the struggles of women against patriarchal oppression at home and at work to the patriarchal oppression which is military power—endless war.

In both cases the walks were bound by nonviolent discipline.

Both walks were interrupted by hatred and rage. The walkers in '64 and again in '83 had to decide whether to continue on their lawful way or accede to the demand of the police chief (or sheriff) to take a different, less visible route; to leave the screaming, cursing men and women with their minds set in a national cement of race hatred, Jew hatred, woman hatred, lesbian hatred, or to insist on the citizens' responsibility to use democratic rights— not just talk about them.

In both cases the walkers decided: We will not attack anyone, we will be respectful, we will not destroy anything, we will walk these streets with our nonviolent, sometimes historically informative, signs and leaflets. We may be pacifists, but we are not passivists. In both cases a confrontation occurred. It was not sought by the walkers, but it was accepted by them.

On that first long journey, men and women walked and went to jail together. Women alone took the second shorter walk, and fifty-four were jailed. Barbara was among them. It was her last action, and those who were arrested with her are blessed to have lived beside her strong, informed, and loving spirit for those few days. That difference between the two walks measures a development in movement history and also tells the distance Barbara traveled in those twenty years.

The direction her life took was probably established by the fact that her first important love was another woman, a hard reality that is not discussed in *Prison Notes* (this is probably the reason she insisted that her letter to Norma Becker be included in any reissue of that book). This truth about herself took personal political years in which she wrote stories and poems and she became a fine artist who suffered because she was unable to fully use the one unchangeable fact of her life—that she was a woman who loved women.

As a writer myself, I must believe that Barbara's attention to the "other" (who used to be called the stranger) was an organic part of her life as an artist—the writer's natural business is a long stretch toward the unknown life. All Barbara's "others" (the world's "others," too), the neighbor, the cop, the black woman or man, the Vietnamese, led her inexorably to the shadowed lives of women, and finally to the unknown humiliated lesbian, herself.

It was hard when this knowledge forced her to separate her life and work from other comrades, most of whom believed themselves eternally connected to her. "Why leave us now?" friends cried out in the pages of *WIN* magazine. "Now, just when we have great tasks." She explained: "Because I realize that just as the black life is invisible to white America, so I see now my life is invisible to you." Of course *she* was not the separator. *They* had been, the friends who wrote, saying, "We know it's okay to be a woman," but hated to hear the word "feminist" said again and again. She stubbornly insisted that they recognize Woman, and especially Lesbian, as an oppressed class from which much of the radical world had separated itself—some for ideological reasons, some with a kind of absentminded "We'll get to that later." (And many did.)

Of course she never separated herself from the struggles against racism and militarism. She integrated them into her thinking. As she lived her life, she made new connections which required new analyses. And with each new understanding, she acted, "clinging to the truth," as she had learned from Gandhi, offering opposition as education and love as a way to patience.

The long letters that Barbara began to write after her terrible automobile accident in '71 have become books. They are studious, relentless in argument; she seems sometimes in these letters to be lifting one straw at a time from a haystack of misunderstanding to get to a needle of perfect communication stuck somewhere at the bottom. At the same time she had developed a style which enabled her to appear to be listening to her correspondent while writing the letter. In our last conversations (by phone), she explained that she had decided to discontinue treatment, the agonizing, useless treatment for her ovarian cancer. She had decided, she said, to die. "I'm happy now, I'm serene and I want to die in that serenity. I don't want to die in a chaos of numbness and nausea."

She left the hospital and went home to Sugarloaf Key to be with her companion, Jane Gapen, and the women of that community. To be present when friends came to visit. They came long distances to say goodbye, to stay a couple of days, to be part of the ceremonies of farewell and passage.

In the end she taught us all something about dying. I thank her for that last lesson and I have written here in the present tense a few other things I learned from her before those last days.

———————

Learning from Barbara Deming:

First: She's a listener.
So you can learn something about paying attention.

Second: She's stubborn.
So you can learn how to stand, look into the other's face, and not run.

Third: She's just.
So you can learn something about patience.

Fourth: She loves us—women, I mean—and speaks to the world.
So you can learn how to love women and men.

—1985

Feelings in the Presence of the
Sight and Sound of the Bread
and Puppet Theater

ADMIRATION

Oh! Ah! The gorgeousness   the solemn size   the humorous disparities

HAPPINESS

Sheer happiness   just plain happiness

RESTFULNESS

In some of the long slow pieces often of holy intention—rest —the spirit—also the body rests inside the event the work- with room and permission for absence. The gathering of knowledge at the "five senses' entry to the soul"—so with rest comes thought—time—room for thinking *during* the work not only after it.

ARTISTIC INSPIRATION

Why not speak the truth directly? Just speak out! Speak to! Why not?

POLITICAL INSPIRATION

Why not speak the truth directly? Just speak out! Speak up! Speak to! Why not?

CORROBORATION

Yes! That's just what's happening.

ENVY

Because the work is so useful the courage of its usefulness in

a long period when usefulness was mocked   Envy as an artist
for the beauty and usefulness of the huge puppet figures like
legends out of history   the gray women of suffering the ridiculous evil Uncle Fatso   the lovely oxen turning round and
round in the dance of silent beasts   the white deer on the hill
under the red ball of the sun   the high birds bravely carried
that have flown before and after us on our demonstrations and
have waited fluttering in the wind outside the jails of New York
Vermont Washington.

To have been useful As an Artist to the important movements of
our times   to have spoken out as artists for the poor, the oppressed
and humiliated in Europe Africa and at home *and been heard*.

AND FINALLY LOVE AND GRATITUDE

for Peter Schuman and Elka Schuman and that solid core of
puppeteers—also for those who came, worked with Peter for a
couple of years, and then went off to Maine California France
Italy Germany Ninth Street New York Brooklyn   Gratitude
for their gifts to us of labor and beauty from the earliest unknown days on Delancey Street when we were sometimes fewer
than they—to these wonderful summer circus days in Vermont
where we, their comrades and friends, meet one another in the
thousands   AND GRATITUDE also for the opportunity generously given to be one of them an ox   a deer   a stilt walker   a
horse   a maintenance man   a washerwoman.

And thanks Peter for the tens of thousands of Loaves of
Bread and the music

—1981

My husband's mother lived in Florida on the sandy shore of a small lake in the middle of an orange grove that looked something like a child's painting, based in the color of sand, with an occasional spear of green green grass bending this way and that. She was dying and wanted to ask a couple of questions about life. We could speak to her only at lunch—briefly—and later at supper. She didn't eat much, but it was the hour of her little strength and she offered it to us.

One evening at supper she asked me about Women's Lib. She and her best friend (also very sick) had been talking about it. She said she thought I might know something about it. What was it like? Did it mean there would be women lawyers?

Yes.

Would they work for women?

Oh surely, I said.

Would women get paid the same? Was that the idea?

One of them, I answered. Equal pay at least.

Would women be free of men bossing them around?

Hopefully, I said. Though it might take the longest amount of time, since it would involve lots of changes in men.

Oh they won't like that a bit, she said. Would people love their daughters then as much as their sons?

Maybe more, I said.

Not fair again, she said slyly.

But that wasn't all, I said. Most of the Women's Libbers I knew really didn't want to have a piece of the men's pie. They thought that pie was kind of poisonous, toxic, really full of weapons, poison gases, all kinds of mean junk we didn't even want a slice of.

She was tired. That's a lot, she said. Then she went upstairs to sleep.

In the morning she surprised us. She came down for breakfast. I couldn't sleep, she said. I was up all night thinking of what you said. You know, she said, there isn't a thing I've done in my life that I haven't done for some man. Dress up or go out or take a job or quit it or go home or leave. Or even be quiet or say something nice, things like that. You know, I was up all night thinking about you and especially those young women. I couldn't stop thinking about what wonderful lives they're going to have.

—1991

Kay Boyle

This is a short tribute to a whole life dedicated and rededicated, day and night, to making good literature. For Kay Boyle it started in 1902.

Kay says, "Should we go out to lunch?"

"What about your back?"

"It's only about six blocks Grace, how's your foot?"

"Oh well, okay, okay, let's go."

Kay is about eighty. I'm about sixty-something. Walk and talk, arm in arm, my favorite way for talk, best for listening, this story and that. The first thing she wants to straighten out with me is this feminism business. Now, I'm kind of adamant on this subject, kind of deep-minded, but narrow. She knows that, and she tells me that in the early eighties her grandmother took her two young children out of Topeka, Kansas, alone in a buggy, and then a train brought her into Washington, where she became the first woman to—

I interrupt, "She was some woman. Her life supported yours. Maybe even invented yours."

Kay laughs. She's able to laugh. It's been a number of years —ten, fifteen probably—since she tried to prevent a group of San Francisco State graduate students who wanted to do their studies on Tillie Olsen. They wanted to organize a women's caucus.

"Why did you do that, Kay, then, why did you do that?" I ask. "But you don't know the facts, Grace. Sometime I'll tell you." "I do know the facts."

But by this time I love her anyway. I knew that many extremely successful self-made women think, until the day they die, that they are self-made. But I'm sad, knowing her work is unknown, was unknown, for years, for important years, to that great reading public: political women. Important years to Kay Boyle and to the women. Because there she was, near, at the end of her story, over thirty-five books, columns, essays, fast book reviews, long critical reviews, novels, potboilers, short stories, a literary writer with a long enough reputation to rise and fall, rise again. A courageous model for women and men in literature and engaged in politics. A woman who had six children, paid attention to them sometimes, ignored them often, supported them frequently with nasty writing jobs, hard times. Hurt their feelings, made them desperately in love with her. Often they were full of the rage and psychological hatred with which our moment in social history comforts us.

Then she told me the story of the McCarthy years, under investigation with her husband in Germany, Joseph Frankenstein, who lost his job, his career in the foreign service. The way in which *The New Yorker* had betrayed her, gone to press with the profile by Janet Flanner. It was hard to think of that magazine in this way, as fearful—of what and of whom? She said her husband wanted nothing to do with the struggle against the accusations. But she insisted. It was essential that they fight back with others. These were events she wanted *me* to know about. She didn't tell me too much about her early life. She didn't speak to me about the periodicals *This Quarter, Broom*, and *The Dial*, all those earlier avant-garde journals, most of them having their first lives in France. That was all in the books anyway and I could read all that.

She was a true worker, too. Apart from her incredible literary productivity, which occasionally upset her publishers, unable to keep up with her at the rate she wanted (which was immediate publication on completion). She was a fine teacher. I saw her at work at Bowling Green and in Spokane at Eastern Washington University, talking in great detail with each student, listening. I was surprised, her listening in that way. Spending hours at her home, which was then a motel room, smoky, cold, cold. She was at least eighty at that time, broke, earning her own living. "It is hard," she admitted, and then she said something she probably said many, many times, "But, Grace, remember this. Depression is cowardice."

There is a way that she was mocked as a person flying from cause to cause, and I know that mockery myself. Maybe that's why I was asked to speak for her today. Otherwise I don't know exactly. But I will say, "Kay, it was luck for me that we met that cold sleety day in front of a fancy Sixth Avenue hotel." Very cold day, side by side, and I think Muriel Rukeyser, her good friend, was with us. While inside, people were talking about peace and Iran, and how long the war would go on. How important to a successful political vigil really nasty weather is.

But I looked at this woman, known by me long ago, long admired, doing work I had barely begun myself. So straight. She had that great posture from standing up, I think, to assorted villains and fools. Sometimes the collective bully of the state (ours); sometimes the single-minded nastiness of fools.

Once, a few years ago, her physical back—of muscle, bone, and cartilage, disks, whatever physical backs are made of—broke. Her back broke. Her spiritual back hustled up all its intransigence and truthfulness to repair its physical self in just a couple of months. It took that much time, but it was after all not such a young back. So that was then, that was when we took a walk. Just after that healing, after her back was broken—and she worried about my foot.

—1994

V / Later

I originally called "The Gulf War" article "Something about the Peace Movement, Something about People's Right Not to Know." I wrote that the Gulf War was brilliantly constructed to prove that hundreds of thousands of men (and some women) could be moved quickly into war and out. The makers of the war believed that American war fervor could last at least three, four months. A longer war and the dreaded Vietnam Syndrome would set in (the name given to intelligent war hatred). I did not emphasize enough the way that the Pentagon needs or thinks it needs a war to test new weapons, to use up old ones, so they can order new ones. I give a couple of examples in the article, but this morning a new one appeared: There is now an ammunition doused or injected with uranium—something that had to be tested apparently; its old awful nature is not described (or remembered), for some reason.

It seems that anyone—a scientist, a military man, an ordinary citizen—would have said, That stuff is dangerous. But like all the endless nuclear tests aboveground, belowground, the awfulness was not awe-full enough.

"Connections" is a talk I gave, a Phi Beta Kappa speech at a Harvard graduation which also happened to be my husband's fiftieth reunion, and I was in the position of addressing his class-

mates, some of whom I considered responsible for the Vietnam War and probably other wars. They were, in fact, the people to whom he wrote during his two-week fast in '65 while he waited to hear their excuses for our bombing of Vietnam's forests and rice paddies. Of course there were as many in his class who were opposed to that war—probably more—and there were many not present; they had been killed in the Second World War.

"Questions" is a preface to a remarkable collection of photographs, Pictures of Peace. As you will see, as I thought about the book, looking into it again and again, a couple of pagefuls of questions about this simple difficult project, this hopeful collection, came into my mind.

I tell, in my piece on menopause, "How Come?," about the writer who called to criticize me for neglecting that subject in my stories. That writer was the wonderful, smart, dream-making, language-loving British author Angela Carter. After I apologized and said I'd surely get it into the next story no matter what, she told me about her severe discomfort and pain. The young doctor, a woman in her early thirties who had examined her a couple of days earlier, had told Angela (white-haired) that she would simply have to accept aging. I think now that her dismissed pain was the beginning of the cancer that killed her in the next couple of years. A friend not to be seen again—three or four books at least (probably already in her head) not to be written, never to be read.

"Across the River," "Life in the Country," and "In a Vermont Jury Room": these come as close as I've been able to come to my Vermont life. In prose, at any rate—I have lots of flower poems, however, and cows, but not enough lifetime left to deepen my understanding of rural life or to sharpen my ear and tongue to speak the language. I have, however, always been involved to some modest degree in the town's troubles and opinions, among my neighbors and at town meetings—school budgets, boards, recycling, river pol-

lution, and the tragedy of the dairy farmer's losses and therefore the town's.

In "Upstaging Time," I didn't know how to write about aging and tried this interview method as a kind of opposition of the two sentimentalities: "Oh, old age! It's so sad!" and "Wow! Is it great! You'll like it!"

" The Gulf War "

One Saturday in late March 1991: The Gulf War has ended. The Iraqis, retreating, have been bombed and strafed on their road home, having unwisely turned their backs to us. The war is not over.

I am walking with my women friends. They are a group that calls itself WIMPs: Women Indict Military Policies. They're a part of the peace movement that thinks about peace even when the newspapers say there's no war. We're walking single file, led by a solemn drumbeat through the streets of our neighborhood in lower Manhattan. Our postwar signs say IS THE MIDDLE EAST MORE STABLE NOW? One sign has a picture of an Iraqi child. Across his chest the words *Collateral Damage* are superimposed.

We're surprised when people thank us for our flyers and for our presence in the streets. Every now and then, some old-fashioned person says, "Go back to Russia." Or a modern fellow says, "Go kiss Saddam's ass." But we're in New York, where the yellow ribbons that have tied our country into a frightened sentimental knot are not so prevalent.

I've been in the U.S. peace or antiwar movement since before the Vietnam War, the mid-1950s. In fact, the Vietnam War interrupted the work many people were doing in trying to end militarism and prevent nuclear war and nuclear proliferation.

In 1961 I was invited to join a group called the Greenwich Village Peace Center, founded by the American Friends Service Committee, which with its customary wisdom left us alone to figure out the consensus, nonviolence decentralized or direct action. We had come from neighborhood concerns: schools, parks, transport. Many of us had children and were worried about the nuclear tests that were sending radioactivity into the air—particularly strontium 90, which traveled through air, to grass, to cows, to our children's milk. We didn't like the arms race, which, during air-raid drills, forced our children to hide under school desks. We were not so much understanding as experiencing the connections. We had, I suppose, been scratching around furiously under the oppression of McCarthyism and were glad to have come together in an autonomous way that was also sensible and communal.

One day our friend and board member Dr. Otto Nathan* said, "You know, there is the beginning of a war in Southeast Asia in a country, very small, called Vietnam. We are now in there with advisers—all kinds of soldiers. Soon—who knows?—we have to pay attention."

We *did* pay attention a couple of weeks later by holding a meeting and discussion (not called a teach-in yet). Just an educational event at a local church, well attended—and then our slow work began as the war itself slowly gathered its political and military determination to slaughter a million Vietnamese as well as 58,000 Americans.

————

* Dr. Otto Nathan, Einstein's executor, an economist, said sadly to me one day, "You know, it isn't guns *or* butter. If THEY wanted it, the country could have guns *and* butter." When I mentioned this to other smart economists, they disagreed. The thirty years of simple American malice since then have inclined me to agree with Dr. Nathan.

Now I will tell you something about the ways we organized against this war—how roughly 3,500 events were successfully hidden from other Americans and the world; how it was shaken by the terrible accumulating speed of the Gulf War. It's as though the war itself was one of those smart weapons, tested in vicious electoral campaigns and used in this case to eliminate the peace movement and its national and historical accomplishment, the Vietnam Syndrome. At this moment of triumph, with 300 Americans and 100,000 Iraquis dead, the President announced that he had indeed extinguished the peace movement and ended the Vietnam Syndrome. Was the main purpose of the Gulf War to bathe the American conscience in blood so as to give it a taste for blood? Well, certainly that was one of its purposes.

The peace movement itself is a valuable old fact, unstable at its broadest constituency, rock-solid at its center. It lives, as many readers know—broad or narrow—in our rich, powerful, somewhat backward, secretly poor, racist, uncomfortably large democratic nation, the United States—which is also cranky and righteous. The elections every four years are considered the final responsibility of citizenship, though usually only about 50 percent of registered voters vote. That's why it takes an awful lot of time and nerve for people to speak up. (That's why a short war is best.) If, on a street corner while giving out flyers, you ask someone why they don't speak up, they are apt to say they don't need to, we're already a democracy. Our two political parties, smiling proudly at one another, enable us to demand lots of pluralism in other countries.*

Now, how should I describe how this war's peace movement happened? There were already women and men innocently joyful about the end of the Cold War (me too), believing we'd come to that moment in our lifetimes when serious expensive internal

* Vermont, where I now live, elected an independent socialist, a terrible shock to the U.S. Congress.

problems could be addressed. The Panama invasion was a bad sign, but if you work in any oppositional movement you will be opposed vigorously. (This surprises some people.) We didn't expect things to be easy, but we had added hope to the personality, if not the character, of our work. The continuing antiwar workers were doing the usual antimilitarism work—opposing the arms budget (much of it hidden in costs of old wars; hidden, too, in the Energy Department budget), fighting underground testing, conducting classes in nonviolence, anti-recruitment drives in high schools. And a boycott of war toys. It seemed clearer with each administration decision that President Bush and his warrior companions had drawn their first line in the sandbox in a tough school, and they hadn't changed too much—in action or in boy language.

Environmental organizations were doing their important work globally and in village toxic dumps. The Central American networks were dealing with decades of exported U.S. repression and war. Feminist groups—radical, socialist, academic, or traditional—were facing the backlashes that often follow success—the anti-abortion moralities of the anti-sexual right as well as the wishful pronouncements of patriarchy that feminism was dead. Blacks and other people of color also hoped that the inner-city disasters of homelessness and poverty would be reversed somehow, although racism, as the most severe inherited illness of the United States, was continuing its nasty life. Gay groups struggled with discrimination and the grief of AIDS. Middle Eastern organizations suffered indifference and faced nearly everyone else's ignorance . . . at a time when their role was about to become central.

I've told you all this to show that radical and social justice organizations had plenty to do. But the experience of Vietnam and the work of decades began to pay off. In general, most of the groups I've described saw their connections to one another—were in fact living those connections. Before the coalition (two in some places—three in Seattle, I've been told—at first anyway) there was a lot of overlapping. For instance, many women in Central American work were feminists. They listened to the radio and watched television and heard the drone and confidence of prowar male experts—even more tedious than some of their political brothers. It's hard to believe that fifteen years ago people opposed to nuclear power and anti-nuclear-war activists didn't understand that they had a common agenda. It took long discussions and a couple of years of political argument and mediation to bring them together. Environmentalists had to learn that war made an ecological mess. Oh? First resistance. Then surprise. Then connection.

On August 29, 1990, Jeff Patterson refused to join his unit; he sat down on the airstrip in Hawaii. He had enlisted in the Marine Corps straight out of high school in California—for the same reason most youngsters do: educational opportunities, maybe some adventure. His experience during deployments to Okinawa, South Korea, and the Philippines changed his outlook entirely. He said, "I have, as an artillery controller, directed cannons on Oahu, rained burning white phosphorus and tons of high explosives on the big island, and blasted away at the island of Kahoolawe . . . I can bend no further." In the next few weeks, others were to join him.

On September 12, 1990, one of the first peace meetings in New York was held at Cooper Union. There were thousands of women and men—the auditorium was full; there were loudspeakers outside. The weather was fine and the plaza around Cooper Union packed with intent listeners. I have been living in white Vermont, and as a true New Yorker I became excited to see once again all the colors of the people of my city. And the numbers! A surprise really. Oh, I thought, this war will never happen.

At the literature table I looked at various flyers and petitions, particularly the flyer and petition issued by the coalition that had put this marvelous meeting together, with its twenty to thirty speakers. I thought it was all right—kind of jargony, but not too terrible. This huge meeting was what mattered.

Still, I did say to the young woman at the lit table: "How come you guys left out the fact that Iraq did go into Kuwait? How come?" She said, "That's not really important." "I know what you mean," I said, "but it happens to be true."

I did know what she meant, and I read their explanation a couple of weeks later. It insisted that if the American people were told about the invasion of Kuwait, they would "become confused." It would "obfuscate" the basic facts and actions. Unfortunately, of course, the American people had already been told and continued to be told day and night about this pathetic little country of trillionaires, and so omitting facts became a lie and did get in the way of organizing people unaccustomed to being held to political lines. It was a stubbornness that hurt work in New York more than elsewhere, but people are used to that, and national—I should say local—organizing all around the country against the frighteningly speedy troop and propaganda buildup continued. Reports of their success vary according to the facts and the disposition of the reporter.

Two coalitions finally had to happen in New York. One was the Coalition to Stop Intervention in the Middle East, which, with its strong cadre of the Workers' World Party, had organized the important New York September 12 meeting; the other became the National Campaign for Peace in the Middle East, with its base in traditional peace and anti-intervention groups. The division was real, a matter of substance, style—and at the same time there were organizations that had simply started to do their anti–Gulf War in one coalition or another—also, it depended on how much they were doing outside the big cities. An example would be Palestinian Aid in the coalition and Palestinian Solidarity in the campaign. The division came to a pointy head over the dates of the major Washington demonstration. The coalition had decided on the nineteenth before a common meeting with the campaign. Reasons for both dates were as good as they were bad. It was good to do it on Martin Luther King's holiday weekend, because . . . Yes, I thought. It was bad to plan it for that weekend, because . . . Yes, I thought. In any event, the vote ran extremely high against the nineteenth.

In late December 1990, the campaign proposed a joint statement supporting both demonstrations. The coalition said no. Many people went to both. The coalition went ahead, had its demonstration on the nineteenth with good representation of people of color—blacks, Hispanics, many Middle Eastern Americans. In San Francisco there were about 150,000 demonstrators. The twenty-sixth brought out about 250,000 people in Washington. The tone and the style of these demonstrations were extraordinary. There were more hand-made, non-organizational signs as well as the big ballooning sky-hiding world hoisted above us all by Greenpeace. The Bread and Puppet marched with its huge puppets, its great music and stilt dancers, and its Vermont cadre of a couple of hundred B. and P. lovers and activist banner carriers. Some of the signs—culled from my head and *The Nation*: WAR IS GOOD BUSINESS; INVEST YOUR SON OR DAUGHTER; GEORGE BUSH IS HAVING A WARGASM; A KINDER GENTLER BLOODBATH; GIVE ESTROGEN A CHANCE; READ MY APOCALYPSE.

These impressive demonstrations happened later, after the war had started but before the rage and drive of the air war and its murderous preemption of hope taught us to say the word "blitzkrieg" and understand where our civilian and military leaders had gone to school.

I want to say a little more about the opposition to the inevitable war before January 15, 1991. Interesting fact: 73 percent of

American women were opposed to the war in the month before it started. Men were split down the middle.

The New York Times printed a letter on August 22, 1990, from Alex Molnar, whose son, a twenty-one-year-old Marine, had been sent to Saudi Arabia. He concluded his letter (to President Bush): "And I'm afraid that as the pressure mounts, you will wager my son's life in a gamble to save your political future . . ." The letter was reprinted many times and created a movement called the Military Families Support Network . . . which by early March 1991 had chapters in thirty-nine states. MFSN supported the use of economic sanctions, opposed massive deployment of U.S. forces and the entire military offensive. Their emphasis on the support of troops has put off a number of columnists. I myself feel that a slogan like "Support the Troops" has to include the words "by Bringing Them Home Now."

Actually, in almost every demonstration I've been a part of or come upon in another city or town, those last words *were* there. There's a kind of critiquing of the events and actions of that hard short period that is not criticism but more like an academic exercise made by people at their desks who are not out on the streets or engaged in the decision-making processes of any noncentralized organization.

Journeys, peace missions to Iraq or journeys of inquiry, have been a part of peace-movement activity from late summer/early autumn 1990, when they began organizing, into February 1991 and the war.

In mid-October a peace delegation organized by the Fellowship of Reconciliation spent two days in Jordan and a week in Iraq. The main purpose of this mission was to bring medicine to Amman and especially to Baghdad. David McReynolds, one of the members of the twenty-person team, returned and reported on the lives of children in Baghdad. I think of one scene he describes: fathers in a small Iraqi village holding their children up to the windows of the Americans' bus. I did not see this report in our newspapers.

The Gulf Peace Team opened a peace camp on the border of Iraq and Saudi Arabia. It remained there for ten days and thousands of sorties of the air war. It was evacuated on January 26, 1991, by the Iraqis. There were eighty-six witnesses living at the camp, many from other countries as well as the United States. They saw the beginning of the environmental destruction by our smart Air Force and the great suffering of the people. I read their reports in the left and pacifist press.

Later—in early February, during the war—Ramsey Clark and a group of well-known photographers and reporters went, including an American Iraqi with family there who was able to bring him into conversation with ordinary civilians and their experiences—beginning with the bombed road from Jordan into Iraq and the destruction of civilian vehicles—food-and-grain trucks. Also the markets, water stations, schools—all the targets, I guess, of our "stupid" bombs.

To return to prewar actions, statements . . . On November 14 the National Council of Churches at a conference in Portland, Oregon, condemned U.S. policy in the Gulf: "As Christians . . . we must witness against weak resignation to the illogical logic of militarism and war." The National Conference of Catholic Bishops wrote to President Bush: "In this situation, moving beyond the deployment of military forces in an effort to deter Iraq's aggression to the undertaking of offensive military action could well violate the criteria for a "just war," especially the principles of proportionality and last resort."

These strong leadership statements stood, but the churches themselves fell into an awful quietness as the war began. I am reminded here that it's important to say that the religious fellowships, the Catholic and Jewish, the Protestant peace churches as

well, did *not* retreat. What happened most to churches and con-
gregations sincerely opposed to the war to begin with is what
happened to representatives and senators who swore they'd never
back down. The sight of a yellow ribbon unnerved them. They fell
before it, just as tyrants and Satans had once fallen before the
cross placed before their terrified eyes.

Meanwhile, in the rest of the country, hundreds of meetings,
vigils, sit-ins, teach-ins were occurring. By early March 1991,
over 3,500 actions had taken place and over 4,000 arrests had
been made. In our valley (between New Hampshire and Vermont)
perhaps a dozen small towns held regular vigils. A newspaper
advertisement was signed by 1,100 people. Who were they? The
women and men who drove in and out of dirt roads were probably
1960s folks, now forty or so, with kids—or not—also Vietnam
vets. But the signers were often old budget enemies from town
meetings, people seen only at the dump or recycling center—or
in church. We were amazed—What? She signed! That one! But
this was before the war . . . Vigils continued through the weeks
of the war. We are going back now to the signers. What will we
find?

Full-page advertisements were taken out by SaneFreeze and
the Ad Hoc Committee, which also organized teach-ins. Communications from other parts of the country tell the same story
—sometimes more original. Seven or eight men and women from
Oakland traveled the train system singing funny anti-Bush lyrics.
They were applauded and cursed. Here are some quotes from
Lucy Lippard's report in *Z* of artists' and just plain creative
people's responses to the prospects of war and to the war itself:

> Our street theater piece "The Bushes Take You For A
> Ride" has George and Barbara in a red cardboard car
> running out of gas and being "serviced" by a soldier/
> gas pump—GI José. A hose from his red satin heart is
> administered by a "Plasmaco nursery" representing Pe-

troleum Multinational. When the soldier collapses, the audience is solicited for more volunteers.

Two of Boulder's most effective cultural groups are satirical. LISP (Ladies in Support of the President) is "an organization of patriotic God-fearing LADIES who deplore nasty war protests" and offer "George is not a Wimp" buttons. An offshoot of the local Queer Cosmos, these men in drag haunt recruitment centers and plead prissily at rallies for "all you homosexuals and commies to please go home." A long-standing socialist feminist group (with anti-racist "Klarette" performances and a public "Sodomy Patrol" among their past credits) are polling crowds.

GRIT (Gulf Response Information Team, "a very private research group") are sending the results to the President. Their questions begin straight, sucking people in, and end with outrageous ones, like "In order to support our troops, how many casualties from your family would be acceptable? (a) 1 (b) 2 (c) 3 or more (d) all of them."

Small groups like GRIT, and individual artists, can be less intimidating and attract less hostility and more dialogue than massive demonstrations, which serve another purpose. For instance, playwright Art Mayers patrolled Maine's state capitol building, in Arab headdress and gas mask dripping blood, muttering over and over, "the horror of it, the horror of it." He was eventually arrested for "terrorizing children," but the charges were dropped.

When I stopped at the office of the War Resisters League to pick up some flyers, they were receiving as many as ninety calls a day asking for military counseling, from reservists as well as active-duty men *and* women. A high-school kid who had just enlisted was speaking to Peter Jamieson, a Vietnam vet (he's a counsellor). Michael Marsh, who has organized the work in this office, is down at Camp LeJeune, North Carolina, where seven Marine COs are being court-martialed on charges of desertion. I was given a sheet of paper listing fifteen resisters. In Germany there are American soldiers at U.S. bases who are resisting deployment. A Military Counseling Network has been in place since early autumn—the American Friends Service Committee, the War Resisters League, and the Central Committee of Conscientious Objectors were major networkers.

A fine project (which, with more money, could have got under way earlier) was MADRE's tour of Women of Courage. MADRE, whose major political work had been about Nicaragua, especially the women, their hospitals, and day-care centers, had undertaken to send about twenty women from different Middle Eastern countries on tour through the United States and Canada. While one group spoke in New England, others were in Toronto—and in California cities. Women from Iraq, Turkey, Palestine, Egypt, and Israel were in the group, I heard. Each city or two visited had to add an American mother whose son or daughter was in the desert.

In going over material I'd gathered for this chapter, I found something I'd written to a friend I work and think with at the very beginning of January 1991:

> Another thing I worry about: Resistance to this war is
> great. So—if we *do* go to war, it will take a lot of hard-
> working repression to keep that anger in check or turn
> it around. We better watch out for it. It will only *start*
> with the suppression of information from the front and

continue by hiding our regional and town actions from one another till we think we or our villages or our families are alone.

This is exactly what happened: the pools. According to the Fund for Free Expression, of the 1,400 journalists in the Persian Gulf only 192—including technicians and photographers—were placed in press pools with combat forces. Journalists "apprehended or threatened with detention or detained include E. Schmitt and Kifner of *The New York Times*, Gughliotti of *The Washington Post*, King and Bayles of the Associated Press . . . These are people who did try to break free of government censors . . ." "A French TV crew was forced at gunpoint by U.S. marines to give up videotape it had shot of U.S. wounded in the battle to retake the Saudi town of Khafji."

Almost overnight, once the war started, the silence began. Having lived for sixty-eight years, a surprising number of them in some political consciousness, I must report that I've never experienced the kind of repression that set in once the air war started. It was not like the McCarthy period—that is, there were no personal direct attacks on well-known people of that kind. It was as though a great damp blanket had been laid over our country with little pinholes for American flags to stick up into the public air.

Here is another paragraph from the February 27, 1991, report of the Fund for Free Expression:

There have been several instances of retaliation against journalists who have questioned the propriety of the war. After he wrote approvingly of an antiwar march, *San Francisco Examiner* associate editor and columnist Warren Hinckle was put on a partially paid three-month leave. "I take the position that I was censored," Hinckle says. The editor of the Kutztown, Pennsylvania, *Patriot* was fired after he wrote an editorial calling for peace. *Village Voice* national affairs editor Dan Bischoff was canceled as a guest on the CBS news "Nightwatch" program. The Pentagon refused to provide anyone to appear on the program if the *Voice* was to be represented among the participants. The program's producer recalls a Pentagon representative as objecting on the grounds that "if someone from *The Village Voice* is on, that raises the possibility that there will be a discussion of the merits" of the lawsuit filed by the *Voice* and other media organizations challenging the Pentagon press restrictions. The Public Broadcasting System postponed a rebroadcast of a Bill Moyers "Frontline" program on the Iran–Contra affair because, according to an internal PBS memo, the program's raising of "serious questions about then–Vice President Bush's involvement and actions" make it "journalistically inappropriate" during the war against Iraq, because "the program could be viewed as overtly political by attempting to undermine the President's credibility."

FAIR—Fairness and Accuracy in Reporting—offered the following report on February 22:

About 1.5 percent of nightly news programs . . . were identified as antiwar protests. Only one leader of a peace organization was quoted in broadcasts surveyed. Seven Super Bowl players were sought out to comment on the war. Half of all sources were connected to U.S. or Allied governments, 3 in 10 from the military.

Another report on television—this time by three academic researchers, Sut Jhally, Justin Lewis, and Michael Morgan—revealed that there was a correlation between knowledge—

information—and opposition to the war. Television viewing was broken down into three groups. The longer people looked at television, the less they knew. The short-time viewers were not well informed, but much better informed than the others. After some protests followed FAIR's exposés, certain programs like the *MacNeil-Lehrer Newshour* (daily) finally allowed Noam Chomsky, Erwin Knoll, and Edward Said to speak their dissenting views.

It's not as though media workers on our side didn't fight back. Paper Tiger/Deep Dish produced a Gulf Crisis TV series—seen on Public Access channels and finally PBS (Public Broadcasting). Tapes were used in university teach-ins.

When peace people (organizers) talked critically of the period, they varied—widely. Frances Crowe, in western Massachusetts, "found a huge antiwar movement waiting to be organized. After ten years of trying to organize around the Middle East, people are ready and willing to learn about the region." Susan Akram asks, "How did the peace movement get so isolated?"

I've tried to describe in these few pages something about what has been happening in the last months in my country. I've left out a lot—by necessity.

If you were part of these events, if you were working in your community, you had a sense of excitement, action, momentum, but at the same time, listening to radio, television news, or reading the daily press darkened you into an unimaginable despair. Not only the sense of a vast damp blanket over the country, but also it seemed that half your neighbors not only didn't know but *wanted not to know*, because if a bit of news squeaked through (the bombing of the Baghdad shelter), there were cries of "Treason!" (the photographers, the anchormen, the television station).

One of the responses to this war that grieved me particularly was the failure of American Jews to see how bad this war was for Israel, how dangerous, how destructive it *had* to be for the hopes for peace and a decent relationship with Palestinians—how it set all that struggle back years and years.

So the war ends—and doesn't end. It never ended for the Vietnamese—all these embargoed years. Not for the Panamanians either, who are worse off than ever. Not for the Middle East, where, as I write, hundreds of thousands of Kurds running, fighting, encouraged by Bush's rhetoric of rebellion, are being slaughtered by Iraq's helicopters and starved and frozen in their tracks. Thousands of Iraqis dead, injured, leave the countryside and the destroyed cities in grief and turmoil. We've learned that *only 7 percent* of our thousands of sorties were so-called smart bombs. The rest were the usual stupid carpet bombs, cluster bombs, etc., used for civilians, ground armies, the earth . . .

Israelis and Palestinians hate each other more than ever—both people having been driven mad: the Israelis by Europeans fifty years ago; the Palestinians by Israelis today. The Palestinians running from the country, Kuwait, which we liberated so that it could continue along its glowing golden road. The oppression of Palestinians in the occupied territories is worse than ever, partly because they made the wrong (foolish) decision to agree with Saddam Hussein, partly because Israel was planning to make it tougher to be a Palestinian anyway.

Why were Bush and friends so determined to jam this war down the originally disinterested throats of allies—the UN and the United States—the American citizenry? We learned—little by little. First everyone said Oil! Of course. Then we learned that we used very little of Kuwait's oil. So we understood next it was about hegemony—that is, being in charge of everyone else's oil. A major purpose was the great Pentagon need to try out all the new, so far unused trillion dollars' worth of airware. How would they perform? Many years ago, in 1969, a North Vietnamese said to me as I was leaving Hanoi, "Please tell the great American scientists to stop using us as their laboratory. Your napalm *does* work. So does your improved white phosphorus." Our government also wanted to teach an important lesson: It was possible to move over 400,000 troops in a few weeks halfway round the fattest part of the earth.

It was also a major necessity to wipe out the historical memory of the 1960s, which moved more powerfully than is usually perceived into the 1970s with the rise of the women's movement, the anti-nuclear-power movement, and the science of ecology with its working arm, environmentalism.

I am reminded of a statement made by Donella Meadows at a Dartmouth teach-in. She explained that there was alternative energy for everything in normal comfortable American life—television, air conditioners, light, heat, cars. There was only one enterprise that required such massive infusion of energy for which no alternative to oil could work—and that was war. A tank, she said, could move only seventeen feet on a gallon of gasoline. So this is the final purpose. This has been a war to maintain turmoil in the world (particularly in the Middle East). This has been a war to ensure that Americans can continue to make war, and like it.

—1991

" Connections "

This is called an oration, which inhibited me a little bit until I realized it just meant I was going to talk.

With that in mind, I called this talk, this oration, "Connections," because that is what it is. A couple of weeks ago I was at a gathering in New York of an organization called Jews for Racial and Economic Justice. They were honoring a couple of older people for their lifelong contributions to organizing—the head of Local 1199 and a teacher from City College—and they were being honored for work in their fields, in thinking about ordinary people. Toward the end of the evening, a young black guy came up to me and said, "Don't you know me, Grace? It's me, it's J.J."

"What? Jimmy?" I could hardly recognize him, because I hadn't seen him in about twenty years.

In 1969, I flew to Vietnam and then spent a month traveling south from Hanoi down to the DMZ with Jimmy and a couple of others. We had this peculiar task. We were bringing three POWs back to the United States. In the middle of the war. The Vietnamese had agreed to send three POWs every month or two. This was in 1969. The bombing of the North had stopped for a while and the Vietnamese thought this might work—that it might be a sign that they wanted the war ended, so we had been asked as peace-movement people to bring these men back, which we did.

The only thing the Vietnamese said was that they shouldn't go back into teaching—they were all fliers, by the way—they could go back into the Air Force, but they mustn't start teaching pilots again, pilots who would then fly to Vietnam and kill Vietnamese. That made a lot of sense. Unfortunately, at that time the United States or maybe Nixon and Kissinger didn't seem to really want the war to end very much so very quickly, so they had these guys teaching pilots. After about nine or ten POWs had been freed, that was the end of the program. And very little is publicly known about it. I would probably know very little about it myself if I hadn't been part of it.

Anyway, this guy Jimmy Johnson whom I met after twenty years, who went to Vietnam with me and five others, had already spent two and a half years in prison. He had spent two and half years in prison—he was about twenty-two or twenty-three—and he had already spent all that time in prison because he was one of a group called the Fort Hood Three. Some of the older people here might remember them.

I had been to his trial in the mid-sixties, maybe 1965 or 1966—you know, you'll notice when you get older you really lose track of dates and you begin to depend on things like the Freedom of Information Act to bring you your records, so you know when you said what and to whom. So I have to look this up, but it was sometime in the mid-sixties. I went to his trial, which was in New Jersey at Fort Dix. And he was a very impressive young fellow. The thing that got me was his parents—they really admired him so much. I mean, there they sat at his trial; he's being tried and God knows how many years he'll get, and they're so proud of him. They just looked at him, and I had to go back into my own culture to feel what it was, as though it was his bar mitzvah and not his trial for near-treason. He was one of three young men who had sat themselves down on the tarmac.

At any rate, he sat down on it, as others have done since (during the Gulf War), but he was one of the first three young men who refused to go to Vietnam. He refused to move toward that plane. And way up in the high reaches of our American world, President Johnson and a whole bunch of people—men—had already decided that the war would go forward and that there would be large troop movements, that there would eventually be 500,000 men in Vietnam and that the bombing of the North would start again. All of this happened around the same time that Jimmy Johnson said he would not be one of those men.

And a lot of those decision-making men came from here. Harvard. I really am sorry to say that. And some of them may be celebrating their fiftieth right now, or some may be celebrating next year, and some may have celebrated a year or two ago. But you needn't feel too bad, because Yale has taken over that job recently with President Bush's men. I mean, good things do happen.

But the reason this war in Indochina had continued in this particular way was because of what was called a crisis of credibility. I don't know how to describe it exactly, but this fear of not being credible, of not being believed unless you are very strong and violent and offering more violence, it's very similar to . . . Well, you know we have often talked about how Asians and Indians and others need to save face, and we have treated that as kind of a backward idea. You know, you want to save face, what are they going to do to their faces after they're saved? But we Americans (some of us) have the same need, really. We like to be credible and it is really pretty much the same thing. And one might say it is really not a facial experience, this need, it's really a testicular one.

But anyway, I'm making these connections in order to get on to our latest war, because a lot of you young people—well, you weren't even born at that time and you keep wondering why people are always talking to you about Vietnam, Vietnam. It's really pretty boring in many ways. Still, actually it turns out that Vietnam is not only on my mind and my friends' minds but it is so much on the President's mind and so much on our leaders' minds that *they* talk about it all the time. They are very much afraid that we'll forget about Vietnam and yet they *want* us to forget about it. They want us to forget—they want you to forget about it, at least about American resistance; they don't want you to think about it. But it's this "credible" thing, and then it's this face-saving thing, and it turns out that we not only went into that war as fiercely as we did for credibility but at the same time that we were making ourselves credible, we were losing face. So we lost our face in Vietnam, and that is why Bush and other leaders and the American public have to keep talking about it. They call it the Vietnam Syndrome. But what the Vietnam Syndrome is about—I'll talk about that a little later.

In any event, once our leader pointed out this loss to all the Americans who really thought they *had kept* their faces for the last fifteen years, the people began to understand they had really lost them. So the yellow ribbon was invented and appeared everywhere easily, as though there had always been a great vat of yellow dye in the middle of the country. And in front of that ribbon organizations, churches, all sorts of authoritative people —Congress and so forth—fell. Then they recovered, held up their yellow ribbon, and were declared present.

It worked like that for a lot of people. But think about the war itself, the war that you have known recently, your most recent war, the Gulf War, which, because it was brilliantly executed, very few of you really had too much to do with! Young recruits were sent over—which most of you were not, although some of you could have been—and old reservists. Really old reservists. For instance, there was a whole group of about fifty-year-old men from Harlem who had been sent by accident into some forward position, which they were not exactly prepared for. What was the Army doing with these old black men down there?

This war really hasn't ended, and it is not going to end so soon. The Vietnam War, to this day, has never ended for the Vietnamese. All these years the Vietnamese have been cruelly embargoed. So we are still at war against them as far as I can see. As for the Panamanians, they are probably worse off than they were before we decided to defend them. And in the Middle East, as we now know, nothing is really much better. If anything, it is less stable than before.

Thousands and thousands of Iraqis are still dead, or injured. The Kurds, well, you know all about them, and we Americans really have a lot of sympathy for them and it's the best part of us in a sense. It's something our country's always done extremely well. I mean, we put them in a position where they are practically slaughtered, but then—I'm going to say something awfully cynical. I don't like to be cynical in front of young people, and I'm not really cynical, but I'm going to say this cynical thing all the same. Which is that once enough of the Kurds had been slaughtered, we became very good-hearted and have probably taken care of them better than almost anybody else could.

And you can compare that in a sense to the wonderful way we took care of Vietnamese orphans. Then we were strong enough. The truth is, we were strong enough to do that—to kill the parents—but we were also good enough to take care of their orphans. And that is in us also—one thing that is there and is a true thing.

But one of the decisions our administration made, one of the worst—as the Gulf War was beginning—was to stretch a great big wet blanket over the country. At least I felt like that. No air and no airwaves. We couldn't see or hear the war, the killing which might have saddened us. I don't remember that kind of silence since the McCarthy days. Our media actually allowed themselves to *not* receive information. We are used to them making a lot of noise. Sometimes we don't like what they say but we're used to that general racket out of which certain pieces of fact and truth often slip out and speak to us. This dampness covered us so thoroughly we couldn't react in our good-hearted way—if I can go from cynicism to sentimentality (which are closely related). Though we saw nothing of the war, the people were generally for it with yellow ribbons and flags flying wildly. But once we saw the pictures of the Kurds on TV, once we saw a few facts and the truth, we were moved, affected by the sight and began to press the government to take some sort of action. So in a sense, the government's strategic decision to hide the truth from us was the smart thing to do from their point of view.

Well, here we are right now, and we are at a point now where the Israelis and Palestinians hate each other more than ever. Both of them are being driven quite crazy. The Israelis were driven crazy by Europeans fifty years ago and the Palestinians are now being driven crazy by the Israelis.* When I say driven crazy, I mean that people who are tormented in these ways are really made crazy with rage. People who have no homes, whose homes are taken away from them. And you don't have to go that far away to see this, because you can walk with me in my own city, and I suppose in Boston, too, but certainly in New York, you can see people who if they were not crazy to begin with are being driven crazy. And that happens in whole parts of the world where people are torn from their homes and their homes destroyed. It isn't just *our* wars that have made people mad—it's all the wars.

I've tried to figure out why this last war was needed so much, why they wanted it, why it was forced on us. Most of our international allies in the beginning didn't think it was a great idea, and Congress was at first opposed or ambivalent. Why did the President and his military advisors stampede us? First I think it wasn't the oil so much (only 5 percent to 7 percent comes from Kuwait) as it was wanting to be the boss of the oil. I think that's called hegemony.

Another purpose was the real Pentagon need to try out all that

* I quote myself—from "The Gulf War."

trillion dollars' worth of unused hardware weaponry. Much of it quite new and much of it really almost as good as an atomic bomb, but without radioactivity, so it was a little healthier, you know. So we had to try them out, because how else are you going to know if it works. Now the funny thing about it—because we really are a free country (at least we acted that way before the war)—is that much of what I've just said was announced by Pentagon people or weapons specialists on TV. I mean, they would say this much: You know, we don't know whether this works, and they were so enthusiastic and cheerful. Does this stuff work? Well, we'll soon find out. So there was a lot of TV enthusiasm about all that.

In a way this is where you all come in, because you are very smart people—you're supposed to be, anyway, and your brains are for something in this world, and you have to decide what you want to do with your brains. Whether you want to be the person to improve the napalm or let it alone. You have to make that decision, because if you don't, the gods and goddesses of this world—whoever they are—are going to begin to think that brains should not be considered an important gene for the continuation of the human race. It will in fact be one of the worst things for the survival of the fittest. So you have to consider all these things when you decide what to do with your smartness. And there is a lot to be done in the world. I think you're the ones who can do it. And you have to protect that biological fact of braininess.

Another major reason for this war was the necessity to prove to the American people and the world that the government could move hundreds and thousands of soldiers very quickly in any direction. Almost more important was the effort to wipe out the historical memory of the sixties, which had become the seventies, with the rise of the women's movement and advances in civil rights, the anti-nuclear-power movement and the science of ecology.

Now, with the establishment of this non-wimpiness settled, the lives and bodies of women have begun to be returned to their rightful owner: the male state. We have seen the direction that certain states and the Supreme Court have been taking in narrowing women's lives. Women's rights, by the way, are human rights!

I want to tell you something Donella Meadows said at a Dartmouth teach-in. She explained that there was alternative energy for everything in normal, comfortable American life. Alternative energy. TV, air conditioners, light, heat, automobiles. That there was only one enterprise that required such massive infusions of energy that no alternative to oil would work, and that was war. A tank, she said to us, could really move not much more than seventeen feet on a gallon of gas. So this made me really think that this might very well be the final purpose of this war, the one we are not quite finished with. It wasn't a war for stability, in other regards, really—its main purpose was to maintain turmoil in the Middle East, and to prove the nastiness of new weapons. Mostly it was a war to make sure that Americans could continue to make war and—most important—like it. That's what it was.*

Since I'm a writer, I will end this talk by telling a story—to go from talk of war and responsibility to a storytelling description of daily life in my city, New York.

Three Days and a Question

On the first day I joined a demonstration opposing the arrest in Israel of members of Yesh Gvul, Israeli soldiers who had refused to serve in the occupied territories. Yesh Gvul means: *There is a limit.*

TV cameras and an anchorwoman arrived and *New York Times* stringers with their narrow journalism notebooks. What do you

---

* This paragraph is almost exactly the same as the one that concluded "The Gulf War." I thought it necessary to this talk.

think? the anchorwoman asked. What do you think, she asked a woman passerby—a woman about my age.

Anti-Semites, the woman said quietly.

The anchorwoman said, But they're Jewish.

Anti-Semites, the woman said, a little louder.

What? One of our demonstrators stepped up to her. Are you crazy? How can you . . . Listen what we're saying.

Rotten anti-Semites—all of you.

What? What? What? the man shouted. How you dare to say that—all of us Jews. Me, he said. He pulled up his shirtsleeve. Me? You call me? You look. He held out his arm. Look at this.

I'm not looking, she screamed.

You look at my number, what they did to me. My arm . . . you have no right.

Anti-Semite, she said between her teeth. Israel hater.

No, no, he said, you fool. My arm—you're afraid to look . . . my arm . . . my arm.

On the second day Vera and I listen at PEN to Eta Krisaeva read her stories, which were not permitted publication in her own country, Czechoslovakia. Then we walk home in the New York walking night, about twenty blocks—shops and lights, other walkers talking past us. Late-night homeless men and women asleep in dark storefront doorways on cardboard pallets under coats and newspapers, scraps of blanket. Near home on Sixth Avenue a young man, a boy, passes—a boy the age a younger son could be—head down, bundles in his arms, on his back.

Wait, he says, turning to stop us. Please, please wait. I just got out of Bellevue. I was sick. They gave me something. I don't know . . . I need to sleep somewhere. The Y, maybe.

That's way uptown.

Yes, he says. He looks at us. Carefully he says, AIDS. He looks away. Oh. Separately, Vera and I think, A boy—only a boy.

Mothers after all, our common trade for more than thirty years.

Then he says, I put out my hand. We think he means to tell us he tried to beg. I put out my hand. No one will help me. No one. Because they can see. Look at my arm. He pulls his coat sleeve back. Lesions, he says. Have you ever seen lesions? That's what people see.

No. No, we see a broad fair forehead, a pale countenance, fear. I just have to sleep, he says.

We shift in our pockets. We give him what we find—about eight dollars. We tell him, Son, they'll help you on Thirteenth Street at the center. Yes, I know about that place. I know about them all. He hoists the bundle of his things to his back to prepare for walking. Thank you, ladies. Goodbye.

On the third day I'm in a taxi. I'm leaving the city for a while and need to get to the airport. We talk—the driver and I. He's a black man, dark. He's not young. He has a French accent. Where are you from? Haiti, he answers. Ah, your country is in bad trouble. Very bad. You know that, miss.

Well, yes. Sometimes it's in the paper.

They thieves there. You know that? Very rich, very poor. You believe me? Killing—it's nothing to them, killing. Hunger. Starving people. Everything bad. And you don't let us come. Starving. They send us back.

We're at a red light. He turns to look at me. Why they do that? He doesn't wait for me to say, Well . . . because . . . He says, Why hard.

The light changes. We move slowly up traffic-jammed Third Avenue. Silence. Then: Why? Why they let the Nicaragua people come? Why they let Vietnamese come? One time American people want to kill them people. Put bomb in their children. Break their head. Now they say, Yes, yes, come come come. Not us. Why?

Your New York is beautiful country. I love it. So beautiful, this

New York. But why, tell me, he says, stopping the cab, switching the meter off. Why, he says, turning to me again, rolling his short shirtsleeve back, raising his arm to the passenger divider, pinching and pulling the bare skin of his upper arm. You tell me— this skin, this black skin—why? Why you hate this skin so much?

Question: Those gestures, those arms, the three consecutive days thrown like a formal net over the barest unchanged accidental facts. How? Why? In order to become—probably—in this city one story told.

—1991

" Questions "

A picture of peace—what is that? Is a picture of peace a peaceful-looking picture, or any photograph taken during the absence of war? Is it that we need to give peace a good name? Why do we have to? Isn't it always better not to be killing others or mutilating them? Are there perfectly good reasons not to be living in peace? When we say peace, do we mean the absence of all conflict, nonviolent struggles, which are often quite fierce? Do we mean no pushing in the playground, no throwing sand in the sandbox? Do we mean peace except for "Oh well, boys will be boys"?

Do we think war is more exciting? Well, hasn't it been made to appear the most interesting moment in the bonding of men? Aren't there novels and autobiographies by men who've been to war that tell the young how interesting and exciting and important it was to have been at some particular battle, even though many of them say they are now opposed to all war?

Haven't we lived through one of the strangest years in our lives and our country's coinciding life? Isn't it true that in the winter of '90–'91 a great many Americans (the majority women) were opposed to going to war and hoped for initiatives for alternative peaceful actions? Wasn't the feeling somewhat pacific even in Congress, which also hated the possibility of losing absolutely all its power to the determined President? Was this really because of the Vietnam Syndrome? Was this particular syndrome a collection of symptoms, like the questioning of authority? Did it also include a preference for mutual consideration and fear of the military and war in general? As syndromes go, wasn't that a good one?

Was it the day the President decided to go to war or a couple of days later that yellow ribbons appeared on trees and doorways and people? Did those ribbons really mean we had suddenly accepted authority? Can it be that overnight the country was wild for war, eager to censor disagreement? Is it true that this included an eagerness to *be* censored? What does all this mean? What is its sorrowful meaning? How long before we take our syndrome back?

This book is called *Pictures of Peace*, a large, hopeful, international project. About twenty-nine years ago our small neighborhood peace group, the Greenwich Village Peace Center, organized an event called exactly that: Pictures of Peace. Since I always think it is worthwhile to tell an old story on the way to the future, this is what we did:

Schoolchildren in the public, parochial, and private schools in the neighborhood were asked to draw an idea of their own peaceful world. There would be no winners. Actually we had planned at first to suggest a little competition, but one of the elementary-school teachers explained our own politics to us. Most of us hadn't grasped it earlier, then we understood it forever. So there would be an exhibition in one of the gyms, and finally Mrs. Kennedy and Mrs. Khrushchev would each be given a painting. These were graciously received at a poorly attended press conference.

What made us undertake this complicated project? We had been thinking mostly of the last decade of deadly nuclear tests and arms buildups. But the nation of Vietnam had just begun to sneak into our consciousness. At the same time, advisors, politicians, generals were sneaking into the Vietnamese countryside and the back pages of our newspapers. We were more worried than usual.

The girls and boys that took part in our project were between six and fourteen years old. The Vietnam War, which had barely begun in their childhood, would last another thirteen years for us and the Vietnamese. Did those labored-over drawings and paintings, those talking, explaining mothers and teachers, the word "peace" said over and over again—did any of that help a couple of youthful idealists against the recruiters and war makers who had been waiting for years for those children to become the right age and size for war?

Modestly, we believe that neighborhood of attention had to have been useful. So, with this book in 1991, these *Pictures of Peace*, rare in our time, we add year by year, image by image, to the struggle for peaceful, just lives. We say, Hold these pictures in your thoughtful heads. If you love this world, make use of them.

—1991

How Come?

About a year ago a friend, a woman, a writer, called long distance
to ask, How come you've never written anything about menopause? I don't mean to be critical, she said, I'm just asking. I
decided it was a critical statement and immediately added it to
other important life facts and worries I hadn't written about yet.
Life is complicated and so short, I thought, and I'm not getting
anything done. But really, what about menopause?

The fact is, I'm sixty-eight and I seem to have forgotten those
years or maybe that year. They happened (in my optimistic re-
construction) between my late forties and my early fifties. On
medical forms I have written forty-nine, fifty-two, fifty—whatever
number was useful to that day's mindset. I *did* write a review of
Rosetta Reitz's fine book on menopause when it came out and
admired Paula Weidiger's as well, so it must have been on my
mind at some point.

I suspect that my menstrual periods simply ceased one month,
having grown lighter and easier. That probable easiness was accompanied by something I do remember: heat, the taking off and
putting on of shirts and sweaters, my face reddening first into
rosy health, then into a fierce faceful of fever. A crazy barometer,
I'd explain to people who thought I was about to faint—or had
they insulted me? Give that barometer two degrees and it takes

twenty, I said. I was joking, and it did have a certain comedy to it. Excess, when not dangerous, often does. I laughed. My friends laughed.

We could laugh, because the kids were just about grown. Something else was coming. We could laugh, because the years were lively, energetic, risky, hopeful; lots of politics, literature, friendship, love.

That was because of luck and the historical moment. This is what luck might have meant for some of us—fortunate family experience—maybe your mother and two aunts say, Oh, it was easy for me that change of life (that's what it was called). Luck also makes itself known by inhabiting a gene or two. (This is how good teeth appear in certain generally toothless families.) But when luck is thickened with good food or bad, with early loving care or neglect, it becomes the historical moment. On the simplest level, when women's lives were counted by their reproducing years, menopause was the end—the year no more children could be conceived. Those whose birth and nurture had used up days and nights were often gone into the life of their own purposes. Poor women! That public and psychological description—quite frequent when I was young—enraged me, disgusted me.

But I want to take the historic moment a little past that ancient idea—well murdered by the women's movement of the last couple of decades, sometimes called the "second wave." All in lucky time for my aging generation.

The historical moment(s) of my change of life* occurred in the late 1960s to early '70s, when those important communities of civil-rights activists and antiwar workers began to break apart dramatically, the women of those movements re-forming, reshaping into feminist organizations, thinkers, wild, delighted activists. Many (me included) retained old, sometimes angry allegiances to

---

* I suddenly and for a short paragraph liked that description. It was certainly real in my mother's time.

the other movements, in fact, brought new people, women people, into those movements, taking other women out. This prepared women and men for the connections they would have to be making in the years ahead.

The women's movement, that world changer, had been scattering consciousness-raising groups all over the country. Concluding that the personal was political gave a way of speaking and writing and thinking, a way for women to make art, educate themselves, work at new kinds of work, rename time and themselves. A book like *Our Bodies, Ourselves* was almost enough to air out the last few dusty centuries.

I have written this little bit of history because I believe that the high anxious but hopeful energy of the time, the general political atmosphere, and the particular female moment had a lot to do with the fact that I can't quite remember my menopause or, remembering it, haven't thought to write much about it. Writing for me has always come from being bugged—agitated by a life, a speaking voice, an idea. I've asked some of my age mates, old friends, and they feel pretty much the same way. We were busy. Life was simply heightened by opposition, and hope was essential.

Now, I write this as the war in the Gulf, the Great American Gulf War, has ended and not ended. Hundreds of thousands have died by our high-flying hand—invisible to each other the killers and the killed. Our antiwar coalitions didn't have time to set out branches and roots. They did well, but the war was so swift, so vicious, that many of us are left with considerable sorrow-despair. I think of women entering their period of menopause now and I wonder, Will it be different for them? I think it must be. Our insides *do* know something about what is happening to our outsides. We live in this world which takes our children and sets terrible barriers before them: war—a new one just for their generation; drugs; narrow nationalisms of hatred, poverty, absurdity. Our bodies live in this world and are picked up, shaken, and what is natural becomes difficult. What is difficult becomes painful and hopeless. If I were going into menopause now, I think I would remember it years later more harshly.

Still, I must remind myself, having said all this, that there *is* now a women's community, women's communities where women stand still, almost breathless to talk to one another, or gather at home or in meeting places—or in a book like *Women of the Fourteenth Moon*, to listen, to say: This is where *my* trouble is; this is where it hurts. And then someone answers, Me too. And listen. This is what I did about it.

—1991

Upstaging Time

I must tell you that at the first upsurge of a contentious or merely complicated concern, I'm likely to slip into a fictional mode. This is a way of thinking, a habit of thought.

For example: A couple of years ago a small boy yelled out as he threw a ball to a smaller boy standing near me, "Hey, dummy, tell that old lady to watch out."

What? What lady? Old? I'm not vain or unrealistic. For the last twenty years my mirror seems to have reflected—correctly—a woman getting older, not a woman old. Therefore, I took a couple of the hops, skips, and jumps my head is accustomed to making and began to write what would probably become a story. The first sentence is: "That year all the boys on my block were sixty-seven."

Then I was busy and my disposition, which tends to crude optimism anyway, changed the subject. Also, my sister would call, and from time to time she'd say, "Can you believe it? I'm almost seventy-eight. And Vic is going on eighty. Can you believe it?" No, I couldn't believe it, and neither could anyone who talked to them or saw them. They've always been about fifteen years older than I, and still were. With such a sister and brother preceding me, it would seem bad manners to become old. My aging (the aging of the youngest) must seem awfully pushy to them.

Actually, they're both so deep into music, archaeology, Russian-conversation lessons, botany, tutoring high-school students, writing, and remembering for grandchildren and great-nephews and -nieces the story of their Russian-language childhood on Chrystie Street and later in Harlem that they may not notice me trailing them at all.

By the time I returned to that first sentence, the boys had become sixty-nine. Most of them were in decent shape, nice-looking older men—those boys whose war was World War II. (There is a war for every boy—usually given by his father's generation.)

But two of them were no longer present, having leapt out of the air of the world into the actuarial statistics that insurance companies keep, where men, in death as in life, have a sad edge over women, often leaving them years of widowhood. (This is pointed out to us in a kind of accusatory way, as though this new longevity is due to a particular selfishness on our part—female life-greed.) The fact is that women may well be owed a couple of years of extra time, historically speaking, since our deaths as young women in various ritual torments and in childbirth are well known. The great men of history, it is recorded, have often been forced to use more than one wife—serially speaking—in order to properly and sufficiently reproduce themselves. This was sometimes unpleasant for them, too, though not always.

In spite of this parenthetical interruption I returned to my work and was able to write the next sentence of what may still become a story: "Two years later, two of the boys had died and my husband said, 'Well, I'd better take this old-age business a little more seriously.'" So we did.

[Poem to Prove Seriousness]

Questions

Do you think old people should be put away?
the one red rheumy eye the pupil goes back
and back

the hands are scaly
    do you think all that should be hidden

do you think young people should be seen
        so much on Saturday night
hunting and singing in packs the way they do
standing on street corners looking this way
        and that

or the small children who are visible all the time
        everywhere
and have nothing to do but be smart
but be athletes
but jump
but climb high fences
    do you think hearts should sink
    do you think the arteries ought to crumble
    when they could do good
because the heart was made to endure
    why does it not endure?
    do you think this is the way it should be?

Dialogue
Don't you think that poem was kind of gloomy?
But don't you have to be truthful?

There's more to getting older than that. What about friendship? All that special energy—you've written about it yourself. What about experience and wisdom?
But did you really want me to say it was all okay and zippy? Still, you may be right, a little bit. Because for me, I'm well, my children are well, my stepchildren are well. And as I pointed out,

even my oldest siblings, with terrifying surgical memories and arteries sticky with the bakeries of the Upper West Side, offer high examples of liveliness, interest in the world, and hope for tomorrow. This is proven by purchases of long season subscriptions to concerts and ballets and the determination to proceed to those events with whatever spiritual and physical equipment is working. So you are right. Several years ago my sister bought me, for my fifty-fifth birthday, ten Arthur Murray ballroom dancing lessons with her favorite partner.

Okay, so now you agree that poem was gloomy.
You're right, and you're wrong, and anyway, that's not the point. The point is that if you insist on saying that old age is only a slightly different marketplace of good looks, energy, and love, you insult lots of others. For instance, I'm not poor. I'm a white woman in a middle-class life, and even there some luck usually has to apply. Also, when I need to knock wood I can just run out my door to a little forest of maple and hemlock to knock on the best living wood for my luck. Also, I'm not alone in this world, I'm not without decent shelter.

All right, I see what you're saying. But people do need to be encouraged. Why won't you admit it? We only want you to be a little upbeat. It's not against your nature.
Okay. I'll try from now on. But I might, just once, slip.

The Relativity of Age
About sixteen years ago at the beginning of the energetic prime of my fifties, in Chile, in the town of Quillota, a few months before the Pinochet coup, the death of Allende, we met a man with an attaché case full of American bills. He was a trucker with a small

pickup. "Come to my house," he said, loving Americans. "Here's a picture of my children. I had fourteen. Twelve live."

We came to his dusty courtyard, on which the American cash had not yet gone to work. "This is my beautiful daughter," he said, introducing us. "She's eighteen. That's my wife." He pointed to an old woman leaning on the outdoor washbasin. She turned away. "Sick," he said. She was thirty-five years old.

In an honest effort to cheer up I asked one of my students to interview any older woman who happened to be passing the stoop where she and I were sitting talking about the apartment situation in New York. She was the kind of kid who's loaded with initiative. She began at once:

Student Interviewer: Excuse me, ma'am. How do you keep busy?

Older Woman: What do you mean by that? I work. I have to keep my place decent. I take care of my aunt. Her kids moved to California. By the way, you don't seem to be doing too much yourself except interfering with us promenaders.

S.I.: Do you *feel* old?

O.W.: Well, middle age in this country comes so late, if it wasn't for the half fares, I'd never give it up.

S.I.: Do you have many friends?

O.W.: Well, I guess I do. We've been meaning to get together and have this group—this women's group on getting older. You know, everything that happens—some things are interesting and some things are not so hot. But the truth is, we're too busy. Every time we say we're going to get it together, two people have a long job to finish. It's a good idea, though.

S.I.: Do you live with your family?

O.W.: My family doesn't live with *me*. They already have lived with me a number of years.

S.I.: Who do you live with?

O.W.: My lover.

S.I.: Oh. So you're still interested in sex, that means.

O.W.: Yes, I am.

S.I. (*shyly*): Would you elaborate?

O.W.: Not to you.

What It's Like

You may begin to notice that you're invisible. Especially if you're short and gray-haired. But I say to whom? And so what? All the best minorities have suffered that and are rising nowadays in the joy of righteous wrath.

Some young people will grab your elbow annoyingly to help you off and on the curb at least fifteen years before you'd want them to. Just tell them, "Hands off, kiddy." Some others with experience in factional political disputes fear the accusation of ageism and, depending on their character, either defer to you with a kind look or treat you cruelly as an equal. On the other hand, people do expect wise and useful remarks—so, naturally, you offer them. This is called the wisdom of the old. It uses clichés the way they ought to be used, as the absolute truth that time and continuous employment have conferred on them.

You are expected to be forgetful. You are. At least as forgetful as you have always been. For instance, you lose your eyeglasses. You have lost your eyeglasses all your life. You have lost your keys, as well as other people's, frequently. It was once considered a charming if expensive eccentricity, proving that your head was in the literary clouds it was supposed to be in. Your family is not too rude, but you don't like the way they look at each other. Pretty soon you stop mislaying your keys—not altogether, but enough to prove you could have always done so.

You are expected to forget words or names, and you do. You may look up at the ceiling. People don't like this. They may say, "Oh come on, you're not listening." You're actually trying to remember their names.

While he could still make explanations, my father explained to me that the little brain twigs, along with other damp parts of the body, dry up, but that there is still an infinity of synaptic opportunities in the brain. If you forget the word for peach ("A wonderful fruit," he said), you can make other pathways for the peach picture. You can attach it to another word or context, which will then return you to the word "peach," such as "What a peachy *friend*," or springtime and peach *blossoms*. This is valuable advice, by the way. It works. Even if you're only thirty, write it down for later.

My father wanted—in general—to tell me how to grow old. I thought that the restoration of those lost words was almost enough, but he had also taken a stand against wrinkles. He applied creams assiduously to the corners of his mouth and his heels. I did not, when I could, pay enough attention, and now I'm sorry, though it's probably a scientific fact that your genes have got you by the shortening muscles of your throat as well as the number of hairs time leaves on your head.

Soon it was too late to ask him important questions and our

conversations happened in the world where people say, "Is that a story or a fact?"

A Story or a Fact

He had fallen, hurt his head, where time is stored. When he spoke, he made the most direct connections. If I listened, I heard his mind taking the simplest synaptic opportunity and making a kind of poem in that necessity. Follow him for a moment, please.

"Come into the room," my father called to me, "come into the room. I have located your second husband," he said. "I have just located him. Not only his body, but his mind. We talked over there on the couch. Does he want my money? Why does he think he can wear old clothes? I have an extra suit. Give it to him. Well, this is the way we are made—getting old—the problem of old men. The problem of old women—we can talk about that later; I'm not interested.

"Do you know these women? The ones I live with in this house. The one who makes my supper, the one that lives in someone's room—the person that's missing. (I told you someone very important was missing. Who? Mama?) Last night they made a party. Very wild music. Not unpleasant, but not usual. Some others came. Men who talked nicely. The women invited me to their party and they said why not dance; they offered me a chance to —well, you know what. I said to them, 'Can't you see how old I am.' Look, I told them they were very handsome women, not to be insulted. But I'm old. I had to explain to them. Feelings can be hurt." Old, he said. Without sadness, but apologetically, as though it were an offense, not the sorrow of human life.

Interviewer: Why did you tell me this story?

Grace: Because I saw you bought a stunning new winter coat and were about to become too sentimental.

Interviewer: Why are you so hard?

Grace: Well, am I? You do have to come out of late middle age into this older time with your muscles of imagination in good shape, and your muscles of swimming against the tides of misinformation pretty strong—as well as the usual back and abdominal muscles, which are kind of easy to exercise in the morning.

Interviewer: You're not so easy to deal with.

Grace: Why should I be? Like most people my age, I've accumulated enough experience to be easy or difficult, whatever the provocation exacts. Your trouble is you don't have a gift, or the character, for normal tragedy.

Interviewer: That's not really fair. I suppose I have to let it go at that, but I do have a few fairly simple questions I'd like to ask you. What have you liked about your life?

Grace: I've liked being Jewish. I've liked being a woman. When I was a little girl, I liked thinking I was a boy. I loved growing up in New York City, the Bronx, my street—and I've tried to give those advantages to my children.

Interviewer: What do you miss?

Grace: My mother, who died before we had all the good talks that are now in books, thanks to the women's movement. I miss my children's childhood. Now that I live in the country, which I love, I miss my political, grass-roots life in the New York streets.

Vigiling in a shopping center in New Hampshire is not quite the same.

Interviewer: Do you mind having to get older?

Grace (*somewhat annoyed, but luckily slips into another story*): When I was twelve and a half, I was walking along Southern Boulevard in the Bronx on the way to the Elsemere movie house with a boy named David, with whom I was in love. He was fourteen and very sophisticated. "What do you think is the greatest age for a woman?" he asked. I pretended to think, though I already knew. "Eighteen," I said. "Oh no," he sighed, "twenty-six, twenty-six—that's the age a woman should be." "That old?" I asked. "That's awful. It's disgusting." David looked at me as though he had never noticed how young I was. He dropped my hand.

By the way, my answer to your question is, I feel great. I like my life a lot. It's interesting every day. But it so happens I *do* mind.

—1989

Life in the Country:
A City Friend Asks, "Is It Boring?"

No! Living in the country is extremely lively, busy. After the gardens have gone to flower, to seed, to frost, the fruits canned, frozen, dried, the days and evenings are full of social event and human communication. Most of it dependent on the automobile or phone, though a few tasks can be accomplished on foot or ski. Even if you are not worried about the plain physical future of the world, there's a lot to do. If you are concerned about your village, there are zoning meetings, water-board meetings, school meetings and school-board meetings, PTA meetings. There's the Improvement Society, whose main task is sustaining the life of the Green or Common as the elms die away from us. There's also the Ladies Benevolent, whose name explains itself. For some there is the interesting Historical Society of their town; there are selectmen meetings. There's the conservation committee, the agricultural committee for those who count the farms each year and find several missing. There are the food co-op meetings: one for ordering, one for distributing, one for the co-op board. For those who love theater, there are groups flourishing in several of the towns of the county, all requiring lots of rehearsal, costume making, and, in the event of a success, traveling to other towns. Of course many of these meetings happen in bad weather, ice, sleet, and require pot-luck suppers, so there is a great deal of cooking and baking.

All of this liveliness happens after the workday world and the meetings of that world, union or managerial. Nor have I mentioned purely social events: returning a neighbor's dinner invitation, going to a church supper, a fair, the high-school basketball game, or a square dance for the pleasure of it.

Many of us, fearing the world's end and saddened by our country's determined intervention, have been involved in political work, and this requires the following: one meeting every two weeks of our affinity group, a meeting every month or two of a coalition, the special legal meetings which usually precede and follow illegal actions. Then the frequent meetings once an action has been decided upon. If these actions include civil disobedience, there will be training meetings as well as legal ones, so that by role-playing and other methods we retain our nonviolent beliefs and strategies.

And then there is ordinary life. For instance, there is keeping the mud and hay out of the house, and stacking the wood in the woodshed. There is also stuffing newspapers and rags into the cracks and chinks that each new descent of temperature exposes. There is also skiing across shining fields and through dangerous woods full of trees one must avoid.

And of course there is standing in the front yard (or back) staring at the work time has accomplished in crumpling the hills into mountains, then stretching them out again only a few miles away into broad river plains, stippling white pink rust black across the wooded hills, clarifying the topography by first aging, then blowing away the brilliant autumn leaves. Although here and there the wrinkled brown leaves of the oak hold tight, and the beech leaf, whose tree will die young, grows daily more transparent, but waits all winter for the buds of spring.

—1991

" Across the River "

There was the pretty town. There was the beautiful farm full of orchards and fields. There was the big barn. It burned. Silo and all. Cattle horses pigs the chicken house one-third of the orchard.

Almost immediately, in order to raise money, the women of the community began to design a patchwork quilt. It would be patched with the old cotton dresses of their little girls and their grandmas' stored remnants. Little by little it became the history of the beautiful farm, with solid-colored dates, polka-dotted outhouses on backgrounds of flowering cattle, light green hills specked with golden dandelions. Raffles were sold at all the banks, but the event itself was saved for Labor Day, so that the summer people could contribute to the good work.

There was also the small, well-endowed college nearby. On its handsome campus, silk-screened posters appeared asking for contributions to help restore the big barn to the beautiful farm.

One day in early June, the trash truck came up the hill to our house. There were a young trashman and an old trashman on the truck. The young trashman shyly worked at our spring cleanup mess. I said to the old trashman, Isn't it hot for May? —No rain either, he said. —Awful day right now, I said. —Desperate for rain, he said.

There must be lots of fires, I said. Many, he said.

I asked, Do you know that big place across the river, burned up, people are collecting money for it?

I do, he said. Terrible fire. Collecting money, that's good of the kids. He looked sideways at our woodpile for a couple of minutes. Have you thought of this? he asked, turning to me. Now what if a poor man's place burned? Small barn, a couple of cows, no insurance. Why, who'd help him? Maybe a couple of fellows from the firehouse or the Legion'd help nail some old boards. Would there be a collection? Would those college boys be running from door to door? No, they wouldn't. The poor farmer would have to begin again like always, like when his last barn went probably when he was young and there was help. And if this farmer was old and his boys disgusted with farming, why—the old trashman shrugged and heaved a great black plastic bag of last summer's junk into the truck—why, it'd be too bad for that poor fool of a farmer, wouldn't it?

—1978

We had been in the jury room of a Vermont county court for hours, waiting for deals to be made and justice to be defined. In the courtroom itself the defendants were probably watching the important backs of the lawyers and the face of the judge. We waited as juries often do when secret information is being exchanged and the area of the case narrows. The idea that the jury's best verdict can be reached by what seems to be the smallest amount of information is amazing to me. My co-jurors agreed. We were all feeling left out, mocked by the rules of the game.

While we waited and talked, a woman taught me how to insert a red thumb in a blue mitten. She had knitted perhaps three hundred mittens. People asked each other where they worked. Two women worked in small textile factories sewing skirts, one woman worked in a furniture factory. Two women worked for welfare, one woman was an aide in the local hospital. One man trucked fuel; another drove for the college. One man leaned back in his chair and was silent.

When I finished my thumb I began to read the business section of *The New York Times*. "Right here on the third page," I said, "it says that people are getting interested in the small farmer."

The eleven other jurors and the two alternates laughed.

Mrs. Crile, the woman who'd taught me mitten thumbs, said

she was a small farmer. Then she corrected herself: her husband was a small farmer. "You, too, are a small farmer," I said.

"Oh, I know what you mean," she said. "You're talking about women's lib, but you know, he won't let me in the barn. He's a loner, you know. And he loves his cows. Milking time, he don't let anyone in. If the inspection man came, he'd keep him out with a hunting rifle. He says it turns the milk, strangers. He knows every cow. You know, they're different. There's some cows don't like their calves. Well, then you have to feed them yourself. But there's cows are adopters. You know, a calf is born, they don't let anyone near. They adopted it. They don't like the mother near it."

"Well," I said, "this is what it says in the paper," and I quoted: " 'Merrill Lynch, Hubbard, and the Continental Illinois National Bank and Trust Company have proposed an Agricultural Land Fund under which pension funds and tax exempt institutions could buy farms and get managers to run them. This would save the small farm, Mr. Mooney, the president of Merrill Lynch, etc., said.' "

Guffaws, this time, from everyone.

"Save it?" said Mr. Fuller, the silent man. He looked sick and left for the bathroom.

Mr. Vann said he'd like a little tax exemption himself; he couldn't run his farm except into the ground.

"Go on there, Vann," said Mrs. Griffith, "you needn't of said that. You didn't do that, you just got squeezed; the milk company squeezed you and you sold off bit by bit."

"And if I had another couple of bits, I'd sell them tomorrow."

"My granddad," the furniture worker said, "did that. He sold out eighteen years ago up toward Warren and he got maybe thirteen thousand for it; it was just sold, I read in the paper, for a hundred and eighty-seven thousand."

"You know, I believe I knew your family," Mrs. Crile said.

"That old farm wasn't too far from where ours was in those days. We rent now, you know."

The furniture worker continued: "And that old hill farm that he nearly killed himself on, there were a couple of owners, and the last one they say is the pilot of the Shah of Iran. I mean it, and he's made a condominium to ski off of. He gave the town two thousand dollars to help pay for the schools, *and* he's got no kids. No road repairs. He got a better road than the county road. Folks like that don't cost the town services."

"Ayup," said Mr. Fuller, who'd just returned. "And when there's no oil and it's too expensive to roll all that food in from California, and when there's a drought like there is now, try gettin' our farms back to planting. When they got those hills scattered every which way with them chalets, why, the game is gone. What're you going to do? Lyman, you don't remember the Depression, but in our village no one starved. Vann, you remember, we went out, every nightfall we brought it home—something for the families, rabbit, deer, possum, what-all . . . no one starved. But now, where's the land, where's the game?"

In the courtroom the lawyers argued and cut the facts to their legal bone. Here in the jury room, the people were talking about their lives with all the information they had, which was not inconsiderable.

—1977

Introduction to a Haggadah

I lived my childhood in a world so dense with Jews that I thought we were the great imposing majority and kindness had to be extended to the others because, as my mother said, everyone wants to live like a person. In school I met my friend Adele, who together with her mother and father were not Jewish. Despite this, they often seemed to be in a good mood. There was the janitor in charge of coal, and my father, unusually smart, spoke Italian to him. They talked about Italian literature, because the janitor was equally smart. Down the hill under the Southern Boulevard El, families lived, people in lovely shades of light and darkest brown. My mother and sister explained that they were treated unkindly; they had in fact been slaves in another part of the country in another time.

Like us? I said.

Like us, my father said year after year at Seders when he told the story in a rush of Hebrew, stopping occasionally to respect my grandmother's pained face or to raise his wineglass to please the grown-ups. In this way I began to understand, in my own time and place, that we had been slaves in Egypt and were brought out of bondage for some reason. One of the reasons, clearly, was to tell the story again and again—that we had been strangers and slaves in Egypt and therefore knew what we were talking about when we cried out against pain and oppression. In fact, we were obligated by knowledge to do so.

But this is only one page, one way to introduce these Haggadah makers, storytellers who love history and tradition enough to live in it and therefore, by definition, to be part of its change.

—1984

VI / Postscript

When my mother and father were fifty-nine, my mother died of breast cancer and my father retired from a heavy neighborhood medical practice. They had both been sick for about ten years. My father's heart trouble meant that he could no longer walk up to the fifth and then fourth floor of our Bronx tenements on house calls. He couldn't imagine doctoring as an office-only occupation.

He must have done some pretty remarkable medical maintenance: my mother lived ten years after a mastectomy (sixty years ago!). After her death, he lived another thirty years, with hospital visits, bedside oxygen tanks, and the nighttime injections I watched him deliver to himself, slowly, slowly, using as little energy as possible in conveying the hypodermic needle from the table to his arm.

When he retired, he probably thought, What will I do now? He remembered being praised in medical school for his anatomical drawings. So he began to draw, then paint, mostly in oils, teaching himself, practicing, working pretty hard. He had, I think, a great deal of happiness at this work. He had a show at the North Bronx Senior Center. Most of the paintings are now distributed among children and grandchildren. One day Donald Barthelme was at supper and looking things over the way he sometimes did. He said,

I like that little painting. My father said, I'll make you one just like it—and he did.

I don't remember when he first realized he had lots of stories to tell. When he did, he sat down and wrote them. (Indecisive, somewhat indolent as I am, I couldn't get over that action immediately following decision.) My sister, generous as always, typed them. Most were about his patients—our neighbors. They were interesting, they were funny. They needed some editing. I was not good at that; he was my father. I should say here that he learned English when he was about twenty-one, a young immigrant, by reading Dickens. (So did my former father-in-law.) That early reading has been evident in his style, in the letters he wrote us from time to time. (He may have learned Italian first—his earliest job was with an Italian photographer on Fourteenth Street.)

The story included here is the only one he wrote about himself as a young man. It's also one of only three or four that he told us about his Russian youth. Why so much silence? I asked this question in the introduction to the first section of this book. Still no answer. As for the young fellow in the Bachmut prison, he's as familiar and dear to me as the old man I watched him become.

My Father Tells a Story:
"I Should Have Been a Lawyer"

I don't know how good a doctor I am. My colleagues—well—you know what professional jealousy is. It makes no difference who is right. I know that I chose the wrong profession. I should have selected law as my life's work.

I began to practice law suddenly, without notice, out of the blue sky. Like Athena, who sprang from Jove's forehead fully armed, I became a lawyer in the twinkling of an eye, without time-consuming study or apprenticeship.

I was then just eighteen. I happened to be in prison in the small south Russian city of Bachmut.

Now! Now! Compose yourself! I see your eyes are bulging. You are horrified and frightened. You cast an apprehensive glance at your silver spoons, which are lying around exposed and defenseless.

I wasn't incarcerated for rape, mayhem, misfeasance, malfeasance, or some other feasance, the prefix of which escapes me at the moment. The reason for my presence in the prison and on the wrong side of the bars, too, was due to an argument between me and the then-ruling dynasty on certain political matters. I lost the argument, and as a result, I had to spend six months in prison, followed by a three-year period of cooling my heels somewhere beyond the Arctic Circle.

In the meantime, I wasn't particularly unhappy. Can you be unhappy when you're eighteen? Being the first political prisoner, I was placed in a solitary cell, which sounds dreadful, but it was not. My casemate was on the ground floor, bearing on the prison yard, with the prison office right across a narrow yard. To the left, the main building reared its incredibly dirty mass. The comings and goings between the buildings kept down my boredom.

The prison was an ancient one. Its sanitary conditions were of the most primitive kind. The management was lax. Rules were sometimes kept. I wasn't surprised, therefore, when the day turnkey, instead of locking my door after I came in from the toilet, followed me into the cell, which was against the rules. He was somewhat embarrassed. He scratched the back of his head with the enormous doorkey.

"They say you politicals are very clever," he said.

I didn't deny it. When I was eighteen, I had no superiors and only a few peers in the intellectual heights I then inhabited. I came in for some rude shocks. But that was later.

"I am but a human being," he continued. "Suppose I did get drunk and missed two days. Must I be kicked out of service like a dog? With five children and a sick wife?"

He brushed away a tear.

I was touched at the injustice, but what could I do?

A shy look appeared on his broad, pockmarked face. "You write for me a petition to the chief warden. You tell him about my poor innocent children, my sick wife . . ."

I was dumbfounded at his request. I had never written any official letters or documents. I told him so.

"You'll know how to write. You politicals have a head on your shoulders. And don't forget to mention that my wife is pregnant, and the way she is carrying, it must be twins!"

I was horrified at the thought of so many people starving for such a small infraction of the rules. The twins, which I accepted in my innocence as a 100 percent certainty, finally swayed me. "All right, Kuzma," I said. "Bring me a sheet of paper and pen and ink."

On the windowsill—there was no table in my cell—I began to draft a petition. And right there and then a legal luminary was born. I whizzed like a meteor across the gray skies of Bachmut's ancient prison.

I put into the petition all the fervor and sincerity of my eighteen years. From the deep recesses of my consciousness swam out shadow forms of legal phraseology. I hadn't been aware that I harbored them.

With a true lawyer's instinct I glossed over, hardly mentioning Kuzma's offense. His two-day drunk I didn't mention at all. But I promised in his name that never, never would a drop of vodka ever cross his lips! I mentioned his five poor children, none of whom, from my description of their helplessness, could have been older than two years. I remarked on his wife's present condition. I was on the point of mentioning the menacing advent of twins, but at the last moment, I desisted. A higher power held my hand.

The petition was an unqualified success. Kuzma was called to the chief warden's office. Obscenities were heaped upon his head, which probably sounded like music to his ears. It was known all over the prison that the chief warden was very dangerous only when he was polite. Kuzma was standing at attention, repeating at appropriate intervals, "Yes, Your Nobleness" and "It's exactly so, Your Nobleness."

He came back to his post, opened my door, and said with a smirk, "Forgiven. Anytime you want to go to the toilet, just knock at the door." This was my reward. In the boredom of prison life, an extra passage through the hall was a lively diversion.

Within twenty-four hours my reputation as a petition writer was firmly established. The trustees, who had the liberty of moving around, were usually the bearers of news in the prison. They hadn't failed to apprise the rest of the prisoners of the appearance in their midst of a legal light whose very first effort was crowned with success.

The facts that Kuzma had only two children and that his wife wasn't pregnant at all did not detract from my fame. As a matter of fact, everybody thought it was very slick on my part to have made things look blacker than they were. And if, in the process of doing so, I had resorted to a lie, what of it? It was the result that counted.

The very next day, Kuzma ushered into my cell a long-faced, melancholy-looking convict, adorned with a sparse, shaggy beard. He was obsequious.

"Here you are, Zinovy (my name). Don't you be scared, Malinikov, speak up!" said Kuzma. To his usually sly look he added the expression of a cat who had just swallowed a canary. I surmised that Kuzma, as a price for allowing Malinikov to see me, must have extorted from him a package of makhorka, a tobacco of unusual venom and acridity. Only a real muzhik could smoke it and survive.

"His wife lives with a discharged soldier." Kuzma guffawed. He left the cell, jangling the keys.

Malinikov's marital troubles were his smallest ones. He was a peasant living in one of the nearby villages. Passing the government liquor store one night, he saw someone had broken in through the window. He looked into the store. There was no one there. But so much vodka! He just couldn't resist.

In the morning he was found with a good deal of evidence inside him, but the incredible number of empty bottles around him and the broken window earned him six years of prison with two years off for good behavior.

But in spite of his good behavior, he was now serving his fifth year, seemingly forgotten. His property was being frittered away. And then he would love to give one swift kick in the pants to the soldier who was living with his wife. Marya was his own wife. He'd had four children with her. Maybe by now there were more than four. Who knew? But he was ready to forgive everything. His last and only hope was my High Nobleness!

I denied my nobleness with indignation; but without the slightest hesitation, I undertook the job of hastening his release.

I drafted a petition to no less a person than the Minister of Justice. I expatiated eloquently upon his helpless wife and numerous children. I added for good measure a decrepit father and mother and drew the attention of His Excellency to his, Malinikov's, exemplary behavior.

Within a month, he was released. I have a lurking suspicion that my petition had very little to do with his release. Most likely there had been some delay in the slow peregrination of the czarist bureaucracy.

But one and all attributed Malinikov's release to my legal acumen.

Kuzma did a land-office business charging for permission to see me. When the chief warden and his assistant were away, he would occasionally smuggle in convicts from the main building, no doubt taking a cut from the other turnkeys. In my later years I visited—never of my own free will—other prisons in Russia, but the Bachmut prison was the freest, or rather, the most loosely governed.

I was deeply interested and engrossed in my new calling. I actually liked to draw up the petitions, complaints, and communications. There was no subject too difficult, no authority too exalted for me to tackle.

Sometimes ill success would dog my legal steps, but my initial glory and reputation stood the stress of adversity and remained untarnished. "If Zinovy couldn't do it! . . ."

When business slackened, I didn't know how to overcome my boredom. My mind had become attuned to the legalistic forms which I had managed somehow to pick up. I thirsted to find my way in complex situations; to present my arguments and refute opposite ones. It became a passion and a game.

To make things more unbearable, the month was May. During the day, if I had no "legal" work, I would read or watch the panorama of the prison yard. But at night, or in the evening, even those diversions were denied me! I couldn't read, because the small kerosene lamp was set so high that I couldn't see the print of the book.

Standing by the window, when the shadows had enveloped everything but the stars and the moon, was almost a torture. The world was beautiful—on the other side of the bars. The air was full of the fragrance of lilacs and jasmine and some other flowers, the names and shapes of which escape me now. Springtime in Ukraine is so much more fragrant than that of the northern United States. Perhaps it only seemed so during "the golden days of my spring," as Pushkin puts it.

I longed to promenade on the boulevards in the soft caressing air of the mild spring. I wouldn't walk, of course, all alone. Yes, there was a girl. And what a girl! And while walking we would discuss perhaps the vestiges of feudalism in England, the institution of the matriarchate in the primitive days of human society . . . We might sit on a bench, perhaps even touch each other with our bodies. We would suddenly become aware of powerful currents, not covered by economics or the history of culture and civilization . . .

The slackening of my law practice made me look around and search for a new line of legal endeavor. What was the matter with my own grievances? Not, of course, as far as my own term of incarceration was concerned, or my impending removal to the Arctic regions. To have contested that would have been a piece of folly, not to be countenanced even by my daring and overconfident eighteen years.

But the prison itself was nothing but a monstrous mass of

hygienic, fire, and building violations. In my soberer moments I was aware that nothing short of razing it to the ground could cure it of its ills, but the temptation to get my legal teeth into something tangible was irresistible. To put down on a sheet of paper an orderly array of arguments, peppering it liberally with "to wits," "whereas's," was like writing poetry. I let myself go. I asked Kuzma for a sheet of paper and pen and ink.

Now, the chief warden's power is almost unlimited. He is like the captain of a ship on the high seas. He can put you on bread and water, confine you to a real solitary cell, damp, dark, and full of rats; he can torture you and, at the least sign of insubordination, shoot you—and go scot-free. But he cannot refuse you paper and ink if you desire to communicate with higher powers.

In my first complaint I described the prison toilet facilities, or rather, the absence of them. I described how offensive they were both to the eye and to the nose, the proximity to the water supply, the possibility, nay, the inevitability of an epidemic.

Before the ink had dried on this complaint, I was ready with another. A Gypsy convict mentioned to me casually that he was suffering from syphilis. Horrible thoughts assailed me! I must prevent the spread of the dreaded disease that was sure to engulf me as well as the other prisoners.

Another sheet of paper. Again pen and ink. To make the complaint stronger, one copy was dispatched to the Inspector of Prisons, another to the Minister of Justice, and a third to the arbiter of my own destinies, the Minister of Interior Affairs. A little later I found out that 20 percent of the prisoners were syphilitic.

An avalanche of complaints and communications bearing on prison life followed. Kuzma regarded my activities without enthusiasm. Where did he come in? There was no makhorka or vodka or any other emoluments in the present line of my legal activity. His shy look was exchanged for a surly one. He wasn't in a great hurry to unlock my door whenever I felt like limbering my legs by a saunter in the hall.

The chief warden regarded my legal efforts on behalf of the convicts with condescension and amusement. Every communication with the higher powers passed through his hands. Perhaps he even had to sign them, but when I started on my new tack, he expressed his displeasure. Not, of course, directly to me. He knew better than to argue with a fresh youth who was in prison because he defied authorities immeasurably more exalted than himself. He couldn't risk an insult.

He sent an emissary to me, the fat office clerk who really ran the prison. He came over to my window one day. He acted nonchalantly, as if he were taking a leisurely walk.

"How are you, Zinovy?" he asked, leaning on the outside sill.

"W-e-ll," I said indefinitely. "And how are you, Anton?"

"Not bad! Not bad at all. Except my wife. Ovaries. I am thinking of taking her to Charkow. There isn't a decent doctor here in Bachmut," he said.

He proceeded to clean his left nostril of numerous clinkers, half of his index finger disappearing into it. Having done a pretty thorough job, he looked at me with an air of intimacy.

"Stop that, Zinovy! You are not doing anybody any good. Peter Mikhailovich (the chief warden) doesn't like it."

A mere chief warden wasn't going to tell me what to do and what not to do. I told Anton to transmit that to his boss.

He sighed. "That's what they told me. You politicals don't respect either age or rank."

He was right in one respect: My legal efforts, as far as prison was concerned, were bare of results. The Regional Inspector of Prisons, the Chief of Gendarmes, and all other pertinent authorities knew perfectly well that the first step in correcting the Bachmut prison would be to demolish it completely.

Whenever the office of the warden was in receipt of an answer to my complaint, I was called to the office, where the warden would read it to me with an impassive face.

"Your petition of such and such a date, addressed to this or that official, has been denied. Please sign your name acknowledging that the answer to your petition has been read to you." This formula occasionally varied. Instead of "your petition has been denied," it might read: "Upon investigation, your complaint was found to be groundless."

But whatever the wording, my legal activity had not changed the archaic prison one little bit.

Still and all, the chief warden was worried. The turnkey, the office, and even the convicts knew very well the reason for his perturbation. He was about to retire on a pension. He had already changed his epaulets to a form indicating that he was a retired officer. The chances that the steady stream of my complaints would hurt him were infinitesimal. So far, all my complaints were turned down. But who could tell when some absurd official would decide to take in earnest the silly complaint of that eighteen-year-old whippersnapper! And before you knew it, your pension, your rest from worries would be jeopardized. Better not take any chances. The emissary was dispatched to me once more.

The fat clerk with his scavenging finger rested his weight on the outer windowsill.

"How are things, Zinovy?"

"W-e-l-l," I said, "so-so."

"How's the food?" he inquired.

I got red in the face. "You call the slops served here food?" The prison food was one of my most frequent complaints. The meat was particularly vile. But the food would improve remarkably when an inspection was impending.

Whenever my mother came to see me, I would complain of the food. Living in another town, she couldn't help me very much. However, she found a cousin in town and arranged to have her send me at least one meal a day. But as luck would have it, my mother's cousin turned suddenly vegetarian, and being a wretched and unimaginative cook, she brought to the prison every day exactly the same meal: thin dairy tasteless borscht and spinach fried in sunflower oil. After a month of this diet, I was ready to chew the bark off the trees rather than eat her monotonous fodder.

Anton looked at me speculatively.

"How would you like to have *zharkoye* with potatoes every single day?" he asked. The above dish is a sort of Irish stew or a goulash, minus the tomatoes. One shouldn't attempt to pronounce it unless one has imbibed a Slavic language with his mother's milk. The first letter is made up of all the sibilants gathered from the whole world and fused into one sound.

I was full of suspicion.

"And who is going to get the meat and the potatoes?" The turnkey, the office staff, and the warden all ate outside the prison. The prison meat would turn the stomach of a hungry dog.

"Peter Mikhailovich, out of his own pocket," answered Anton.

He must really be in a panic, I thought. His offer couldn't come at a more opportune time. I was about to discontinue anyhow the dispatching of complaints connected with the prison. The authorities had turned down every one of those complaints. (I was on the point of stopping them of my own account.) I was being offered a divine *zharkoye* every single day!

Strange as it may seem, the last consideration was the least important one. It's true I had subsisted for months on black, soggy rye bread and tea, but recalling my state of mind in that remote era, I cannot honestly say that I was particularly distressed by the horrible diet. I complained; I felt hungry always, but it was of minor importance in the greater scheme of things.

Another suspicion crossed my mind. "And who is going to cook?" I knew perfectly well that the regular cooks would steal the meat, the potatoes, and the pot.

"Don't you worry!" answered Anton. "Peter Mikhailovich wasn't born yesterday. He assigned a convict who is going to cook and eat with you."

I meditated for a while as if considering whether to accept the peace offering or to refuse it. Noticing my seeming hesitation,

Anton added with alacrity, "Peter Mikhailovich said you can draw up for the convicts all the petitions you want. He likes to read them. He said you write with passion and sincerity, but he does not think you know any criminal law."

"Very well, Anton, let's try the arrangement, but I reserve the right," I added haughtily, "to terminate it if any grave injustice should crop up."

Anton shrugged his shoulders. "I don't understand you, Zinovy. At times I believe you are a very clever fellow, and then you talk like a child. Did you really expect to change anything in the prison?"

I wouldn't lower myself by arguing with him. The nerve of a man who doesn't know what surplus value is, who is ignorant— absolutely ignorant!—about such elementary matters as dialectical materialism, daring to criticize me!

The very next day at twelve o'clock, when I was expecting my slops, there was the clang of Kuzma's keys, and the door was widely opened, ushering in the shifty-eyed Grishka Koval (a pickpocket who had spent almost all his life in prison) bearing a steaming and odoriferous pot of *zharkoye*. He placed it on a box, which served me as a table. The stew looked very good. The potatoes were brown. The meat looked like real meat and not like trimmings consisting of dirty fat, tendons, and often disgusting and unmentionable things.

I anticipated a Lucullan repast. I looked inside the pot—we dispensed even with wooden plates—there wasn't too much of the stew.

Grishka understood my questioning glance. He said, "I ate my part." I had a sense of momentary nausea. Did he at least use a fork or spoon? Or did he use his fingers?

I looked closer at the stew. What the dickens! It was chockful of laurel leaves and aromatic pepper. The odor was pleasant at the beginning, but there was a little bit too much of it.

I began to eat the aromatic *zharkoye*. I shoved aside the masses of laurel leaves and the aromatic pepper. The meat and the potatoes were permeated with spicy odors.

I puckered my nose and said to Grishka, who was watching me benevolently, "Don't you think it is overspiced?"

"It's just right!" You can't get *zharkoye* like that in the best restaurant!"

Halfway through the meal I was almost suffocated by the aromatic odor. I couldn't finish it.

"I'll tell you what you do, Grishka," I said firmly. "Don't put in so much of the laurel leaves and the pepper."

"Goodness gracious! I didn't expect that!" Grishka was offended. "Even the head cook . . ."

For hours the pungent odor hung not only in my cell but also in the corridor through which the *zharkoye* had traveled twice.

Next day I was still in an anticipatory mood when Grishka arrived with the steaming pot. I glanced into it. The same amount of laurel leaves, the same mass of aromatic pepper.

I looked up from the pot and said with indignation, "Didn't I tell you yesterday that I don't like the *zharkoye* overspiced?"

"But it is much tastier like that."

"That's what you say!" I remarked, but my sarcasm was lost on Grishka.

"I just love it like that," he said.

"But you are cooking for me! And I want you to put in as little spice as possible or, better still, don't put in any spice at all!"

"But how will it taste?" He stretched his hands pleadingly.

"It tastes like medicine now! Listen, Grishka, I want a plain, ordinary *zharkoye*! Did you get that?"

He sighed deeply, his face full of grief. I fished out a few pieces of meat, but I could not finish the meal. I stopped eating. I was thinking hard. What should I do? The vast experience of my eighteen years did not cover this situation. An idea suddenly occurred to me.

"Say, Grishka! Can you cook anything else but *zharkoye*?"

He did not answer me at once. He gazed at the ceiling. He scratched his head with all his five fingers. He rubbed his hands together. He had finally come to a conclusion.

"No, Zinovy! That's all I can cook." He fastened his crafty eyes on me. They said quite plainly, "Whether you believe me or not, *zharkoye* is all you are going to get. *I* like it."

"Take it away," I said, "and remember tomorrow, just a touch of spices!"

When I saw him coming into my cell the next day, I caught a sly expression on his face. A feeling of hatred began to well up in my chest.

But when he set the pot in front of me, I looked into it and exclaimed, "Thank God!" There were no laurel leaves, nor any aromatic pepper. But my nostrils were at once assailed by the same strong pungent odor. I tasted the food. It had exactly the same medicinal taste. He must have picked out the leaves and the pepper after stewing the meat and the potatoes together with them.

"You are laughing at me, Grishka," I exclaimed. "I told you twice."

"You can ask anybody you want, Zinovy. Anyone will tell you that this is the best way to make *zharkoye*. Why, when I pass by Kuzma, he always grabs a piece of meat out of the pot."

What upset me particularly was not the fact that, as of yore, I would have to satisfy my hunger by eating black bread, but the utter stubborn stupidity of the man!

"Did it ever occur to you, Grishka, that you would be out of luck if I refuse to eat your stuff?" I inquired.

"But why should you refuse to eat it? The Czar would not refuse to eat *zharkoye* like that."

And then he added innocently, "When you get used to it, you will like it."

I made an effort to eat the stew, but it got stuck in my throat, and it was an even toss whether I would swallow it or vomit it up.

"Take it away!" I said angrily.

"Some people are never satisfied. You do the best you can, but instead of gratitude . . ." he grumbled.

Next day it was exactly the same. Apparently he had made up his mind that I would have "to get used to it." It never entered his mind that I might return to my black bread and tea. Most likely the spices were supplied by the cook, who liked overspiced food and who probably took his cut of the *zharkoye* first of all. I also had no doubt that my hardly tasted portion was sold by Grishka or exchanged for the vicious makhorka.

He knew, of course, that if I complained to the chief warden he would be replaced at once by another convict. He either took a chance on that or he judged correctly that I wouldn't complain.

He was right in the last supposition. Day after day, exactly at twelve o'clock, Grishka would appear with his steaming pot of aromatic stew, only to take it away hardly touched. I ruminated on the steps I should take. Complaining to the chief warden was out of the question. I could just imagine the hilarity of everyone connected with the prison when it became known that a highly respected "political" ran to the warden like a petulant baby complaining of too much spice in his *zharkoye*! Outside of the ridiculousness of the complaint, telling on another convict, however truthful, was always viewed by both "political" and "criminal" offenders in the light of "informing," than which there is no greater crime.

In addition, I began having qualms about my agreement with the warden. I felt that I had traduced my principles for a pot of *zharkoye*. "Never mind that you were 100 percent unsuccessful! No fight is ever wholly lost," my conscience stormed at me. Would my conscience have bothered me if the *zharkoye* had been exactly to my taste? I do not know.

I was also vexed at myself for brooding about such an inconsequential matter as food, while there were such important things to do, or at least to read, like the *Principles of Psychology* by William James, just translated into Russian. I recalled with nostalgia the good old days when my pen was unfettered and my mind was busy with the fashioning of all kinds of legal barbs.

I might have hesitated another week or two if it had not been for an occurrence that resolved my doubts and prompted quick action.

I do not recall whether it was on the third or fourth week of my *"zharkoye"* era. It was about twelve o'clock and I was awaiting Grishka with his aromatic stew. I came closer to the window. A foul odor took my breath away. I asked a passing turnkey what the matter was.

"The sewer broke down again. This dump!" he said contemptuously. The same thing had happened two months ago. It gave me then a reason and an opportunity to compose one of my most brilliant legal papers.

A heavy weight was suddenly lifted off my chest. I saw clearly where my duty as well as my inclinations lay.

I turned sharply at the sound of the opening door through which Grishka and his stew were coming and hardly gave him a chance to cross the threshold.

"Away! Take it away and never bring it again," I shouted. While the bewildered Grishka was backing out, I spied the turnkey standing behind him.

"Kuzma!" I said firmly, "I want a sheet of paper, pen and ink. At once!"

" " *My Father at Eighty-five*

My father said

> how will they get out of it
> they're sorry they got in

My father says

> how will they get out
> Nixon   Johnson   the whole bunch
> they don't know how

goddamnit he says

> I'd give anything to see it
> they went in over their heads

he says

> greed   greed   time
> nothing is happening fast enough

My Father at Eighty-nine

His brain simplified itself
saddening everyone   but he
asked us   children
don't you remember my dog Mars
who met me on the road
when I came home   lonesome
and singing   walking
from the Czar's prison

Publication History

These essays have also appeared in the following publications: "Injustice": *Global City*, 1955; "The Illegal Days": *The Choices We Made*, 1991; "Six Days: Some Rememberings": *Alaska Quarterly*, 1994/1995; "Traveling": *The New Yorker*, 1997; "Peacemeal": *Greenwich Village Peace Center Cookbook*, 1973; "Other Mothers": *Esquire*, December 1995; *Feminist Studies*, 1978; "Two Villages": *WIN*, 1969; "Report from North Vietnam": *WIN*, 1969; "Everybody Tells the Truth": *WIN*, 1971; "The Man in the Sky Is a Killer": *The New York Times*, 1972; "Thieu Thi Tao: Case History of a Prisoner of Politics": *American Report*, 1974; "Conversations in Moscow": *WIN*, 1974; "Other People's Children": *Ms.*, 1975; "Demystified Zone": *Seven Days*, 1980; "Some History on Karen Silkwood Drive": *Seven Days*, 1979; "Cop Tales": *Seven Days*, 1979; "Women's Pentagon Action Unity Statement": *Seven Days*, 1982; "The Seneca Stories: Tales from the Women's Peace Encampment": *Ms.*, 1983; "Pressing the Limits of Action": *Resist Newsletter*, 1984; "Of Poetry and Women and the World": *TriQuarterly Review*, 1986–87; "El Salvador": *A Dream Compels Us*, 1989; "Some Notes on Teaching: Probably Spoken": *Writers as Teachers, Teachers as Writers*, 1970; "One Day I Made Up a Story": *War Resisters Calender*, 1985; "Note in Which Answers Are Questioned": *WRL Calender*,

1977; "Christa Wolf": *What Remains*, 1992; "Coat upon a Stick": *Jewish Publication Society*, 1987; "Language: On Clarice Lispector": *Soulstorm*, 1989; "Isaac Babel": *By His Side*, 1996; "About Donald Barthelme: Some Nearly Personal Notes": *Gulf Coast*, 1990; "Thinking about Barbara Deming": *Prisons That Could Not Hold Spinsters Inc.*, 1985; "Feelings in the Presence of the Sight and Sound of the Bread and Puppet Theater": *WRL Calendar*, 1983; "Claire Lalone": *Long Walks and Intimate Talks*, 1991; "The Gulf War": *The Gulf Between Us*, 1991; "Questions": *Pictures of Peace*, 1991; "How Come?": *Fourteenth Moon*, 1991; "Upstaging Time": *Lear's*, 1989; "Life in the Country: A City Friend Asks, 'Is It Boring?' ": *Long Walks and Intimate Talks*, 1991; "Across the River": *Seven Days*, 1978; "In a Vermont Jury Room": *Seven Days*, 1977; "Introduction to a Haggadah": *The Shalom Sedevz New Jewish Agenda*, 1984; "My Father at Eighty-five": *New and Selected Poems*, 1991; "My Father at Eighty-nine": *New and Selected Poems*, 1991.

"Like All the Other Nations" was a talk given at a Tikkun Conference in December, 1988; "The Value of Not Understanding Everything" was a talk given at Barnard College in the mid-1960s; "Imagining the Present" was a talk given at the Teachers & Writers Collaborative in 1996; "Kay Boyle" was a talk given at a tribute to Kay Boyle organized by the Academy of Arts and Letters in 1994; "Connections" was a talk given at Harvard University in 1991.